Technology, Globalization and Development Series

Series Editor: **Anthony P. D'Costa**, Professor in Comparative International Development, University of Washington, USA.

The series examines technological change in the larger global context by identifying where the markets are, who is specializing in what areas of technology and why, what is the nature of global trade in technologies, and what are some of the social and political challenges posed by such change. Relationships between the OECD and rapidly growing Asian and Latin American economies are brought out by this series. At the same time, the series will also address the issue of why some regions such as Africa and the Middle East lag behind. The question of whether technology is important for development, and how various governments have targeted technology development, whether through education, skill development, or R&D also adds to the diversity of the series. The series includes comparative and regional studies, including single-country case studies of large economies such as India, China, Japan, South Korea, and Brazil. While no single approach or methodology is used exclusively, scholars within the series rely on political economy approaches that are sensitive to institutional and historical realities when analysing specific countries/regions or technologies.

Titles include:

Anthony P. D'Costa (*editor*)
THE NEW ECONOMY IN DEVELOPMENT
ICT Challenges and Opportunities

Govindan Parayil (*editor*)
POLITICAL ECONOMY AND INFORMATION CAPITALISM IN INDIA
Digital Divide, Development and Equity

Technology, Globalization and Development Series
Series Standing Order ISBN 1–4039–3591–2

You can receive future titles in this series as they are published by placing a standing order. Please contact your bookseller or, in case of difficulty, write to us at the address below with your name and address, the title of the series and one of the ISBNs quoted above.

Customer Services Department, Macmillan Distribution Ltd, Houndmills, Basingstoke, Hampshire RG21 6XS, England

---

The New Economy in Development

ICT Challenges and Opportunities

Edited by

Anthony P. D'Costa
Professor in Comparative International Development,
University of Washington, Tacoma, USA

Foreword by

Matti Pohjola

in association with

UNITED NATIONS
UNIVERSITY

UNU-WIDER
World Institute for Development
Economics Research

First published in 2006 by
PALGRAVE MACMILLAN
Houndmills, Basingstoke, Hampshire RG21 6XS and
175 Fifth Avenue, New York, N.Y. 10010
Companies and representatives throughout the world

PALGRAVE MACMILLAN is the global academic imprint of the Palgrave
Macmillan division of St. Martin's Press, LLC and of Palgrave Macmillan Ltd.
Macmillan® is a registered trademark in the United States, United Kingdom
and other countries. Palgrave is a registered trademark in the European
Union and other countries.

ISBN-13: 978–0–230–00146–6 hardback
ISBN-10: 0–230–00146–7 hardback

This book is printed on paper suitable for recycling and made from fully
managed and sustained forest sources.

A catalogue record for this book is available from the British Library.

Library of Congress Cataloging-in-Publication Data

The new economy in development : ICT challenges and opportunities /
edited by Anthony P. D'Costa; foreword by Matti Pohjola.
p. cm.—(Technology, globalization and development)
Includes bibliographical references and index.
ISBN 0–230–00146–7 (cloth)
1. Information technology – Developing countries.
2. Communication in economic development. I. D'Costa,
Anthony P., 1957 –. II. Series.

HC59.72.I55N49 2006
303.48'33091724—dc22   2006043245

10 9 8 7 6 5 4 3 2 1
15 14 13 12 11 10 09 08 07 06

Printed and bound in Great Britain by
Antony Rowe Ltd, Chippenham and Eastbourne

To my father, Camille, and Olivia
who unwittingly live in the new economy

Contents

List of Figures

List of Tables

Box

Acknowledgements

In addition to the individual contributors, this volume is the result of the work of many organisations and individuals. First, I would like to acknowledge the key role played by the United Nations University – World Institute for Development Economics Research (UNU-WIDER) in Helsinki for launching a major initiative to better understand the relationship between development and the new economy. This volume is a partial result of three of WIDER's interrelated research projects between 1998 and 2003: 'Information Technology and Growth', 'Production, Employment and Income Distribution in the Global Digital Economy' and 'Information Technology and Global Economic Development'. Both Anthony Shorrocks, Director of WIDER, and Matti Pohjola at the University of Helsinki who directed the three projects, deserve special mention. I thank Matti also for writing the Foreword to this book. Adam Swallow, Publications Manager at WIDER, did a stupendous job of managing the administrative and editorial aspects of the volume from beginning to end; without his efficient handling I doubt the manuscript would have met the deadline.

Second, at Palgrave Macmillan, it was Amanda Hamilton, Senior Commissioning Editor for Economics, who first brought WIDER's projects to my attention. In 2004 as a Sabbatical Fellow at WIDER, I met Amanda in Helsinki and found her to be an enthusiastic supporter. Jennifer Nelson and Alison Howson, also at Palgrave Macmillan, administratively saw the project through. I thank them all.

Third, I gratefully acknowledge the financial support received in 2003 from the South Asian and South East Asian Studies Programs at the Jackson School of International Studies, University of Washington, Seattle, to examine various public-sector ICT projects in Bangkok. I also thank Dr Chadamas Thuvasethakul, Director of Thailand's National Information Technology Committee Secretariat, and her staff, who organised my interview schedule with numerous Thai ministries and government departments engaged in designing and implementing ICT projects for development purposes.

At home, my family members have gracefully put up with my extended overseas research trips. I owe them a special thank you. Janette Rawlings continues to review my work with a professional disposition. My father, in India, provided a congenial environment to work through

the editing of the individual chapters. In the end, none of the organisations and individuals mentioned here is responsible for my errors and omissions.

Anthony P. D'Costa
Tacoma, Washington

Permissions

Chapter 4 was previously published as 'The Internet and Economic Growth in LDCs: a Case of Managing Expectations?' *Oxford Development Studies*, 31, 1, and is reprinted with the kind permission of Taylor and Francis, http://www.tandf.co.uk.

Chapter 5 has been printed with copyright permission from the journal *Information Technologies and International Development*: Marcin Piatkowski, 'Can ICT Make a Difference?', *Information Technologies and International Development*, 3(1) (Fall, 2005) © 2006 by the Massachusetts Institute of Technology (forthcoming).

Chapter 7 is a slightly revised and updated version of a paper that appeared in the *Journal of Information Technology for Development*, 11(1) (2005): 59–75.

An earlier version of Chapter 10 appears in the *Philippine Sociological Review*, 49 (2001): 1–17, while an expanded version is available in Czarina Saloma-Akpedonu (forthcoming), *Possible Worlds in Possible Spaces: Knowledge, Globality, Gender and Information Technology in the Philippines* (Ateneo de Manila University Press).

Foreword

The global distribution of income and wealth is highly unequal and the gap between the rich and poor is growing. The *Human Development Report* states that 2.5 billion people live on less than $2 a day while 10 per cent of the world's richest population receives 54 per cent of global income. In the last 20 years over 80 per cent of the world's population has experienced rising inequality. Notwithstanding measurement difficulties, it is clear that the divide between rich and poor is real within and between countries. Genuine global efforts such as Millennium Development Goals to reduce poverty and inequality are not making much headway either. Paradoxically, the benefits of greater global integration and an explosion in new information technologies are captured mainly by the OECD economies and a few developing countries.

The development process is no doubt complex. History and institutions matter; as do good macroeconomic and social policies. A favourable international environment is equally important if effective global participation is to be realised. In the contemporary context an additional factor for economic development has been identified, namely technology. The history of economic development is a story of rising productivity. Notwithstanding the structural and institutional barriers to access to innovations, developing countries desire new technologies on the assumption that productivity growth could lead to greater social welfare in terms of income and wealth. Today, the availability of information and communication technologies (ICT) has raised new hopes of many poor countries of extricating themselves from the low-productivity, low-growth trap. This optimism is not without merit. After all many East and South East Asian economies, India and Brazil, among others, have been successful in developing and deploying innovations in ICT. Not only is there greater production and exports of ICT but there is also the growth in consumption and the use of such technologies across many sectors, including government. But what of the other developing countries, which have neither an old economy industrial foundation nor the knowledge base to participate effectively in the globalised new economy of services and ICT? What are their possibilities for economic development using new technologies?

Anthony D'Costa has put together a set of chapters that includes contributions to a UNU-WIDER conference on the New Economy in

Development, held in Helsinki in May 2002, which examine theoretically and empirically both opportunities and challenges faced by some of the lesser-studied developing countries and regions in their production and consumption of ICT goods and services. At the macro-level the volume addresses several issues. Because ICT is integral to the new economy, which also includes the service sector, there are theoretical and conceptual challenges to measuring it and thus policy implications. At the same time, the new economy operates in a global setting, which means that changing international governance mechanisms are critical for global information infrastructure. While some poor countries can proactively adapt foreign innovations, they often remain peripheral to the global economic engine. The adoption of ICT in developing and transition economies is hampered by the lack of physical and human capital and appropriate institutions. These are quintessentially old economy development problems. Simultaneously, micro-studies on ICT production and deployment suggest that the ICT-based productivity growth strategy is not completely closed. Some of the chapters broach the issues of export competitiveness in ICT goods and services, the deployment of ICT in small and medium-size enterprises and the significance of spreading the benefits of the new economy to agricultural populations for broader development. No doubt challenges remain but these chapters suggest that the new economy need not be alien to poor countries nor should the old economy problems be ignored in the pursuit of economic and social welfare.

Matti Pohjola
Professor of Economics
Helsinki School of Economics

Notes on the Contributors

Birgitte Andersen is Reader in the Economics and Management of Innovation in the School of Management and Organisational Psychology, Birkbeck College, University of London, UK, where she is also Director of e-business programmes. She has a Ph.D. in Economics. Her research profile is within evolutionary economics and industrial dynamics with respect to innovation and institutions, services dynamics and productivity, and the economics and management of intellectual property rights. She has published extensively within those fields: her books include *Intellectual Property Rights: Innovation, Governance and the Institutional Environment* (2006); *Technological Change and the Evolution of Corporate Innovation: the Structure of Patenting 1890–1990* (2001); *and Knowledge and Innovation in the New Service Economy* (with Howells, Hull, Miles and Roberts 2000). She has directed, owned and/or worked on research programmes funded by the EU, the Economic and Social Research Council of the UK, the Economic and Social Research Council of Denmark, the British Academy, the Danish Research Academy, and the Arts and Humanities Research Board of the UK. She has advised and/or collaborated with economists and policymakers of national governments inside and outside Europe, international agencies including the EU, ILO and UNCTAD, as well as leading interest organisations.

T. A. Bhavani is Associate Professor, Institute of Economic Growth, Delhi, India. Her M.Phil. and Ph.D. in Economics are from the Delhi School of Economics, and she was a Ford Foundation Post-Doctoral Fellow at the University of Illinois at Urbana-Champaign, USA, during 1992–93. She has worked extensively on the issues related to Indian small-scale industries. One of her papers in the area won a GDN research medal in 2003. Some of her studies involved collaborations with international institutions such as Hitotsubashi University, Japan, and Erasmus University Rotterdam, The Netherlands, and are sponsored by the Japanese Science Research Fund, IDPAD Netherlands and GDN. Currently, she is working in the areas of political economy and institutional aspects of Indian economic performance and economic reforms.

Daniel Chudnovsky has a D.Phil. in Economics (Oxford University) and is Full Professor at the University of San Andrés and Director of the Centro de Investigaciones para la Transformacin (CENIT). He has

written extensively on foreign direct investment, innovation, sustainable development and regional integration.

Derrick L. Cogburn is Assistant Professor of Information at the Syracuse University School of Information Studies, and Senior Research Associate at the Moynihan Institute of Global Affairs at the Maxwell School. He directs the Collaboratory on Technology Enhanced Learning Communities (www.cotelco.net) and serves as a principal in the Internet Governance Project (www.internetgovernance.org). Dr Cogburn also serves as Visiting Professor of International Relations at the American University School of International Service and as Visiting Senior Fellow at the University of the Witwatersrand. Professor Cogburn holds a Ph.D. in Political Science from Howard University and is the former Executive Director of GIIC Africa, with the Global Information Infrastructure Commission, as well as former Director of the Centre for Information Society Development in Africa at the Council for Scientific and Industrial Research (CSIR) in South Africa. Dr Cogburn attended his first ICANN meeting in March 2000 in Cairo and has been active in the WSIS (www.itu.int/wsis/) since Prepcom-3 of the Geneva Phase. He is a member of the WSIS Civil Society Internet Governance Caucus and served as an invited expert at the ITU Internet Governance Symposium in Geneva.

Marva E. Corley is an Economist with the United Nation's International Labour Office in Geneva, Switzerland. She holds a Ph.D. in Economics from Howard University in Washington, DC. Dr Corley's research interests are in the areas of labour markets and employment issues, productivity growth and measurement (with a specific focus on services), and conflict and economic growth. She was one of the main researchers for the ILO's *World Employment Report 2004–05* and has been extensively involved in other ILO publications such as *Key Indicators of the Labour Market* (KILM) and *Global Employment Trends*. She has published articles in the *Journal of African Economies* (2005) and *International Review of Labour Economics* (2003), and has worked on research programmes funded by the EU, and at the national level for the government of the United States' Bureau of Labor Statistics and the Board of Governors of the Federal Reserve System.

Anthony P. D'Costa, Professor of Comparative International Development at the University of Washington, Tacoma, has written widely on the political economy of global and Asian steel, auto and software sectors. He is the author of *The Global Restructuring of the Steel Industry: Innovations, Institutions and Industrial Change, The Long March to Capitalism: Embourgeoisment, Internationalization, and Industrial Transformation in*

India, and co-editor with E. Sridharan of *India in the Global Software Industry: Innovation, Firm Strategies and Development*. He serves on the Board of Trustees of the American Institute of Indian Studies and the editorial board of *Asian Business and Management*.

P. D. Kaushik is working as a Senior Fellow at the Rajiv Gandhi Foundation, New Delhi. He was awarded the International Jawahar Lal Nehru Fellowship during his Ph.D. Currently his area of interest is electronic commerce and the World Trade Organisation. He has a wide experience of industry and academia, he is associated with consultancy work for the FAO and the World Bank, and he is a visiting Faculty to the reputed Management Institutions on Strategic Management. He has a long collection of publications on policy issues emerging from electronic commerce and international trade, and has also authored two books on the World Trade Organisation.

Charles Kenny is a Senior Economist in the Global Information and Communications Technology Department of the World Bank. He works on a number of projects related to telecommunications, post and broad-casting policy and investment, including coordination of the bank's information infrastructure activities in Afghanistan, Iran and Kenya. He also coordinates a departmental research and analysis programme. He has published papers and book chapters on issues including the role of information and communications technologies in development, the impact of reform in the telecommunications sector, the 'digital divide', what we know about the causes of economic growth, the link between economic growth and broader development, and the link between economic growth and happiness.

Andrés López, a Doctor in Economic Sciences from the University of Buenos Aires, is Principal Researcher at CENIT, and Associate Professor at the Facultad de Ciencias Económicas, University of Buenos Aires, Argentina. He specialises in industrial economics and the economics of technical change.

Samia Satti Osman Mohamed Nour is a graduate of the MERIT/UNU-INTECH (United Nations University – Institute for New Technologies) Ph.D. Programme in Economics and Policy Studies of Technical Change in Maastricht, the Netherlands, and the University of Khartoum, Sudan. Her publications include *Technological Change and Skill Development in the Arab Gulf Countries* (Maastricht University 2005), 'Deficiencies in Education and Poor Prospects for Economic Growth in the Gulf Countries: the Case of the UAE', in the *Journal of Development Studies* (with

Joan Muysken 2005) and 'Science and Technology (S&T) Development Indicators in the Arab Region: a Comparative Study of Arab Gulf and Mediterranean Countries', in *The Journal of Science, Technology and Society* (2005; 10(2): 249–74).

Marcin Piatkowski is Advisor to the Executive Director at the International Monetary Fund, Washington, DC. Previously Research Director at TIGER (Transformation, Integration, and Globalisation Economic Research), an economic think tank based in Warsaw, Poland, in 2002–3 he served as an advisor to Poland's Deputy Premier and Minister of Finance. He has conducted research studies at Harvard University, UNU-WIDER, OECD Development Centre and the London Business School and his research interests include the impact of information and communication technologies on growth and productivity in post-communist countries, the development of information society and financial markets in emerging economies.

Czarina Saloma-Akpedonu is Assistant Professor and Chairperson of the Department of Sociology and Anthropology, Ateneo de Manila University. She earned her academic degrees from University of Bielefeld (Dr.rer.soc.), Peking University (MA) and University of the Philippines in Diliman (BA). Her first book, *Possible Worlds in Impossible Spaces: Knowledge, Globality, Gender and Information Technology in the Philippines* (forthcoming), examines the 'doing' of information technology in a so-called developing country.

List of Abbreviations

ABT	Agreement on Basic Telecommunications
ACMA	Automotive Components Manufacturers' Association
AHDR	Arab Human Development Report
AISI	African Information Society Initiative
APEC	Asia-Pacific Economic Cooperation
B2B	business-to-business
B2C	business-to-consumers
BPL	below poverty line
BPO	business process outsourcing
C2C	consumer-to-consumer
ccTLDs	country code top level domains
CEE	Central and Eastern Europe
CEER	Central and Eastern Europe and Russia
CMIE	Centre for Monitoring the Indian Economy
CRM	customer relationship management
DCSSI	Development Commissioner Small Scale Industries
DGP	Director-General of Police
DNA	domain name authority
DOT force	Digital Opportunity Taskforce
DRDA	District Rural Development Agency (India)
DTI	Department(s) of Trade and Industry
ECA	United Nations Economic Commission for Africa
ECASA	Electronic Commerce Association of South Africa
ECD	electronic data interchange
ECLAC	Economic Commission for Latin America and the Caribbean
ERP	enterprise resource planning
ESCWA	Economic and Social Commission for Western Asia
EU	European Union
FDI	foreign direct investment
FSIA	Faridabad Small Industries Association
G2C	government-to-citizen
G7	Group of Seven industrialised countries
G8	Group of Eight industrialised countries
GAC	Government Advisory Council
GCC	Gulf Cooperation Council
GDN	Global Development Network

GII	Global Information Infrastructure
GIS	Global Information Society
IC	intellectual capital
ICANN	Internet Corporation for Assigned Names and Numbers
ICC	International Chambers of Commerce
ICT	information and communications technology
IFPRI	International Food Policy Research Institute
ILO	International Labour Office
IMD	Institute for Management Development
IP	Internet protocol
ISAD	Information Society and Development
ISIC	International Standard Industrial Classification
ISO	International Standards Organisation
ISP	Internet services providers
IT	information technology
ITA	Information Technology Agreement
ITR	International Telecommunications Regime
ITU	International Telecommunication Union
JIT	just-in-time
KIBS	knowledge-intensive business services
LDCs	least developed countries
LINK	Learning, Information, Networks and Knowledge Centre, University of Witwatersrand
LP	labour productivity
MIEM	Ministerio de Industria, Energía y Minería (Argentina)
MNEs	multinational enterprises
MPCICs	multi-purpose community information centres
MSN	Microsoft Network
NC	numerically controlled (machinery)
NECTEC	National Electronics and Computer Technology Centre (Thailand)
NGOs	non-governmental organisations
OAP	old age pension
OECD	Organisation for Economic Cooperation and Development
OEMs	original equipment manufacturers
OLS	ordinary least squares
PCs	personal computers
PDS	public distribution system
PITs	public information terminals
PMP	phased manufacturing programme
PMRY	Prime Minister's Rozgar Yojana

PTO	public telecommunications operator
PTT	post, telegraph and telephone
R&D	research and development
RoW	rest of the world
S&T	science and technological
SADC	Southern African Development Community
SADoC	South African Department of Communications
SAMOS	South African Multiple Option Settlement
SARB	South African Reserve Bank
SARS	South African Revenue Service
SIDBI	Small Industries Development Bank of India
SIS	software and information services
SMEs	small and medium-sized enterprises
SMMEs	small, medium and micro-sized enterprises
TARA	Technology and Action for Rural Advancement
TFP	total factor productivity
TFPG	total factor productivity growth
TIGER	Transformation, Integration, and Globalisation Economic Research, Poland
TNCs	transnational corporations
TPRC	Telecommunications Policy Research Conference
TQM	total quality management
TRIPS	Trade-Related Aspects of Intellectual Property
UAE	United Arab Emirates
UNCITRAL	United Nations Conference on International Trade Law
UNCTAD	United Nations Conference on Trade and Development
UN-DESA	United Nations Department of Economic and Social Affairs
UNDP	United Nations Development Programme
UNESCO	United Nations Education, Scientific and Cultural Organisation
UNU	United Nations University
USA	Universal Service Agency
USP	unique selling proposition
WDI	World Development Indicators (World Bank)
WEF	World Economic Forum
WIDER	World Institute for Development Economics Research, of the UNU
WIPO	World Intellectual Property Organisation
WITSA	World Information Technology and Services Alliance
WSIS	World Summit on the Information Society
WTO	World Trade Organisation

1
Introduction: Charting a New Development Trajectory?

Anthony P. D'Costa

1.1 Introduction

The last three decades have witnessed a sea change in the character and functioning of the world economy. Both quantitatively and qualitatively the OECD and a handful of newly industrialising economies have been transformed by global flows of trade, foreign direct investment (FDI), technology and technical talent. Within national economies the ensuing structural change is nothing short of remarkable, with the speeding up of the relative decline of the industrial sector, the rise of the services economy, and the growing ubiquitousness of information and communications technologies (ICT) such as computers, software, satellite communications, e-mail and the Internet in the wider society. This twin sectoral development and structural change, combining ICT and services, is labelled the 'new economy' and considered integral to a 'knowledge-based, information society'. There is increasing recognition that knowledge-based economic activities are key to international competitiveness and productivity growth, and that industrialisation, particularly manufacturing, is no longer viewed as the principal driver of economic growth. This poses a fundamental question: what are the implications of the new economy for developing countries?

This volume takes a broad look at the new economy both theoretically and empirically to understand the development possibilities and the attendant challenges associated with ICT. As services comprise a significant sector in the new economy, the book begins with some conceptual issues pertaining to the measurement and performance of services. Andersen and Corley (Chapter 2) argue that the 'productivity paradox' associated with ICT exists not because of a lack of productivity growth but rather due to flaws associated with the measurement of total factor

1

productivity (TFP). As services are intertwined with new technologies such as telecommunications and the Internet, they are not only difficult to measure but they require new global rules of engagement because of their network characteristics. Consequently, whether developing countries can work effectively with the changing global regime, how they might utilise the open access to knowledge and information, and how they can adopt best practices (such as telemedicine, distance learning and e-government) are significant questions for development (Cogburn: Chapter 3).

Developing countries are structurally disadvantaged in seeking the best from the global regime of ICT infrastructure, which, *inter alia*, is related to their lack of key ingredients such as human capital, physical infrastructure, and lack of venture capital to exploit ICT (Kenny: Chapter 4; Chudnovsky and López: Chapter 7). But that does not mean the doors are completely shut. Poor countries such as the Philippines, which have unwittingly created human capital, are better placed to interact with the global economy, adapt imported ideas and know-how and localize them (Saloma-Akpedonu: Chapter 10).

The empirical studies in the volume show that the impact and potential of ICT for development are at best mixed and there is considerable variation within and among countries. Small domestic markets limit the adoption of ICT and thus productivity growth. This can be seen in the case of several transition economies of Central and Eastern Europe (Piatkowski: Chapter 5) and Argentina, which has made limited progress in leveraging the domestic market for software service exports (Chudnovsky and López: Chapter 7). Similarly, the Arab region is characterised by a high degree of uneven adoption and diffusion of ICT due to income differences and low levels of human capital development (Nour: Chapter 8).

The transition economies also display wide variation in ICT diffusion, mainly due to weak economic and institutional environments. This suggests that the old (non-ICT) economy and the traditional development concerns are equally important to secure the benefits of the new economy (Piatkowski: Chapter 5). Previously emphasised development needs, such as infrastructure investments and domestic market stimulation, are still relevant. However, the selective adoption of ICT in the developing world introduces a new set of contradictions. For example, while ICT in the form of automation suggests not only increasing competitiveness of small and medium-size enterprises (SMEs) due to productivity growth (Bhavani: Chapter 9), it also results in labour displacement, especially of the unskilled (Nour: Chapter 8). At the same

time, productivity-led opportunities thrown open by economic integration suggest that the vast rural poor and illiterate populations may miss out on the benefits of ICT if appropriate social policies are not aimed at improving the quality of their lives (Kaushik: Chapter 6).

It is important to underscore that both *production* of ICT goods and services and their *local consumption* are critical to securing the full benefits of the new economy (D'Costa 2005a; Parayil 2006). However, most poor countries are not poised to take advantage of ICT hardware manufacturing nor do they necessarily possess a large and strong science and technology base to offer skill-based services. But they can introduce ICT in SMEs and the public sector to improve the quality of service delivery and increase productivity. This is all the more necessary under a WTO-inspired world economy, under which few companies in the future will be immune from global competition. This could very well spur local economic activities, leading to adaptation of technologies and even export competitiveness of higher-value goods and services. That said, there is also the danger that ICT will display urban, English-speaking, middle-class and gender biases (Arun and Arun 2002; Meng and Li 2002; Wong 2002; D'Costa 2003a).

1.2 The new economy and globalisation

The notion of the new economy itself is contested. What exactly is new and how it differs from the 'old' economy are weighty questions. Some view the new economy as simply an intensifying form of capitalist exploitation where workers are subject to 'flexible' work demands and a 'race to the bottom' in terms of wage pressures brought about by the global workings of neo-liberalism, deregulation and privatisation (Harvey 1989: 121–200; Gadfrey 2003). Others, based on the US and OECD experiences, disproportionately play up the qualitatively new features of contemporary capitalism, where services, with their weightless character, become the economic engine and ICT is perceived to be critical for productivity growth (Alcaly 2003; OECD 2003). The sources of growth vary but arise from increasing returns to scale and network externalities (OECD 2000: 17).

While the conceptual understanding and measurement of the service sector remain problematic, services themselves have qualitatively changed. Previously, most services were classified as non-tradable, that is, the service was consumed at the point of production. Thus international trade in services remained low. Also, most services were embedded in the production process; hence they were included in the value of

manufacturing. Today, however, services are becoming increasingly tradable, thereby not only making cross-border multinational activity in services a reality but also facilitating their outsourcing to third parties. With innovations in ICT it is now possible to conduct global outsourcing or 'offshoring' of services in commerce, engineering, accounting, management, law, finance, insurance, health, advertising, entertainment, retail and logistics areas (UNCTAD 2004). Consequently, export opportunities have arisen for developing countries with a good supply of technical and professional talent such as India, the Philippines and China.

As markets become more open, the new economic spaces are hotly contested, with low-wage countries competing in labour-intensive manufacturing, while workers in affluent societies, particularly in older industries, face retrenchment (Castells 2002). In rich countries, where social and political responses have been weak, the new economy is characterised by anti-union, anti-statist and anti-welfare developments (Gadfrey 2003). However, workers in rich countries can still resort to some forms of state-supported income transfers while their economies adjust to the new economy by specialising in high-technology manufacturing and high-value services. Both extensive and intensive deployment of ICT in business and in society at large, such as the access to, and use of, the Internet and convergence technologies, in general facilitates renewed productivity growth in rich countries (Cohen *et al.* 2004: 11–29). Both new and old sectors such as ICT, biotechnology, automobile production and education benefit, albeit selectively, from the deployment of ICT.

The new economy notwithstanding, developing countries must still contend with traditional development problems such as poverty and inequality as well as structural transformation from agriculture to industry (Cypher and Dietz 2004). These countries continue to be plagued by low levels of economic development and low living standards (Castells 2000; Hoogvelt 2001). Increasing export competition in labour-intensive manufactures means declining terms of trade and a reduction in social protections due to endemic fiscal crisis. Whatever job growth exists is accompanied by the ever-expanding informal sector in urban self-employment or low-value services, open unemployment due to privatisation of the state sector and, paradoxically, by productivity-enhancing new technologies. China, and to some extent India, known for recent robust growth and massive expansion in the production and consumption of ICT goods and services, is also faced with rising unemployment and regional inequality (Meng and Li 2002: 277; D'Costa 2003a). The

continued emphasis on investment in old development spheres such as education, literacy, basic health and physical infrastructure is necessary (D'Costa 2003a; Gadfrey 2003).

Furthermore, the evidence of productivity growth based on ICT diffusion is not robust, certainly not for developing countries (Heeks 2002). For example, the data on adoption of ICT by SMEs in Kenya, Tanzania and India show a negative or weak relationship between adoption and productivity (Chowdhury and Wolf 2006; Bhavani: Chapter 9). Also, there are considerable productivity lags with the diffusion of ICT (Andersen and Corley: Chapter 2). Consequently, it may not seem realistic or attractive for poor countries to participate in the new economy, which rests heavily on a highly skilled and educated workforce, a developed communications infrastructure, high investment in fixed capital and high income (Pohjola 2001; Clarke 2003).

At the same time it would be foolhardy to ignore the benefits of ICT in poor societies. If anything, ICT is an enabling carrier technology, applicable in both new and old economies (OECD 2003: 92). While ICT is not a panacea for poverty, developing countries, if they fail to actively engage in the use and production of ICT goods and services, are likely to be impoverished further and experience a pronounced form of global digital divide (Clarke 2003).

1.3   Participating in the new economy

What then are the areas in which developing countries could conceivably enter to foster the production and consumption of ICT? As outlined in Figure 1.1, telecommunications, information technology (IT) and information content are three broad areas in which developing countries could selectively insert themselves. As the prices for cellular phones decline, wireless rather than ground lines are generally easier and less costly to introduce. Even low-income economies have been witnessing the growth of such services, though teledensity as a whole still remains very low compared to OECD economies (ITU 2005).

In general the production of telecommunications and IT equipment is beyond the manufacturing capability of most developing countries. The limited market size, large investment requirements and manufacturing inexperience in sectors that are subject to short product and innovation cycles are inherent barriers to entry (Piatkowski: Chapter 5; Chudnovsky and López: Chapter 7; Nour: Chapter 8). A handful of East and South East Asian and Latin American countries are manufacturing telecommunications equipment and components. Japan, China, Taiwan, South

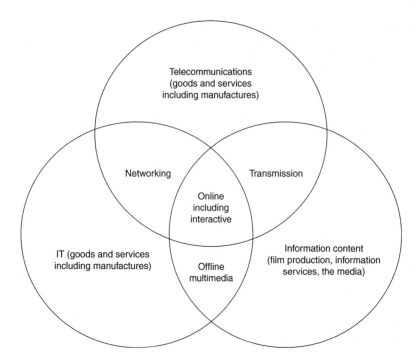

Figure 1.1   Areas of ICT opportunities and challenges
Source: OECD (2005: 99)

Korea and Singapore are key global centres of electronics goods production, while the bulk of software products and services are produced
mostly in the US with Western Europe (including Ireland), Israel and
India among other contributors (D'Costa 2004a). However, this division
between ICT hardware and software production is compounded by the
division between production and consumption. The ability of Japan and
the four East Asian economies to capture a large share of the global electronics market has not necessarily led to a greater adoption of ICT use
there compared to OECD economies (Wong 2002; also Piatkowski:
Chapter 5). This suggests that export success in ICT manufacturing must
be complemented by domestic consumption of ICT goods and services,
or productivity growth, based on network externalities, may not be
realised.

   In the area of IT services, which includes a range of software services,
India, China and the Philippines are becoming important global export
centres. For smaller countries, including some in Africa, opportunities

exist for offering labour-intensive IT-enabled services such as call centres and back office operations. Both India and China are economically expanding, integrating internationally and regionally, becoming efficient, and reducing poverty. Their use of ICT is also increasing, even as the benefits accrue mostly to those with the college degrees, technical skills and middle-class position (D'Costa 2003b). Businesses both large and small are investing in IT in a range of domains such as finance, retail, banking, education, manufacturing industries and design.

Information content is one area in which developing countries could have some control. For example, due to local tastes and culture film production, information services and media (radio, TV, the Internet) could also have a large domestic component. However, the power of the US entertainment industry combined with capital-intensive technologies for transmission and networking are significant barriers to entry. Generally the larger developing countries with a visible industrial experience and relatively strong domestic cultural industries are likely to maintain some autonomy.

From a development perspective, the option of not participating in the new economy does not exist. However, given the experience of global ICT production it is clear that only the larger, industrially stronger countries can manufacture for export markets. These include but are not limited to China, East and South East Asia, and to some extent Brazil and India. Where the supply of technical talent is not a major constraint, wage arbitrage could work in favour of such countries to export ICT-based services. India, the Philippines, Thailand, China, Brazil and Argentina are good candidates. That leaves virtually the entire developing world to figure out how to insert themselves into the new economy favourably. One basic fact should not be forgotten: old economy challenges such as education, literacy, health, inequality and infrastructure still remain and hence must be aggressively pursued.

Poor countries must foster e-development to complement a development strategy to meet basic needs. Based on the extensive and intensive use of ICT, public sector services can be efficiently provided to citizens, different levels of government arms and businesses. The expected benefits are lower transactions costs, efficiencies in delivery of services, transparent governance and productivity growth (Singh 2004).

1.4 New economy policy thrust

Consistent with national industrial policy the production of ICT goods is an option for the larger developing economies. With rising

investment costs in electronics and semiconductor production facilities, and increasingly the commoditisation of much manufacturing, ICT goods production is unattractive for late entrants. Due to small markets most developing countries are unlikely to reap the benefits of network externalities and scale economies at this time. However, the export of ICT-based services is one option for countries with a science and technology skill base. Both small and large countries such as Ireland, Israel, the Philippines, China and India have been successful in this area. Yet heavy reliance on a few export markets could lock the nation's industry into low-end activities and induce a variety of distortions (D'Costa 2004b, 2005a; Joseph 2006). Hence, when it comes to choosing a strategy the challenge is to find a balance between ICT goods and services production, between domestic and export markets, and among export markets.

What all developing countries ought to foster, beyond those who can produce ICT goods and services, is the use of ICT as a tool to provide critical information-based services and thus, over the long haul, productivity growth. Several sectors such as education, industry, government administration and agriculture could come under the ambit of ICT. Computers and the Internet can be used for a wide range of service applications: to obtain and store information, access libraries remotely, send e-mail, order industrial inputs for manufacturing, organise the logistics of complex production, manage inventory, schedule delivery of finished products and provide price, weather and health information to various constituencies. Many developing countries have launched such ICT-based services, even in rural areas (author's field visit, Bangkok 2003;[1] for India, Kaushik: Chapter 6).

The challenges to the implementation of such projects should not be underestimated as it requires resources, long-term commitment, public acceptance and intra-government coordination. For example, in some rural areas in India the deviation of expected from actual benefits from the use of ICT has been largely due to imposition of ICT projects without a good understanding of the intended beneficiaries' needs (Sreekumar 2006). In other rural areas, it has been pointed out that only by removing old obstacles such as unequal landownership, illiteracy and financial duress can ICT act as a potent force in the development process (Thomas 2006). Similarly, in Thailand, the telemedicine programme to provide health-care services to rural areas has faltered due to overspending in satellite communications and failure to anticipate the reluctance of urban doctors to consult with their rural counterparts (interview, Ministry of Health, Bangkok 2003; see note 1).

It is apparent that ICT cannot be seen as a technological fix to what are essentially social and political problems. At the same time, the economics of ICT suggest that developing countries can increase their long-term economy-wide productivity if they do not remain outside the new economy. In the end ICT must diffuse in both old and new production sectors, in manufacturing and agriculture, in education and social sectors, to generate employment and to increase the efficiency of basic services for the public at large.

No doubt the principal barriers to the development of, and access to, ICT-based services are investment and inequality, widely known as the digital divide. Addressing them is consistent with old economy challenges (see Figure 1.2). Furthermore, effective participation in the global economy increasingly points to the importance of creating technological and commercial knowledge through both the endogenous process of human capital development and international technology transfers. Other intrinsic benefits of ICT-led productivity and growth include inducing expatriate technical talent to return home and encouraging others not to leave (D'Costa 2005b; Rai 2005). Much of the investment for public sector services and the necessary ICT infrastructure must

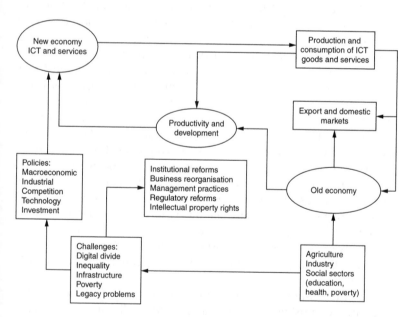

Figure 1.2 New economy development trajectory

Source: Compiled by the author; Clarke (2003)

come from governments. This must be complemented by an enabling environment of business growth and employment through market development, competition policy, intellectual property rights and appropriate equity-based social policies. The role of the government and other institutions cannot be overemphasised, especially in areas of regulatory reform (OECD 2005: 297–313; Piatkowski: Chapter 5).

1.5 Conclusion

The general lessons obtained from the theoretical and empirical materials presented in this volume suggest that structural change towards services is significant for both OECD and select non-OECD countries, many such services rely heavily on ICT, and increasingly they are becoming tradable. This calls for better measurement techniques and suggests that developing countries ought to promote the more value-adding ICT-based services, especially for the rural and urban poor. This in turn suggests the continued emphasis on knowledge workers, information literacy and communications infrastructure vital to participating effectively in the new economy. At the same time, developing countries must find a political voice at the global level so that they are not excluded from the multilateral negotiations on the emerging global information society. At the very least, such participation could create the space for a global consensus on the modes of governance of the new economy and poor countries' involvement (Cogburn: Chapter 3) and in a limited way generate a sense of national identity (Saloma-Akpedenu: Chapter 10).

However, too much emphasis on the new economy could be misplaced. After all, past radical technological developments such as the railways, telephone and television have not fundamentally transformed the economic structures of developing economies. Far from convergence, the 50 years of development experience and the more recent diffusion of ICT demonstrate the uneven character of global and regional outcomes even as some countries in some narrow sectors have closed the technology gaps. Also, at the industry level, the Indian experience suggests that the mere adoption of ICT does not produce international competitiveness. Rather the transformation of business and management practices and work reorganisation are complementary to ICT adoption.

Since the all-important new economy coexists with a vast old economy comprising both agriculture and traditional industries it is imperative to continue to address old economy problems but address them with new economy approaches. Thus fostering knowledge workers

and establishing communications infrastructure is consistent, though in conflict resource allocation-wise, with basic education and human capital development and with infrastructure spending on rural roads and irrigation. Also consistent with industrialisation, the production of ICT goods and services, especially those that have significant spillover effects, could be a viable strategy for some of the larger developing economies. Export markets will no doubt be critical for developing countries, but building up competitiveness will call for familiar policies of protection, promotion and performance in various degrees. Both macroeconomic policies sustaining an open economic system and sectoral policies within the framework of a national innovation system will be critical. Thus FDI, technology transfers, local learning efforts, SME development and revamping of education will remain critical in the years to come. The adoption of ICT is likely to compel reorganisation of business, new management practices and increased research and development spending, which are critical for many developing and transition economy firms plagued by legacy problems and global competition. However, the fruits of ICT adoption such as enterprise competitiveness may remain mixed at best.

More importantly, in an age of runaway globalisation, the role of the government is even more salient, especially when it comes to addressing the more fundamental development challenges of literacy, basic education, alleviation of poverty and inequality, health and the rural–urban gap. These are areas where ICT adoption could complement collective efforts in providing a variety of critical services to underserved constituencies. The Indian ICT projects aimed at the rural poor are promising. By being a major consumer of ICT goods and services, the state could begin to address the legacies of the old economy such as inefficiency, lack of transparency and lack of accountability. In the process it could nurture the backbone of an information society, create the conditions for growth and in a virtuous way induce more organisations to adopt ICT. And the ensuing 'good' governance will indubitably strengthen democracy.

Note

1 Field research was conducted in the greater Bangkok area with several ICT-implementing public sector agencies during August–September 2003. These included Ministries of Health and Education, Customs and Revenue Departments, Election Office for voter registration smart card as well as Thailand's National Electronics and Computer Technology Centre (NECTEC) and the public sector software technology park.

References

Alcaly, R. (2003) *The New Economy*, New York: Farrar, Strausand and Giroux.

Arun, S. and T. Arun (2002) 'ICTs, Gender and Development: Women in Software Production in Kerala', *Journal of International Development*, 14 (1): 39–50.

Castells, M. (2000) *End of Millennium*, Oxford: Blackwell Publishers.

Castells, M. (2002) *The Rise of the Network Society*, Oxford: Blackwell Publishers.

Chowdhury, S. and S. Wolf (2006) 'Investments in ICT-capital and Economic Performance of Small and Medium Scale Enterprises in East Africa', *Journal of International Development*, 18 (4).

Clarke, M. (2003) 'e-Development? Development and the New Economy', Policy Brief 7, Helsinki: UNU-WIDER.

Cohen, D., P. Garibaldi and S. Scarpetta (eds) (2004) *The ICT Revolution: Productivity Differences and the Digital Divide*, Oxford: Oxford University Press.

Cypher, J. M. and J. L. Dietz (2004) *The Process of Economic Development*, 2nd edn, London: Routledge.

D'Costa, A. P. (2003a) 'Uneven and Combined Development: Understanding India's Software Exports', *World Development*, 13 (1): 211–26.

D'Costa, A. P. (2003b) 'Catching Up and Falling Behind: Inequality, IT, and the Asian Diaspora', in K. C. Ho *et al.* (eds) *Asia Encounters the Internet*, London: Routledge, pp. 44–66.

D'Costa, A. P. (2004a) 'The Indian Software Industry in the Global Division of Labour', in A. P. D'Costa and E. Sridharan (eds) *India in the Global Software Industry: Innovation, Firm Strategies and Development*, Basingstoke: Palgrave Macmillan, pp. 1–26.

D'Costa, A. P. (2004b) 'Export Growth and Path-Dependence: the Locking-in of Innovations in the Software Industry', in A. P. D'Costa and E. Sridharan (eds) *India in the Global Software Industry: Innovation, Firm Strategies and Development*, Basingstoke: Palgrave Macmillan, pp. 51–82.

D'Costa, A. P. (2005a) 'Exports, University-Linkages, and Innovation Challenges in Bangalore, India', paper presented for Universities as Drivers of Urban Economies in Asia project, 17–18 November, Washington, DC: World Bank.

D'Costa, A. P. (2005b) 'The International Mobility of Technical Talent: Trends and Development Implications', paper presented for International Mobility of Technical Talent and Development Impact project, 26–27 May, Santiago: ECLAC.

Gadfrey, J. (2003) *New Economy, New Myth*, London: Routledge.

Harvey, D. (1989) *The Condition of Postmodernity, an Enquiry into the Origins of Cultural Change*, Oxford: Basil Blackwell.

Heeks, R. (2002) 'i-Development Not e-Development: Special Issue on ICTs and Development', *Journal of International Development*, 14 (1): 1–11.

Hoogvelt, A. (2001) *Globalization and the Postcolonial World: the New Political Economy of Development*, 2nd edn, Baltimore, Md: Johns Hopkins University Press.

ITU (2005) International Telecommunications Union: http://www.itu.int/ITU-D/ict/statistics/at_glance/basic04.pdf, accessed 28 December 2005.

Joseph, K. J. (2006) 'The Perils of Excessive Export Orientation', in G. Parayil (ed.) *Political Economy and Information Capitalism in India: Digital Divide, Development and Equity*, Basingstoke: Palgrave Macmillan, pp. 88–108.

Meng, Q. and M. Li (2002) 'New Economy and ICT Development in China', *Information Economics and Policy*, 14 (2): 275–95.

OECD (2000) *A New Economy? The Changing Role of Innovation and Information Technology in Growth*, Paris: OECD.

OECD (2003) *ICT and Economic Growth: Evidence from OECD Countries, Industries and Firms*, Paris: OECD.

OECD (2005) *OECD Communications Outlook: Information and Communications Technologies*, Paris: OECD.

Parayil, G. (2006) 'Introduction: Information Capitalism', in G. Parayil (ed.) *Political Economy and Information Capitalism in India: Digital Divide, Development and Equity*, Basingstoke: Palgrave Macmillan, pp. 1–10.

Pohjola, M. (2001) 'Information Technology and Economic Growth: Introduction and Conclusions', in M. Pohjola (ed.) *Information Technology, Productivity, and Economic Growth: International Evidence and Implications for Economic Development*, Oxford: Oxford University Press for UNU-WIDER, pp. 1–30.

Rai, S. (2005) 'For Indian Diaspora, No Place Like Home', *International Herald Tribune*, http://www.iht.com/articles/2005/12/25/business/brain.php, accessed 5 January 2006.

Singh, N. (2004) 'Information Technology and India's Economic Development', in K. Basu (ed.) *India's Emerging Economy: Performance and Prospects in the 1990s and Beyond*, Delhi: Oxford University Press, pp. 223–61.

Sreekumar, T. T. (2006) 'ICTs for the Rural Poor: Civil Society and Cyber-Libertarian Developmentalism in India', in G. Parayil (ed.) *Political Economy and Information Capitalism in India: Digital Divide, Development and Equity*, Basingstoke: Palgrave Macmillan, pp. 61–87.

Thomas, J. J. (2006) 'Informational Development in Rural Areas: Some Evidence from Andhra Pradesh and Kerala', in G. Parayil (ed.) *Political Economy and Information Capitalism in India: Digital Divide, Development and Equity*, Basingstoke: Palgrave Macmillan, pp. 109–32.

UNCTAD (2004) *World Investment Report: the Shift Toward Services*, New York: UNCTAD.

Wong, P-K. (2002) 'ICT Production and Diffusion in Asia: Digital Dividends or Digital Divide', *Information Economics and Policy*, 14 (2): 167–87.

2
Theoretical and Conceptual Foundations of Total Factor Productivity Measurement in Services: Looking Back and Ahead

Birgitte Andersen and Marva E. Corley

2.1 Introduction

For a few decades services productivity was widely discussed but little understood. This was mainly initiated by the productivity slowdown in the US from the 1970s to well into the 1990s. The essence of the debate was that the economy in general was experiencing a development and diffusion of a new technological revolution or techno-economic paradigm that was not being reflected in standard performance indicators, such as productivity. This was puzzling, particularly since the *new* key factor in creating and widening investment opportunities for productivity gains was information and communications technology (ICT) and microelectronics. At this time, ICT and microelectronics were (i) rapidly increasing supply and available in unlimited supply over longer periods, (ii) readily available in low and rapidly falling relative cost, and (iii) widely expanding their scope and pervasiveness in the sense that there was a clear potential for the use (or incorporation of) the new set of inputs throughout the economic system. Such factors had during previous technological revolutions in new key factors input for the economic system, spurred a jump in productivity levels and sometimes productivity growth rates. Previous technological revolutions include for example (i) the early mechanisation period (1770–1840) with mechanisation as key factor input, (ii) the steam power and railway period (1830–90) with steam-powered transport as key factor input, (iii) the

electrical and heavy engineering period (1880–1940) with steel as key factor input, and the Fordist mass production period (1940–90) with oil as key factor input for wide applications (Freeman and Perez 1988). However, regarding the information and communication technology (ICT) period (from about 1990), with microelectronics as key factor input, we did not experience the jump in productivity levels or productivity growth rates, as expected.

Furthermore, there is a tendency for firms to concentrate in those branches where the key factor is produced and most intensively used (Freeman and Perez 1988). The main carrier branches, acting as engines of this current technological revolution, are the computer and software industry and knowledge-intensive service sector branches. Although visible in the *computer producing* branches, productivity gains were not apparent in the *computer using* branches. Thus, one of the most alarming facets about the arrival of the new economy was that those industries that used new technology the most were determined as having the lowest levels of measured productivity. For example, Bosworth and Triplett (2000) researched America's total factor productivity by industry between the period 1989–99 and showed that banking, health care and business services had negative productivity growth rates, and that retail, communication, transport and insurance, although positive, had productivity growth rates that were significantly lower than those of mining, manufacturing and public utilities. Those results were found despite the fact that the service sectors' *information technology (IT) intensity* (measured as spending on IT as per cent of output) was higher than, or equal to, that of the mining, manufacturing sectors and public utilities. The situation of the inadequate services was subsequently termed 'the productivity paradox'.

This paradox provided further foundation for the arguments already put forward by Solow (1987) on computers and the productivity paradox, and Baumol (1967) on the urban crisis of the service sector, that the service sector may not be as productive as we think. However, this view has subsequently been contested, as history has shown that it just took technological change a longer time in the service sector to have an impact on productivity than in other sectors (such as manufacturing).

Currently, we see that many of the service industries are in fact leading developed economies in terms of productivity gains and that ICT has impacted on productivity in practically all sectors of the economy. David (1990) led the view that the lag in the productivity gains from the most recent technological revolution in electronic computing was due to learning and adjustment. Brynjolfssen (1993) and Triplett (1999)

agreed with this view, but also took a broader perspective moving beyond the focus on the technological revolution, arguing that there is a fundamental methodological problem in our key tools when measuring the performance of the service sector and that measurement difficulties in the service sector may account for the lion's share of the gap between our expectations of technology impact and its apparent performance.

Why is it important to focus attention on productivity in the service sector? One obvious reason is the large and growing share of service sector activities in most economies. The service sector accounts for about three-quarters of output in many of the industrialised countries, and has been steadily increasing over the years (see Table 2.1). The developing countries are already showing the same development trajectory. However, our ability to identify and measure the constituency of service industries from the statistical standpoint is lagging behind the growth of this sector. And because services represent an overwhelming chunk of output, any errors in output measurements impact greatly on the national accounts figures in the form of official measures of GDP. Thus, mismeasurement of the service sector has implications not only for productivity measurement of services, and the sectors using services as input, but for the economy as a whole. The situation is further exacerbated by the emergence of e-commerce and e-business, global networks, intellectual capital such as knowledge (as opposed to physical capital), where our current productivity measurement tools are inadequate to account for the new ways in which services are being produced and delivered. The various sections of this chapter will look into those particular problems and others.

In particular, this chapter critically reviews the theoretical and empirical form, function and impact of the service sector in the

Table 2.1   Service sector share in the economy (% of GDP)

	Services share (% of GDP)	
Income level	*1980*	*2004*
Low-income countries (≤ $735)	38	52
Lower middle-income countries ($736–$2935)	39	51
Upper middle-income countries ($2936–$9075)	48	64
High-income countries (≥ $9076)	58	71*

Note: $ = US$; * 2001 value.

Source: World Bank (2005).

economy. The principal objective of the chapter is to provide an in-depth, systematic and thought-provoking overview of the theoretical and conceptual foundations and difficulties of total factor productivity measurements in services. The technological revolution in ICT and microelectronics challenge to such measurements will also be discussed within the framework of total factor productivity (TFP) measurement. In this context, the inadequacy of the existing mainstream thinking and analytical frameworks dominating the theoretical and conceptual literature on productivity measurements in the service economy is highlighted.

Section 2.2 discusses the conventional meaning of the TFP measure and examines the historical development of economic statistics for service sectors. Section 2.3 critically reviews the productivity output measures, and section 2.4 reviews the input measures, focusing on the special characteristics and measurement problems of the service economy. Section 2.5 concludes.

2.2 The conventional meaning of the productivity measure

In this section we explore the conventional meaning of multi- and partial productivity measures. We will also introduce the historical development of such measures and discuss industry classification schemes in this context. We will emphasise the challenges that ICT raises to the usefulness and applicability of such measures and schemes.

2.2.1 The elements of the productivity measure

Measures of productivity are used to gauge the efficiency of the production process by relating output to inputs used in production. The most commonly used measures are labour productivity (LP) and total (or multi) factor productivity (TFP). LP is a measure of the efficiency of workers and is defined as output produced per unit of labour. LP is, however, a partial productivity measure, and it takes into consideration only one of the factors used in production. This is not a criticism, as partial measures of productivity can be useful. However, such partial measures do not fully answer the question of how productivity actually increased in the first place. For example, increased LP could be attributable to improved worker training and education (increased human capital), increased investment in machinery (capital deepening), increased usage of ICT, or improved materials used in production (increased intermediates).

Thus, partial productivity measures can be deceptive by providing only a 'snapshot' view of the productivity of the production process.

TFP takes into consideration all factors of production: capital (K), labour (L), energy (E), materials (M), and service intermediates (S) and reflects the efficiency of the entire production process. In simplest terminology, TFP is the increase in output (Y) that cannot be attributed to increases in all the factors of production.

Partial productivity (e.g. labour productivity): LP = Y/L
Total factor productivity: TFP = $Y/(K+L+E+M+S)$

TFP growth is commonly measured using the 'growth accounting framework', which can be attributed to Solow (1957). The growth accounting framework assumes that any changes in output that cannot be attributed to changes in the factors of production are the result of productivity growth, that is:

$$\Delta\text{TFP} = \Delta Y - (\Delta K + \Delta L + \Delta E + \Delta M + \Delta S)$$

where Δ denotes percentage change. Applying such a dynamic perspective to productivity, we can illustrate alternative cases applying the growth accounting framework; see Table 2.2. For example, we can have a case where LP has increased, but TFP has decreased (Case 3), or a case in which LP has increased, but there is no change in TFP (Case 2), or a case in which both LP and TFP increase (Cases 1 and 4).

The above example illustrates that as long as output is growing faster than the resources of production, productivity will continue to grow. Accordingly, an increase in both measures of productivity (TFP and LP) will occur if with the same resources employed firms are able to produce a larger output, or if we sustain the same output with less resources employed. From the equations above, one can see that because TFP takes into consideration more factors of production than LP, TFP growth is generally less than LP.

Table 2.2   Alternative cases of the growth accounting framework (%)

	ΔY	ΔL	ΔK	$\Delta I (E + M + S)$: Intermediates	ΔLP	ΔTFP
Case 1	20	10	8	0	10	2
Case 2	0	−5	5	0	5	0
Case 3	−5	−10	5	−5	5	−5
Case 4	20	5	5	4	15	6

Both TFP and LP can be measured at all levels of the economy, that is, firm, industry or the country level. However, the more disaggregate the level the more difficult measurement becomes mainly due to data availability.

2.2.2 Productivity and economic performance

Macroeconomists and policymakers have a strong interest in productivity growth because theory tells us that gains in productivity will lead to increased standards of living, and keep inflation at bay. Benefits start at the firm level where increased productivity lowers the cost of production for the firm enabling it to produce more output with the same or less labour. This of course increases profits for the firm, which can be passed along to workers and consumers in the form of higher wages and lower prices. Thus, as productivity increases, the costs of goods can be kept down and due to the stability of prices inflation remains low. Also, the increase in wages contributes to greater consumption and worker welfare. Furthermore, as firm profit increases there is more money available to invest in new resources such as computers, machinery and equipment and to hire more labour. This can create a virtuous circle of increased growth, increased production, investment, wages and increased employment, which encourages more spending on the part of consumers and leads to an expanding economy. Thus, it is no coincidence that those economies with the strongest growth in productivity also have strong performance in other social and economic indicators. For example, since the 1980s those regions of the world where LP growth has been the most impressive (e.g. East Asia) have seen the most gains in employment as well as in poverty reduction. While those regions where productivity has been in decline, namely in sub-Saharan Africa and Latin America, are the regions of the world where poverty and employment have been the most entrenched (ILO 2004).

2.2.3 Services productivity: the heritages from the past

The *Physiocrats* introduced the concept of 'productive' and 'unproductive' or 'sterile' labour in which the agricultural sector was regarded as the only sector capable of producing a surplus over replacement costs and therefore the only real source of wealth creation. The farmers, therefore, formed the 'productive class', as opposed to (i) the 'sterile' unproductive manufacturing class (whose role was regarded as manipulation and not creation of wealth) and (ii) the class of landlords, or distribute class whose economic role was to consume the surplus created by the productive class and to begin, by the expenditure of the rents, the circulation process of

money and goods among the economic sectors (see e.g. Quesnay's *Tableau Économique* from 1758, or for an overview, see Screpanti and Zagmagni 1995: 44–8).

Adam Smith, in his *Wealth of Nations* (1776), and Karl Marx, in *Das Kapital* (1867), adopted the *physiocratic* concept of productive and unproductive labour (although Adam Smith rejected the view that manufacturing, trade and transportation were sterile occupations). In their framework the service sector was also implicitly viewed as being immaterial and unproductive. Their argument was that the sector cannot create wealth to the nations by adding value to materials (as in the case of agriculture and manufacturing). Furthermore, they asserted that services output is non-durable, as the value of services cannot be recaptured by sale due to instantaneous consumption (i.e. the service production process cannot be separated from consumption). Another feature of this assumed simultaneously production–consumption process is that services are assumed to have a fixed division of labour and therefore not very knowledge intensive.

In the context of present time it should be noted that the physiocrats', including Adam Smith's and Karl Marx's, notion of services is generally based upon what we today determine as 'consumer services' or 'personal services', although financial and insurance services were already increasingly important at the time Adam Smith wrote. This understanding of the role and impact of services in the production system has impacted on the way conventional economists today theorise, conceptualise and measure services' role in the economic system. It is quite plausible that such views may be one of the reasons for the persistently negative or otherwise ignorant view of the service sector throughout the eighteenth century, and even into the twentieth century (see for example Baumol 1967).

2.2.4 Services: a distinct activity

Classification schemes are important, because they present what governments formally recognise as being a distinct and productive activity in the economic system. Consequently, all economic analysis is based upon such schemes. For example, the input–output measurements underpinning productivity statistics (in terms of output sector (Y) and intermediate input (I)) are derived using those classification schemes. Standardised schemes are also important, as analysis made using those schemes can show development trends over time, and allow for comparative studies across industries and countries. Finally, industrial policy is based upon such schemes.

The first specific attempt to define services as a distinct activity was characterised by Fisher (1933, 1935, 1939) and Clark (1940). They

subdivided the economy into three categories: primary (agriculture, fishing), secondary (mining and manufacturing) and the residual tertiary (immaterial service) sector. The basis of Fisher and Clark's approach was to describe distinctive features of each of the three sectors (e.g. distribution of workforce, income elasticity and structure of consumer demand, technological progress and economic development). This is basically still how the aggregate service sector is regarded today in mainstream economics and national accounts (i.e. as everything that is not agriculture or manufacturing).

Empirical studies in the economic literature and most statistical accounts in industrialised countries have broken down what Fisher and Clark termed the tertiary or service sector into general structures. For example, the International Standard Industrial Classification (ISIC), which is used by OECD and Eurostat, is categorised in Table 2.3.

Classification schemes differ by country and can change over time due to new frontier possibilities in services. These changes hamper a direct comparison of service activities across countries and time. For example, Japan's Ministry of Finance in the early 1980s revised their service classifications due to the microprocessor revolution. This was especially in relation to taking in new tertiary industries associated with software, information, business services, culture and sport (Clairmonte and Cavanagh 1984).

Differences in opinion have arisen among academics in relation to (i) which industries to include as sectors, (ii) defining the boundaries between the three sectors in the Fisher–Clark model, and (iii) defining the boundaries between several of the subsectors (Clairmonte and Cavanagh 1984; Petit 1986). Stigler (1956) asserted that there exists no authoritative consensus on either the boundaries or classification of services.

Table 2.3 ISIC for services

Classifications	
ISIC G	Wholesale and retail trades
ISIC H	Hotels and restaurants
ISIC I	Transport, storage and communications
ISIC J	Financial intermediation
ISIC K	Real estate, renting and business services
ISIC L	Public administration and defence
ISIC M	Education
ISIC N	Health and social work
ISIC O	Community, social and personal services

In addition enterprises are classified only according to their 'primary product'. For example, an enterprise that has an output that spans across several classification codes will only be grouped into one category. Consequently, instead of classifying services activities into the 'producers' of such, some academics instead classify services activities into 'users' of the services products (Petit 1986; Walker 1985). This has led to somewhat broader schemes, as specified in Table 2.4.

Classification schemes may provide some analytical convenience in pursuing product groups, markets or users. However, a major problem is that these types of classification schemes ignore the growing complexity of service activities in the economy as a whole, particularly the impact that ICT has had on the new organisation of services activities in our economy. For example, one can no longer treat services and non-services (i.e. manufacturing) as independent creators of output and productivity, as knowledge-based business service activities have become increasingly outsourced due to the integration of network-based ICT systems (see section 2.4.3.1). What seems to be relevant when considering intermediate input from some sectors into others, and vice versa, is their mutual interdependence in establishing activity and performance for both manufacturing and services. Furthermore, one must question to what extent *any* service product boundaries are meaningful today. Most large multinational enterprises have corporate structures which transcend the sectoral model of Fisher–Clark, not to mention the great extent to which they even transcend subsectors across as well as within services and manufacturing (Clairmote and Cavanagh 1984). Such new corporate structures have especially emerged due to the impact of ICT and microelectronics.

Table 2.4 Service markers or 'users'

Classifications

Producer services or business services: finance, insurance, real estate and other business services (e.g. research and development, advertising) for intermediate demand

Consumer services or personal services: e.g. hotels and restaurants, miscellaneous repair and maintenance services, motion pictures, amusement, recreation, private households, personal care for final consumption

Collective services: e.g. health, education, non-profit organisations

Government: public administration, military

Distributive services: e.g. transport, communication, utilities, wholesale

Retail: shops

2.3 Output (*Y*) measurements in services

In most economies the system of national accounts operates with a 'volume' measure of output (*Y*), where volume is defined as the price (*P*) multiplied by the quantity of the good (*Q*). Whereas volume in manufacturing is based on more quantifiable 'goods or materials produced' in services it is measured as number of service 'transactions undertaken':

Manufacturing $(Y) = Q_{produced} *(P)$
Services $(Y) = Q_{transacted} *(P)$

2.3.1 Deconstructing services output and realising heterogeneity

The argument from the Adam Smithian and Karl Marxian heritage is that due to its intangibility service output can only be considered as a transaction. This argument is based on the view that (i) a service does not involve or result in some change of state in materials, and (ii) the service delivery is indistinguishable from the consumption of the service itself. That is, all services are defined as instantly consumed and non-durable in nature. These views have become embedded in the way mainstream economics and many associated statistics today conceptualise services (see section 2.2.3).

Hill (1977) proposed an alternative concept of services, defining it as 'a change in the condition of a person, or of a good belonging to some economic entity, brought about as the result of the activity of some other economic activity, with the approval of the first person or economic entity'. Along these lines, we have introduced an even broader definition of services as objects (material or immaterial/tangible or intangible) that experience transformations (permanent or not permanent/durable or non-durable) within certain transformation spheres (see Table 2.5).

As an illustration of Table 2.5 it becomes clear that the service sector is very heterogeneous, and does not necessarily follow the mainstream

Table 2.5 Services production deconstructed*

Objects	Nature of transformation	Transformation sphere
Artefacts	**Physical**	Time
Actors	Biological	Space
Nature	Social	**Instantaneously**
Symbolic material	Abstract	

* Mainstream view is in bold.

characteristics of services:

- First, there are many different *objects of services*. They can be cat-egorised into 'artefacts' (food, waste, goods such as cars), 'actors' (firms, people, animals), 'nature' (water, air, energy), 'symbolic material' (information, ownership rights, performing art).
- Second, there are many different *natures of the transformation*. They can be 'physical' (haircut), 'biological' (waste disposal), 'social' (change in social relations such as ownership rights (retail)) as well as 'abstract' (education).
- Finally, the service *transformation sphere* can be 'over time' (storage services in general), 'across space' (transport and logistic services) and 'instantly' (i.e. services production and consumption cannot be separated over time or across space such as haircutting, live enter-tainment, food consumption in a restaurant).

Furthermore, there are many different routes in which services objects experience transformations within certain spheres:

- For example, broadcasting services may constitute a musical compo-sition on a compact disc (object = symbolic material and artefact), which through satellites or cables (transformation = physical) are broadcast (transformation sphere = space). However, if we consider a live concert performance instead, the object of the service may be both the musical composition and the performing artists (object = symbolic material and actors), and the transformation may be ways in which the artists deliver the musical composition (transformation = abstract), and finally, the service transformation (i.e. delivery) and consumption cannot be separated in time and space (transformation sphere = instantly).

Another complexity is that a service may typically involve a mixture of service object entities (e.g. a business service may involve a mixture of actors and symbolic material); a mixture of types of transformations (e.g. cooking and gene therapy involve both physical and biological transformations); and a mixture of transformation spheres (e.g. space and time in air transport as well as storage services).

A general point we wish to make here is that services output involves a broader and more complex spectrum of objects, types of transforma-tion, and spheres, than has been addressed in the mainstream literature. The ways in which mainstream literature and conventional statistics

have dealt with services with respect to these issues are highlighted in bold in Table 2.5. This, in turn, has created an imperfect picture of the way services have been conceptualised and ultimately measured in the economy, i.e. (i) by recognising only measures which can be quantified, (ii) by requiring a physical transformation in order to add value to physical materials while treating all services as intangible by nature and (iii) by treating services as non-durable, recognising only those services with instantaneous transformation spheres in which service delivery and service consumption cannot be separated.

2.3.2 Defining services units and implications for measurements

2.3.2.1 Services units and role of customer involvement

Quite often, the units of service transactions are not clearly definable in measurable terms as in manufacturing where the physical state of output can be more clearly measured in tangible elements of production. This is especially due to the intangible nature of some (though not all, see subsection above) services.

This intangibility makes it difficult to quantify and sometimes even *identify* an industry's output in terms of transactions, often because it is not always clear what the output of the industry constitutes. For example, if one considers the output of a bank, it must be clear what service the bank actually provides. Is its primary service the provision of customer accounts, loans, or providing an optimal portfolio? Depending on which way the primary service is viewed will determine a different mix of outputs and inputs (Sherwood 1994).

Sherwood brings out another difficulty in determining a service, that is, the role of customer involvement. As mentioned earlier, 'goods'-producing industries manufacture an output, which is then sold to the market. Even if no one purchases the product, the industry has still generated an output, which can be stored in inventory. But in the case of a service the role of the consumer is assumed to be implicit in determining the output. One example Sherwood uses is the case of a teacher who teaches to an empty classroom; in this extreme case there is no output because there was no consumer involvement. This is distinct from measurement of output in manufacturing in that even if no one buys the good, the value of production is still counted. Thus, by definition, not allowing for service delivery and consumption to be separated can underestimate the output of a service industry (and ultimately productivity) in comparison to manufacturing.

2.3.2.2   *Aggregation of heterogeneous units*

The heterogeneity of services occurs due to the personalised aspects of business and consumer services. This is particularly a problem when measuring volume, which is based on aggregation of (assumed homogeneous) transactions. It is subsequently a problem when calculating productivity, which ultimately is based upon an assumption of homogeneity of services. In this regard, productivity measures are less accurate for industries with a high degree of heterogeneity and must be viewed in sharp contrast to manufacturing where output is generally identical due to mass production.

A further complexity involves aggregating services that are already a part of a service package, that is, 'bundled services'. For example in the banking industry, a current account may provide a package of services such as online banking, the use of ATM and bankcards, and the safekeeping of funds. In the output measurement of bundled services each component of the service must be separated out, properly priced and then reaggregated. This of course is a difficult process, since a particular service may not be individually priced in the overall price of the total 'bundled service'.

2.3.3   Managing price (*P*) levels and quality of services

In order to compare the output of any good or service across industries over time the price component of output must be removed (i.e. the relative prices are held constant). This is usually done by deflating a nominal output measure (such as nominal GDP, sales, revenue) with a price index (e.g. PPI). However, price indices are often not available for many of the intangible services. Additionally, as mentioned above, when services are bundled (which is the case for most services), each individual service must be priced separately. Such detailed statistical coverage to manage price levels perfectly (or even satisfactorily) would be unrealistic for most services.

In addition, quality changes are often not reflected in the change in the price index (e.g. the price of online computer services has declined steadily over the years, while the quality has increased). This price/quality distortion has led to the concept of *hedonic pricing*. Basically, this is a statistical technique that is used to derive the relationship between a product's price and its characteristics. It is used to adjust the price index so that it takes into consideration the variation in quality over time. Triplett (1996) provides us with this example of a hedonic function for semiconductors:

$$P_s = h_s(s)$$

The function takes into consideration the specific characteristics of semiconductors where P_s is the vector of prices for semiconductors with different capabilities that are defined by the vector of characteristics quantities, s. To calculate such a function one must be able to count the quantities of the characteristics produced and consumed, as well as price the characteristics. In practice this would amount to determining the quantity of characteristics as well as their prices, which is a difficult process indeed.

Hedonic pricing is more widely used in some countries than others (e.g. the US) to deflate output in industries where rapid technological changes have occurred in branches, such as computer technology, health services and telecommunications. For example, within health services one could even expect services transactions in health to decline due to more accurate surgery as a result of the ICT revolution and use of electronics. This would lead to a decreased productivity level if we do not use hedonic pricing.

In general, hedonic pricing is of particular importance for services as the revolution in ICT and electronics has led to considerable service quality increases over the years in the branches that are heavy users of such technology. Thus, when estimating productivity for these industries hedonic pricing provides one with a more realistic picture of output changes, which in turn becomes reflected in higher productivity figures. An effect of using hedonic pricing is also to raise the average rate of productivity growth for a country.

2.3.4　E-business and the transaction multiplier effect

The problems regarding the 'transaction' perspective for measuring output and productivity in the services literature has become aggravated with the emergence of electronic business (popularly termed e-business). However, the measurement issues regarding e-business-based sectors have been taken seriously by some national governments. The UK National Statistics has set up a new division called the 'New Economy Measurement Department' that specifically focuses on issues regarding measuring e-business. They are in particular concerned with the 'micro-aspects' of measuring e-business performance, as they believe that this is the key to understanding the dynamics and value added of the new sector. In the US (see for example Mesenbourg 2000), e-business performance has so far been measured in terms of the services notion 'transactions undertaken'.

As many knowledge-intensive business services are mainly processing and managing information (rather than producing tangible output),

such activities have seen a great scope for integrating e-business into their core business operations. It has even been identified that e-business output (measured as 'transactions undertaken') and e-business labour are growing faster than traditional manufacturing (Cisco Systems and University of Texas 2001). In this respect, there is of course a great overlap in activities between e-business (which is a process – that is, way of doing business) and the service sectors. Hence, the growth of services also reflects the implications of ICT and the growth of e-business processes, and vice versa. Therefore, just as measuring output and productivity in the services literature has become aggravated with the emergence of e-business, there is also much to learn from this literature in order to understand the role and scope (e.g. value added, growth, productivity and overall performance) of e-business to the economy as a whole.

An additional complication to using the transaction notion for measuring e-business is that e-business can include 'multiple e-business transactions', even if it is done via the 'one click' system. For example, the purchase of a book online via for example, amazon.com, includes the following transactions: (i) purchase of the book; the firm separates transactions with third parties to obtain fulfilment of services, which includes: (ii) acquiring the book, (iii) securing credit confirmation service, (iv) providing payment processing service, (v) arranging for delivery, and many more. The complexity is that such online network integrated transactions involve many parties and some play multiple roles.

Mesenbourg (2000) argues that in the future any business-to-consumer transactions will involve a much larger number of related business-to-business transactions. Although this transaction multiplier effect is not unique to e-business, it is expected to increase with e-business. Today we have e-business transactions between 'brick' firms, 'click' firms and 'brick and click' firms. The measurement challenge here is to account for the increased volumes in transactions, to identify the business players and their roles and their respective industries and to avoid double counting the value of related transactions. While comprehensive measures of e-business may be useful to profile all of these transactions, such detailed business statistics coverage would be unprecedented if not unrealistic.

2.4   Input measurements in services

In this section the specific components of productivity inputs are discussed: labour, capital and intermediates.

2.4.1 Labour force (*L*) measurements in services

The measure of labour used in the estimation of productivity is generally quantified in terms of either total hours worked (*H*) of all employed (*E*), if one wants to measure output (*Y*) per hour worked; or total number of employed persons (*E*), if one wants to measure output per person employed:

Output per hour worked (*LPH*) = *Y* / (*E* * *H*)
Output per employed (*LPE*) = *Y* / *E*

This methodology for valuing labour in productivity measurement is not adequate to capture the particular characteristics of labour in the service sector; therefore productivity indicators for services are often miscalculated.

2.4.1.1   *The impact of the ICT revolution on patterns of work*

The ICT revolution in digital technology has increased opportunities for new such ways of working, particularly in knowledge-intensive business services (KIBS), which account for about one-third of the workforce. It is well known that many service employees are working more hours than are documented in the official numbers. It can be argued that actual 'hours worked' should include work performed after hours – work at home, work during travel as well as usage of cell phone for working activity – all of which are activities directly associated with work. However, none of the measures are taken into consideration in the estimates of hours worked. The omission of these additional working hours could overestimate productivity growth measures in the new knowledge-based service economy (by underestimating the hours worked input). This is to be seen in sharp contrast to the previous mass-production techno-economic paradigm, where the bulk of workers toiled along the assembly line. They were totally off work when they left the factory, in the sense there was a clear distinction between work and leisure.

2.4.1.2   *Measuring human capital*

In addition to the problem of accounting properly for the hours worked, the quality (knowledge embedded) in the workforce is also an important factor that is generally not recorded in productivity measures. The heterogeneous nature of the hours worked may indeed make a huge difference to the quantity and/or quality of the output. For example, if one were to measure the hours worked of employees at a law firm should the hours worked of someone straight out of law school be counted as the same as a more experienced attorney? At which point do the skills of workers begin to diminish? Is this impact different across industries and sectors?

From an empirical viewpoint, Jorgenson *et al.* (1987), Jorgenson and Fraumeni (1989) and Rosenblum *et al.* (1990) have all done pivotal work in the area of taking into consideration the human capital component of labour in productivity measures. From a conceptual and theoretical point of view, many institutional and evolutionary economists, starting with Thorstein Veblen, have criticised how human capital in the mainstream production function (and hence in productivity measures) is treated as a 'tangible' asset, and always embedded in each person separately. They suggest, along with Veblen (1919) and Polanyi (1962), how the amount of human capital must be measured as 'intangible' or 'immaterial'. In this context, productive human capital can be embedded in (i) each individual and (ii) in organisational routines, as follows.

(i) Embedded in the individual.   Both the explicit and tacit knowledge embedded in human capital add to the productivity of the workforce, and this is especially relevant for the services industries. Consider for example workers in the health-care sector, and the financial and business service sectors that rely on tacit knowledge to improve the service provided. In contrast, within some manufacturing industries, the knowledge tends to be more embodied in machines rather than the workers along a resample line. In this context, hours worked may be more suitable for manufacturing productivity, whereas the measure is inappropriate to use within services where the quality of the workforce is more determinant of efficiency of output.

(ii) Embedded in organisational routines.   Evolutionary economists (Winter 1975; Nelson 1991a,b; Lundvall 1988, 1992), building upon the resource-based theories (Penrose 1959), argue that the collective aspect of tacit knowledge is perhaps the most important as this is embedded in the organisational routines within the firm. In this sense, the firm as a team is 'more' than the sum of its parts. Applying such a holistic interpretation to the labour productivity measure indeed has serious implications for management and policy, where hiring or laying-off workers may not always be the solution to making the firm more efficient or productive.

2.4.2   Capital (*K*) measurements in services

The capital quantity measure used in the calculation of productivity is generally quantified in terms of net capital stocks. Net capital stocks can be derived from flows of net investment based on various methodologies. The perpetual inventory method is the most widely used:

Capital quantity $(K) = i + (1-\delta)K,$

where i is net investment and δ is the rate of depreciation.

Valuing the capital stock for productivity measures using the perpetual inventory method has its limitations and is not necessarily the best measure to use when capturing the capital stock input in the service economy, particularly if one considers the compositional changes in investment that have taken place in recent decades. In addition the meaning of the capital measure itself has been subject to dispute. This section argues that some of the most important non-physical factors of production are not included in the capital index.

2.4.2.1 The intellectual capital (IC) discourse

The *intellectual capital* discourse criticising the way capital is measured has dominated the debate from the 1980s to the present. With the impact of the ICT revolution on the service economy, it is evident that there have been some relative changes in the configuration of the asset bases of firms. Whereas the relative and absolute importance of intellectual capital (IC) has increased, the relative importance of physical capital (K) has decreased. Non-physical corporate assets are a particular feature of the new knowledge-based service economy, and the emergence of e-business. However, even asset bases of manufacturing firms are dematerialising into value-driven IC and intangible assets (Andersen *et al.* 2000). In the knowledge-based ICT-driven service economy this type of intellectual capital can play a more important role as a factor of production and in productivity measures, than conventional physical capital, such as bricks and mortar.

2.4.2.2 Organising institutions and social technologies

As discussed in section 2.4.1.2, the productivity index actually reflects a holistic measure of how well all the physical factors of production (capital K, labour L, energy E, materials M, services input S) are organised. This implies that we can never measure the efficiency of any of those factors of production in total isolation, as the efficiency of one factor of production depends on its relationship with the other factors. Evolutionary economists (building upon Rosenberg 1976, 1982) refer to the mistreatment of the firm as a 'black box' or merely a production function within mainstream economics. Their basic argument is that the efficiency of production cannot merely be valued from the most efficient (in terms of price and quantity) combination of the factors of production, where the specificities of technology and the social distribution of labour are given. Rather, corporate value creation, and hence productivity, is generated from the technological capabilities and social

modes of coordination, embedded in those factors of production, both of which take time, effort and resources to build.

Nelson and Sampat (2001) assert that organising institutions for value generation should not only be built upon a theory of 'physical technologies', but should also recognise business practices as important routines. Thus, we need a theory of the firm and a division of labour plus a 'mode of coordination', and it is the latter that Nelson and Sampat describe as 'social technologies'. Whereas the advance in physical technologies is often listed as the key driving force for the productivity increase within firms, 'social technologies' are crucial when changes in the modes of interaction and coordination are called for and as new technologies are brought into productive use.

For example, investment and advances in ICT create an important physical technology calling for new 'social technologies'. Although ICT is embedded in hardware, the efficiency of its interplay with organisational structures is of key importance. Appropriating from the way ICT is integrated in business practices is one of the most essential aspects of the efficiency of value generation and competition within many knowledge-intensive business services.

However, productivity may also be determined outside the unit from which it is measured. In this context social capital is crucial to the productivity debate. Social capital includes the productive assets embedded in 'networks' (Bourdieu 1983) and 'social communities' (Putnam 2000; Dasgupta and Serageldin 2000).

Both social and organisation capital are areas that the productivity measurement does not take into account. Productive efficiency is indeed embedded in social relations and this should also be reflected in the interpretation and reporting of the productivity statistics and in relation to associate input–output relationships underpinning such statistics. This is indeed crucial for management and policy for productivity enhancement.

2.4.3   The impact of services intermediates (I)

The intermediate (I) volume measure used in the calculation of productivity growth is generally quantified in terms of quantity of all intermediates used in production (Q_i = energy (E), materials (M) and services (S)) times the price (P) as specified below:

Intermediate volume (I) = $Q_i * P$

Materials and energy normally play a more significant role in manufacturing, which relies on raw materials and heavy energy

consumption for production, than in the service sector. However, as we discuss below, the technological revolution in ICT has provided an increasingly important role for services, as a knowledge-based specialised intermediate input for much of the manufacturing sector, and indeed also for many service industries.

2.4.3.1 The impact of the specialised knowledge base in services intermediates (I)

As services are assumed to be instantly produced (i.e. simultaneously with the consumption process) they are also assumed as having a fixed division of labour and not being very knowledge intensive (see section 2.2.3). However, the development of ICT hardware and software has transformed many services to become divisions of specialised knowledge, many of which have in turn been outsourced from manufacturing creating new service industries (Andersen *et al.* 2000). Such outsourced specialised knowledge sectors in particular involve KIBS including finance, accountancy, law, insurance and other business services. It also includes communications, transport (logistics), industrial or high-scale cleaning and many administrative tasks.

When services become knowledge intensive this poses considerable problems for the identification and measurement of advancements and quality increase in such specialised knowledge. Since many knowledge indicators are based upon science and technological (S&T) knowledge or developed through research and development (R&D), the question of appreciating other forms of knowledge types as an alternative to the traditional measurements arises. The basic problem is that the types of knowledge that might be important for some, and perhaps even most, service objects and service transformation processes are very different from manufacturing. Such knowledge bases include:

1. Aesthetic knowledge, that is, knowledge and appreciation of craft-related services;
2. Know-how, that is, practical knowledge regarding how to do certain tasks;
3. Cultural knowledge, that is, knowledge and appreciation of institutionalised cultural aspects of services, which is also intertwined with market awareness and appreciation of the dynamics and interests of subcultures and associated practices as well as intertwined with knowledge about symbolic material;
4. Social, organisational and strategic management knowledge, that is, knowledge about organisational dynamics in a changing world, including knowledge about administrative structures and procedures;

5. Information-based knowledge, that is, knowledge associated with services whose key competence is knowing and handling a lot of information material, such as for example institutional and legal knowledge.

However, S&T knowledge is of course important for some services. This includes knowledge about problems that may be presented by technological change concerning service production, service delivery and service consumption, as well as technical ways of capturing returns from services. This also includes knowledge in how to apply new science and technology to those aspects of services, as well as knowledge concerning future possibilities for such applications.

It is a major problem that we have not found more adequate ways of accounting for measuring the knowledge base of sectors within non-science-based fields, because otherwise we may miss many of the most central aspects of the human resources and dynamic capabilities in the new service economy. The increased outsourcing of the services knowledge base from manufacturing may also be a reflection on how the opportunities and requirements of the services knowledge base have become higher-skilled and increasingly specialised knowledge, a type of knowledge which is very different from that of manufacturing.

Drawing upon input–output tables, Tomlinson (2000) points out the great extent to which services today function as input into both manufacturing as well as other services activities. The increased contracting out of services in recent history in improving efficiency is also now well recognised by policymaking organizations (ILO 2004; European Foundation for the Improvements of Living and Working Conditions in collaboration with Huws *et al.* 2004). However, the impact those changes have on the productivity measures is not reflected accurately in the statistics.

Productivity measures are 'macro measurements' where it is difficult to determine where productivity gains arise – do they come from input industries or output industries? Conventionally, or in the mainstream view, productivity measures are always interpreted as coming from the output firm or industry. For example, when the relative increase in the quality of intermediate services inputs is not reflected in their calculated input measure, but instead shows up in the output sector, as productivity increase in the manufacturing or other sectors using the cheaper and better services inputs. In this context, Griliches (1992) argued that measuring GDP by industry and hence productivity correctly requires at the minimum a set of input–output tables in order to understand where the productivity increase originated.

2.4.3.2 *Services productivity impact on global systems producing goods and services*

Services impact on, and their role in, global systems of production is also a highly topical issue in the productivity debate. Basically, services role in global production systems challenges the argument that services are inherently unproductive because they cannot add value to materials, are inherently fixed in labour productivity/specialisation, and their transformation sphere cannot be separated over time and space (see sections 2.2.3 and 2.3.1). Services productivity is not only about efficiency in terms of adding value to materials, but also the efficiency in facilitating, creating or adding value to intangibles such as networks and global systems supporting production of goods and services. Furthermore, the integration of ICT within services has opened up the role of services in the social division of labour within and across firms and industries in global production systems.

For example, services have historically been regarded as non-tradable internationally, in the sense that services themselves cannot move (only labour which provides the service can move). However, services have more recently become non-localised and a part of traded products, partly due to heavy usage of ICT integrated within strategic information systems and e-business. This includes business as well as cultural, educational and entertainment services that have become more 'internationalised' due to the way ICT has altered the way that such services are created, delivered (e.g. broadcasting) and consumed.

Also, there are many types of services that do not enter international trade. In such cases, multinational enterprises (MNEs) have, in particular, been the preferred route for organising cross-border activities involving services (Dunning 1989). It is especially the rise in real income and technological advances in telecommunication, which have increased the demand and encouraged the international supply of services. MNEs relative to other firms have been well placed to benefit from these developments (Dunning 1989), particularly those services where (i) international transaction costs (either by consumer or provider) are in practice too high or (ii) local bound services which require simultaneous service production and consumption (e.g. car hire chains, chain hotel and other tourist facilities). Also, there are intermediate services, which are widely transferred with MNEs such as FIRE and other business services. A point made by Clairmonte and Cavanagh (1984) is that, whereas economies of scale generally can be realised in manufacturing industry by the production of a large number of standardised units in one location, in services economies of scale

are achieved by organising individual units (e.g. into chains) and managing them through centralised or decentralised (or both) networks, such as those of MNEs.

Overall, services (and especially the role of ICT in services) as well as the rise in real income (economic wealth) have provided global networks for most service sectors of the economy, including service trade and services production and consumption. Basically, the role of services in the social division of labour within and across firms and industries is essential for understanding how services enhance productivity, not only for themselves, but also for other sectors.

2.5   Conclusion

The derivation of productivity indicators is only as good as the indicators used in their estimation, and this chapter has illustrated that most productivity measures are imperfect measures. It is the services productivity measurements that are in a crisis – not the service sector as such. One way of making the general point is that, what is uniquely challenging about the new service economy lies in the difficulty of defining unambiguous measures of intangibles and microeconomic relationships. Some go so far as to link this to a new economic paradigm, which has been named the 'post-industrial society', the 'fifth Kondratieff', the 'weightless economy', the 'network economy', the 'knowledge economy' or the 'service economy'.

The elements of the TFP productivity measures (K, L, E, M, S) are difficult in and of themselves to measure in manufacturing industries, but when doing so in the service industries, it becomes that much more problematical. The emergence of the technological revolution in ICT and microelectronics – which have changed the way services are produced and delivered, changed the organisation of service activities in the economy, and changed the structure of the human and intellectual capital underpinning service activities – has brought with it further difficulties in measurement. Even with the recent improvements in the measurements of the variables of the TFP index, there is still much work that needs to be done before we are able to take into account the changes and current characteristics caused by this latest technological revolution.

An important aspect of this chapter has also been to highlight the inadequacy of the existing mainstream thinking and analytical frameworks dominating the theoretical and conceptual literature on productivity measurements in the service economy. This is relevant

because the conventional approach has dominated the textbook view on productivity measurement as well as policymaking throughout the world economy. Our traditional productivity measurements are inherently flawed – mainly due to the way service industries are perceived, that is, they are not treated as very important value creators. The main reason for this is that services are assumed immaterial and intangible by nature, as not being able to add value to materials and services production is not distinguished from services consumption. Thus as services are assumed instantly consumed (i.e. simultaneously with the production process) they are treated as non-durables. As they are also assumed to be instantly produced (i.e. simultaneously with the consumption process) they are also assumed as having a fixed division of labour and not being very knowledge intensive. Other problems arise when associated mainstream analytical methods measure services input and output and related performance indicators using the same conceptual framework and indicators as those that are applied for problem solving for agriculture and manufacturing.

Such entanglements in the way we theorise and conceptualise have other and wider consequences for understanding the empirical impact of the service sector on the new economy and for designing appropriate policy and management. This is not just a data collection and analytical problem, but also a political issue; for example, this discussion raises the question of governments not being able to design policies based on illusive statistics.

Understanding productivity measurements is important in order not only to achieve economic growth and sustainable development, but also to provide 'a higher quality of life for communities worldwide'. This latter point must be the greatest aim of productivity research and calls for a new way of thinking about productivity goals in the framework of a new economy.

Note

All opinions expressed in this chapter rest solely with the authors and do not constitute endorsement by the International Labour Office or any other institution.

References

Andersen, B., J. Howells, R. Hull, I. Miles and J. Roberts (2000) *Knowledge and Innovation in the New Service Economy*, Cheltenham: Edward Elgar.
Baumol, W. J. (1967) 'Macroeconomics of Unbalanced Growth: the Anatomy of Urban Crisis', *The American Economic Review*, 3: 415–26.

Bosworth, B. and J. Triplett (2000) 'Numbers Matter', Policy Brief, Brookings Institution, July.

Bourdieu, P. (1983) 'The Form of Capital', in J. G. Richardson, *Handbook of Theory and Research for the Sociology of Education*, Westport, Conn.: Greenwood Press.

Brynjolfssen, E. (1993) 'The Productivity Paradox of Information Technology: Review and Assessment', *Communications of the ACM*, December.

Cisco Systems and University of Texas (2001) *Measuring the Internet Economy*, www.internetindicators.com

Clairmonte, F. F. and J. H. Cavanagh (1984) 'Transnational Corporations and Services: the Final Frontier', *Trade and Development: an UNCTAD Review*, 5: 215–73.

Clark, C. (1940) *The Conditions of Economic Progress*, London: Macmillan.

Dasgupta, P. and I. Serageldin (2000) *Social Capital: a Multifaceted Perspective*, Washington, DC: World Bank.

David, P. (1990) 'The Computer and the Dynamo: an Historical Perspective on the Modern Productivity Paradox', *The American Economic Review*, 80 (2): 355–61.

Dunning, J. H. (1989) 'Multinational Enterprises and the Growth of Services: Some Conceptual and Theoretical Issues', *Service Industries Journal*, 9 (1): 5–39.

European Foundation for the Improvements of Living and Working Conditions in collaboration with U. Huws, S. Dahlmann and J. Flecker (2004) *Outsourcing of ICT and Related Services in the EU. A Status Report*, Luxembourg: Office for Official Publications of the European Communities.

Fisher, A. G. B. (1933) 'Capital and the Growth of Knowledge', *Economic Journal*, September.

Fisher, A. G. B. (1935) *The Clash of Progress and Security*, London.

Fisher, A. G. B. (1939) 'Production, Primary, Secondary and Tertiary', *The Economic Record*, June: 24–38.

Freeman, C. and C. Perez (1988) 'Structural Crises of Adjustment: Business Cycles and Investment Behaviour', in G. Dosi *et al.* (eds) *Technical Change and Economic Theory*, London: Pinter Publishers: pp. 38–66.

Griliches, Z. (1992) *Output Measurement in the Service Sector*, Chicago and London: The University of Chicago Press.

Hill, T. B. (1977) 'On Goods and Services', *Review of Income and Wealth*, 23 (4): 315–38.

ILO (2004) *World Employment Report 2004–05*, Geneva: ILO.

Jorgenson, D. and B. Fraumeni (1989) 'The Accumulation of Human and Nonhuman Capital, 1948–1984', in R. E. Lipsey and H. S. Tice (eds) *The Measurement of Saving, Investment, and Wealth*, Chicago: University of Chicago Press: pp. 227–82.

Jorgenson, D., F. Gollop and B. Fraumeni (1987) *Productivity and U.S. Economic Growth*, Cambridge, Mass.: Harvard University Press: pp. 211–60.

Lundvall, B-Å. (1988) 'Innovation as an Interactive Process – from User–Producer Interaction to the National System of Innovation', in G. Dosi *et al.* (eds) *Technical Change and Economic Theory*, London: Pinter Publishers.

Lundvall, B-Å. (ed.) (1992) *National Systems of Innovation: Towards a Theory of Innovation and Interactive Learning*, London: Pinter Publishers.

Marx, K. (1867 [1906]) *Das Kapital* (edited by F. Engles), *Capital: a Critique of Political Economy*, Vol. I. *The Process of Capitalist Production*, translated by

S. Moore and E. Aveling from the 3rd German edn, Chicago: Charles H. Kerr and Co.

Mesenbourg, T. L. (2000) *Measuring Electronic Business Definitions, Underlying Concepts, and Measurement Plans*, Assistant Director for Economic Programs, Bureau of the Census: http://www.ecommerce.gov/ecomnews/e-def.html

Nelson, R. R. (1991a) 'Why do Firms Differ, and How Does It Matter?' *Strategic Management Journal*, 12: 61–74.

Nelson, R. R. (1991b) 'The Role of Firm Differences in an Evolutionary Theory of Technical Advance', *Science and Public Policy*, 18 (6): 347–52.

Nelson, R. R. and B. N. Sampat (2001) 'Making Sense of Institutions as a Factor Shaping Economic Performance', *Journal of Economic Behavior and Organization*, 44 (1): 31–54.

Penrose, E. T. (1959) *The Theory of the Growth of the Firm*, Oxford: Blackwell.

Petit, P. (1986) 'Services: Problem or Solution', *Slow Growth and the Service Economy*, 1–18.

Polanyi, M. (1962) *Personal Knowledge*, London: Routledge.

Putnam, R. (2000) *Bowling Along: the Collapse and Revival of American Community*, New York: Simon and Schuster.

Quesnay (1758) *Tableau économique* (Economic Table). [This book provided the foundations of the ideas of the Physiocrats.]

Rosenberg, N. (1976) *Perspectives on Technology*, Cambridge: Cambridge University Press.

Rosenberg, N. (1982) *Inside the Black Box: Technology and Economics*, New York: Cambridge University Press.

Rosenblum, L., E. Dean, M. Jablonski and K. Kunze (1990) 'Measuring Components of Labor Composition Change', presented at the annual meeting of American Economic Association, December.

Screpanti, E. and S. Zagmagni (1995) *An Outline of the History of Economic Thought*, Oxford: Clarendon Press.

Sherwood, M. K. (1994) 'Difficulties in the Measurement of Services', *Monthly Labor Review*, March: 11–19.

Smith, A. (1776 [1937]) *An Inquiry into the Nature and Causes of the Wealth of Nations*, New York: Modern Library.

Solow, R. (1957) 'Technical Change and the Aggregate Production Function', *Review of Economics and Statistics*, 39 (3): 313–30.

Solow, R. (1987) 'We'd Better Watch Out', *New York Times* Book Review, 12 July: 26.

Stigler, G. J. (1956) *Trends in Employment in Service Industries*, Baltimore: Princeton University Press.

Tomlinson, M. (2000) 'The Contribution of Knowledge Intensive Business Services to the Manufacturing Industry', in B. Andersen *et al. Knowledge and Innovation in the New Service Economy*, Cheltenham: Edward Elgar: pp. 36–48.

Triplett, J. (1996) 'High-tech Industry Productivity and Hedonic Price Indices', in OECD Proceedings, *Industry Productivity: International Comparison and Measurement Issues*, Paris: OECD.

Triplett, J. (1999) 'The Solow Productivity Paradox: What do Computers do to Productivity?' *Canadian Journal of Economics*, 32: 309–34.

Veblen, T. B. (1919) *The Place of Science in Modern Civilisation and Other Essays*, New York: Huebsch; reprinted 1990 with a new introduction by W. J. Samuels, New Brunswick: Transaction Publishers.

Walker, R. A. (1985) 'Is There a Service Economy? The Changing Capitalist Division of Labour', *Science and Society*, XLIX (1): 42–83.

Winter, S. (1975) 'Optimization and Evolution in the Theory of the Firm', in R. H. Day and T. Groves (eds) *Adaptive Economic Models*, New York: Academic Press.

World Bank (2005) *World Development Indicators*, Washington, DC: World Bank.

3
Emergent Regime Formation for the Information Society and the Impact on Africa

Derrick L. Cogburn

3.1 Introduction

International relations is a complicated, interdisciplinary field, encompassing issues as diverse as why states go to war to how the balance of payments is sorted out in international telecommunications. One of the more enduring questions in international relations is the question of global governance and under what conditions can cooperation occur in a world system comprised of sovereign and equal nation states. For more than three decades, this question, sometimes called the 'anarchy problematique', focuses on the evolution of cooperation at national, regional and global levels (see, *inter alia*, Krasner 1983; Keohane 1984; Axelrod 1985; Keohane and Nye 1989). International regime theory has been one of the most resilient mental models for addressing this problem, and has been formulated from a wide variety of epistemological and scholarly traditions.

In a special issue of the journal *International Organization* (1982) Stephen Krasner and his colleagues attempted to forge a consensus definition of an international regime. Krasner suggested that if the expectations of actors involved in a given area of international relations could converge around 'sets of implicit or explicit principles, norms, rules, and decision-making procedures', then an international regime might be emerging. For Krasner, and most international relations experts steeped in the realist tradition, the key 'actors' in international relations are states. So from this perspective, if states can begin to agree on the fundamental principles and values supporting a particular issue area in international relations, that convergence could lay the foundation for global governance. While many

scholars disagreed with the international regime theory approach, some even within the same special issue (*International Organization* 1982, Strange: 479–96), this classic definition created an environment for significant scholarly work in the area of global governance.

Using this theoretical lens, scholars from around the world have documented the emergence and efficacy of international regimes in a broad spectrum of international relations phenomena, including: (1) international shipping; (2) international air transport; (3) international post; (4) international atomic energy and weapons; (5) international environmental issues; (6) the global 'commons' (e.g. the high seas and outer space); and (7) even for commodities (e.g. diamonds). In 1990, Peter Cowhey (1990) documented one of the oldest and most successful of these institutional arrangements, the International Telecommunications Regime (ITR).

Based on the International Telecommunication Union (ITU) and an epistemic community that supported the concepts of the preferred natural monopoly for telecommunications, and the 'clubby' and 'cartelised' relationships between ministries and officials of monopoly post, telegraph and telephone entities (PTTs), ITU officials (many of whom are former PTT officials) and a limited number of upstream suppliers to the PTT in the national capitals, the ITR was highly successful (Cowhey 1990; Freiden 1996).

However, in the mid 1990s, the ITR began facing tremendous internal and external shocks. From the growing dot.com boom and the importance of global electronic commerce, to the institutional pressures emerging from the WTO for rapid and widespread privatisation and liberalisation of telecommunications through the Agreement on Basic Telecommunications (ABT), the 'convergence of expectations of actors' diverged significantly. The Internet became increasingly important, and new policy actors came increasingly onto the stage. Non-governmental and civil society organisations joined governments and the private sector as key players around which any new regime needed to coalesce. In 1998, driven largely by the demands for global electronic commerce, the US government privatised the primary functions of Internet governance, by creating the private, non-for-profit corporation called the Internet Corporation for Assigned Names and Numbers (ICANN). ICANN was established to privatise and internationalise the process of managing the more important scarce resources of the Internet, and was explicitly multi-stakeholder and non-governmental (governments, with the exception of the US, participate only through the Government Advisory Council – GAC, whose decisions are non-binding on ICANN).

3.2 The problem

With these pressures for continued multi-stakeholder participation in the global governance of the Internet, telecommunications and information and communication policy more broadly, the old ITR is being eroded and a new regime to govern the global information society is slowly coming into being. However, there is significant contestation around the fundamental norms, principles, values, decision-making procedures and enforcement mechanisms of the newly emerging regime. Will the new regime focus on open access to knowledge and information and the sharing of best practices in a wide variety of information society applications (e.g. telemedicine, distance learning, e-government); or will it focus more narrowly in the requirements for global electronic commerce, coupled with perceived national security needs? The primary location for these ongoing contestations are the international conferences and meetings convened by a collection of key international organisations, including the ITU, ICANN, WTO, World Intellectual Property Organisation (WIPO) and UNESCO. Most important of these international meetings in recent years has been the UN World Summit on the Information Society (WSIS) organised by the ITU, with the first phase held in Geneva (2003) and the second phase in Tunisia (2005).

3.3 Research questions

What are the emerging 'principles, values and norms', of this new regime, and what stakeholder interests are best represented by them? What will be the rules of this new regime, and how will they be decided upon and enforced? Who wins and who loses from this emerging regime, and how are developing countries and non-governmental organisations responding to the opportunities and challenges of these processes? And, what can be done, if anything, to influence the direction of this regime to ensure the development of a more just and equitable global information society? These are the research questions that this chapter seeks to address.

3.4 Theoretical framework

This chapter draws heavily on the literature exploring international regime theory for its theoretical framework. Regime theory provides a lens through which to understand the institutional role being played by international conferences such as WSIS, which end with the primary

formal accomplishment being the adoption of a *WSIS Declaration of Principles* and a *WSIS Action Plan*.

There are three dominant schools in international regime theory: (1) liberal/neo-liberal; (2) realist/neo-realists and Marxist/neo-Marxist; and what might be called (3) postmodernist. In the liberal/neo-liberal school, there is a focus on the importance of functions. Theorists working in this school focus on the impact that international regimes have in the creation of peace and in reducing transaction costs. These scholars argue that while regime actors have self-interests, they are able to see the possibility of creating a global environment where the majority of good can be created for the majority of actors through cooperation. In this approach, no single actor would get the exact regime that it wants, but that through interdependent cooperation it can achieve enough of its aims, while allowing other actors to achieve a sufficient amount of their aims. This approach is designed to create an international regime based on peace and stability.

If this perspective were correct, we would find an international conference such as WSIS to be actively involving multiple stakeholders and perspectives, and where many different voices could be included in the conference outcomes. We would see a number of actors voicing satisfaction with the process, regardless of their sector and an outcome that reflects some of the key interests of most of the active players in the process.

Those theorists working within the realist/neo-realist and Marxist/neo-Marxist schools tend to focus on the importance of power in the formation and maintenance of international regimes. These global power dynamics can take the form of hegemonic states against weaker ones, or of a global power-wielding corporate elite against the unorganised global working class.

From this perspective, we would expect to see one or a few dominant players getting what they want out of the policy formulation processes. Economically and militarily powerful states, such as the US, either alone or in coalition with powerful corporate actors, will overwhelmingly dominate the process of decision-making, and their principles, values and norms will be most evident in the final conference outcomes.

Finally, there is a school of regime theory that might be considered postmodernist. Theorists working in this tradition focus on the formation of cognitive frameworks and the ability to set global agendas through the use of media and other tools. These scholars see the regime formation dynamics as based on what forces can influence the acceptable forms of problem definition and solution. These forces form the

'epistemic community' for the particular issues in international affairs, and create its 'accepted' belief system.

Through this lens, we would expect to find organised groups of scientists, scholars, research institutes or other transnational networks of experts involved in global policy processes – epistemic communities – working actively within these international conferences to shape how the issues get formed and make it onto the international agenda.

While international regime theory provides a very useful theoretical framework to help us understand this period of rapid transformation, there are some problems with its use. In some cases, those that have used regime theory have approached the state as a unitary actor, and ignored domestic contestation to the regime formation processes. Also, in most cases, there is a very heavy focus on state actors, at national, regional and global levels. This focus ignores the increasingly important role played by non-state actors, at each of these levels, particularly by global NGOs representing the interest of the private sector. Also, there are often insufficient linkages between the processes of global economic restructuring and its influence on domestic actors and political–economic processes. Finally, there is often insufficient attention paid to the factors that affect 'state autonomy', or the ability of the state to exercise de facto sovereignty.

In this study, we have primarily adopted the Krasner (1983) approach to international regimes. This causes us to look at the issues of regime transformation, and the emergence of consensus in four critical areas: (1) principles and values; (2) norms; (3) rules; and (4) enforcement mechanisms. However, in our use of regime theory, we will also have an important focus on the impact of non-state actors in the regime formation process. Also, we plan to explore the expectations generated by each of these contending schools of international regime theory, to assess the relative influence of multi-stakeholder cooperation, power and knowledge on the regime formation processes.

3.5 Methodology and data

The methodology adopted in this study is qualitative in nature and uses a theory-driven case-study approach. After defining our terms, theoretical framework and research questions, all of which are grounded in the extant literature, multiple qualitative data collection techniques were employed, including: (1) participant observation; (2) observer observation; (3) in-depth interviews; and (4) content analysis of primary and secondary sources. Data collection was focused primarily on developing

a thick-narrative case study of the impact of regime transformation on an emerging economy. The case selected for analysis was the Republic of South Africa. South Africa was chosen for a number of reasons, including:

1. In 1996 it implemented a fairly wide-ranging restructuring of its telecommunications sector (see, *inter alia*, Cogburn 1998);
2. It was a founding member of the WTO;
3. It plays a strong political and economic leadership role in the African region, and within the broader developing country context;
4. It participated in, and made an acceptable offer to, the WTO ABT;
5. It has developed a merged telecommunications and broadcasting independent regulatory body;
6. It went through a Green/White Paper process to develop an electronic commerce policy; and finally
7. There has been significant activity from non-state actors in South Africa, at both the national, regional and global levels, including significant South African governmental and non-governmental participation and leadership in the WSIS processes.

3.6   Findings and discussion

3.6.1   The emerging GII/GIS regime and its principles, values and norms

Our theoretical framework would suggest that evidence of an emergent regime would come initially from the development of a global consensus on the principles, values and norms around a particular issue area of international affairs. In this case, we are analysing the data from multiple international conferences focused on information and communication policy to assess the degree to which a consensus is emerging around the principles, values and norms of an information society.

One of the most successful international regimes in history was the ITR (Cowhey 1990). This regime was based primarily on a specialised agency of the UN, the ITU. However, due to various social, political, economic and technological factors, this regime is being eroded and new regimes are emerging, the broadest of which might be called the Global Information Infrastructure/Global Information Society (GII/GIS) regime.

The ideas around the development of a GII/GIS were given global prominence in 1994 when US Vice President Al Gore gave a keynote address on the GII to the First World Telecommunications Development Conference, held in Buenos Aires, Argentina. This event was followed closely by the European Commission's release of its report entitled

Recommendations to the European Council: Europe and the Global Information Society, known more popularly as the Bangeman Report, in reference to the chair of the high-level commission that produced the strategic recommendation. Following these meetings, in February 1995, the European Commission hosted a ministerial meeting of the Group of Seven (G7) on the information society. South African Deputy President Thabo Mbeki was the only significant participation by the developing world, and he urged the G7 leaders to take a more inclusive approach to the GII/GIS. He offered South Africa as host to such an initiative. The resultant initiative, known as the Information Society and Development (ISAD) conference, was held in South Africa in June 1996.

In 1998, ICANN was formed in order to provide a new global, multistakeholder mechanism for Internet governance. Specifically, ICANN's mandate was to establish the effective international allocation and distribution of the primary scarce resources of the Internet, the Internet protocol (IP) addresses and domain names, and to administer a system of registrars for new domain names, and to arbitrate domain name disputes.

Most recently, the UN WSIS, organised by the ITU, attempted to forge a global consensus on the principles and values of an emerging information society, with the first phase of WSIS, held in Geneva (2003), concluding with a globally accepted 'Declaration of Principles and an Action Plan', and the second phase held in Tunisia (2005) concluding with a 'Tunis Agenda and Commitment' that included the creation of a 'Global Alliance for ICT for Development' and a new global, multi-stakeholder 'Internet Governance Forum'.

Out of these various global and regional initiatives, there are a number of issue areas around which primary norms, principles and values are emerging around information and communications policy to promote the GII/GIS. Table 3.1 illustrates the broad spectrum of application areas driving the GII and GIS.

Table 3.1 An applications-driven global information society

General application	Specific examples	Global epistemic support
Education, research and training	Distance education Collaboratories† Asynchronous training	WTDC* G8 Conference ISAD WSIS
Digital libraries	Library of Congress University of Michigan Digital Library	WTDC G8 Conference

Continued

Table 3.1 Continued

General application	Specific examples	Global epistemic support
	Internet Public Library J-Stor	WSIS
Electronic museums and galleries	Louvre	WTDC G8 Conference WSIS
Environment management	GIS applications	WTDC G8 Conference
Emergency management	Environmental Management Services	WTDC G8 Conference
SMMEs, employment creation and e-commerce	PeopLink African crafts market	WTDC G8 Conference ISAD WTO
Maritime information	Early warning systems	WTDC G8 Conference
Electronic government services	E-passports Sharing and reuse of records	WTDC G8 Conference WSIS
Debt management and financial services	Debt management systems Electronic bill payment	WTDC G8 Conference
Tourism	Hotel and package booking Promotion and data mining	WTDC G8 Conference
Health care	Telemedicine Health education and information	WTDC G8 Conference
Legislation and legal services	Parliament information systems Legal database access	WTDC G8 Conference
Transportation of people and goods	Transportation system management	WTDC G8 Conference
Business development and trade efficiency	Trade promotion B-2-B e-commerce	WTDC G8 Conference
Universal access	Community information centres Public Internet Terminals	WTDC G8 Conference ISAD WSIS
National systems of innovation	Collaboratories Geographically distributed research teams	WTDC G8 Conference
Entertainment and leisure	On-line gaming Adult-oriented material	WTDC G8 Conference

*World Telecommunication Development Conference.
†Collaboratories are a new institutional form that emerged out of the US National Science Foundation (NSF) in the mid 1980s. It blends the words 'collaborate' and 'laboratory', to invoke the image of a 'centre without walls'.

This broadly based, applications-driven approach to the GII/GIS holds tremendous hope for the countries of the developing world. They hope to enhance the quality of life of their citizens and to meet these strategic challenges through a range of initiatives such as the African Information Society Initiative (AISI) developed by the United Nations Economic Commission for Africa (ECA). The process of developing a GII/GIS based on this diversity of applications and the movement towards a global knowledge-based economy is unleashing tremendous transformative pressures on the existing international telecommunications regime. The ITR was highly suited for the industrial economy. However, the mechanisms to govern this new economy and a GII/GIS will be qualitatively different. Table 3.2 presents a comparison of some of the key elements of the 'old' ITR and the 'emerging' GII/GIS regime.

However, there is a high level of tension at play in the transition to this new regime. The transition is not easy. A significant degree of contestation is occurring, and being fought primarily over whether or not principles, values and norms of the GII/GIS will represent the broad perspectives articulated by the information society approach or

Table 3.2 Comparison of the international telecommunications regime (ITR) and the global information infrastructure/global information society (GII/GIS) regimes

ITR	GII/GIS regime
Limited competition: natural monopoly for telecommunications	High competition: liberalisation and privatisation for telecommunications
Single issue: telecommunications	Multiple issues: telecommunications, broadcasting, health, education, SMMEs, debt management, etc.
Single ministry: telecommunications, PTT	Multiple ministries: broadcasting, education, health, trade and industry, finance, etc.
Single industry: telecommunications and equipment suppliers	Multiple industries: content providers, ASPs*, ISPs, e-commerce, etc.
Limited stakeholders: telecommunications employees and experts	Multiple stakeholders: nurses, educators, small-business owners, etc.
Epistemic community: narrow	Epistemic community: wide

*Application service provider.

represent those of narrow and somewhat more limited interests of global electronic commerce.

At present, it appears that the latter is occurring. The momentum towards a truly GIS appears to be waning, with the WSIS conference now concluded, and many of the key actors quickly working to return to the *status quo ante* WSIS. Nonetheless, those stakeholders having an interest in the development of global electronic commerce are working to develop a global consensus on the key issues of a new regime that will facilitate the more rapid development and potential of electronic commerce.

Some of these key norms, principles and values include the following:

1. Telecommunications and information infrastructure – the importance of liberalisation, privatisation and a pro-competitive environment;
2. Customs/taxation – that the Internet and e-commerce should continue to be a 'tax free' zone;
3. Electronic payments – that multiple options should continue to emerge (both inside and outside money) that are interoperable and allow for both anonymous, pseudonymous and traceable methods;
4. Commercial code – that a common global commercial code should emerge to provide for the global rule of law and protection for contracts and private property;
5. Intellectual property protection – that IPR regulation needs to be revised to reflect the realities of the digital economy, while still providing an incentive for the production of information goods;
6. Domain names – an important and contested commercial asset, and famous marks should be protected while not allowing them to abuse smaller enterprises, and that ICANN is the legitimate body charged with the responsibility to deal with domain name issues;
7. Personal data – should be protected, while at the same time allowing for legitimate corporate uses of data profiling and targeted advertising;
8. Security and encryption – an important national and personal security concern that has to be balanced with personal privacy concerns;
9. Awareness/trust – a limiting factor for the growth of e-commerce;
10. Trust – might be enhanced with the widespread use of authentication and digital signatures;
11. Technical standards – should be technology neutral and industry driven to the fullest extent possible;

12. Local content – should be promoted and protected, if e-commerce is going to reach its full potential;
13. Labour and society – will be affected by the move towards a digital economy and we should work to minimise the negative impact, while harnessing the potential;
14. Universal service/access – or lack thereof, as characterised by the 'digital divide', is one of the most potentially limiting factors for global e-commerce, and finally
15. Human resources and capacity – require immediate global attention.

3.6.2 Decision-making, rules and enforcement of a new GII/GIS regime

If we now agree that the old regime is being transformed, and a new regime is emerging, complete with its own set of principles, values and norms, a key question surfaces. What are the rules of this newly emerging regime and what international body will enforce these rules?

To answer the second question first, there is little doubt that the centrepiece organisation of a new GII/GIS regime will be the WTO. However, unlike the ITR that was based primarily on a single intergovernmental organisation, the ITU, the emerging regime will rely on a host of governmental and NGOs to enforce its rules. Thus, in addition to the WTO, the ten most important organisations for the 'governance' of this emerging regime will be the following: (1) WIPO; (2) OECD; (3) ICANN; (4) GII Commission/Global Business Dialogue; (5) Group of Eight (G8) industrialised countries; (6) World Economic Forum; (7) World Bank Group; (8) European Commission; (9) ITU; and (10) bilateral aid agencies. Table 3.3 illustrates several aspects of these organisations, including their organisational type and primary function within the regime.

These organisations are working together formally and informally to formulate global information and communications policy, to make decisions, and to formulate rules for the new GII/GIS regime, and seek to enforce them. To illustrate this point, we take the example of South Africa, as it attempts to develop its new e-commerce policy.

3.6.3 South African responses to the emergent GII/GIS regime

As this new GII/GIS regime emerges, who wins and who loses, and how are developing countries, particularly South Africa and others in Africa, responding to its opportunities and challenges?

Global e-commerce is being driven in many ways by the leadership of the private sector. However, there are very important information policy

Table 3.3   GII/GIS regime enforcement organisations

Organisation	Organisation type	Regime component(s)
WTO	Intergovernmental (global)	Principles, values, norms, rules, enforcement
WIPO	Intergovernmental (global)	Principles, values, norms, rules, enforcement
OECD	Intergovernmental (regional)	Principles, values, norms
ICANN	Global non-governmental	Principles, values, norms, rules, enforcement
GIIC/GBD	Global non-governmental	Principles, values, norms
G8	Intergovernmental	Principles, values, norms
WEF	Global non-governmental	Principles, values, norms
World Bank Group	Intergovernmental (global)	Principles, values, norms, rules, enforcement
European Commission	Intergovernmental (regional)	Principles, values, norms
ITU	Intergovernmental (global)	Principles, values, norms
Bilateral aid agencies	Governmental	Principles, values, norms, rules, enforcement

issues that will facilitate its optimal growth, both within South Africa and around the world. This reality presents a fascinating and challenging paradox. While the scope of electronic commerce is clearly global, national regulation continues to provide the legal and regulatory basis for its operation.

The South African government has taken these responsibilities very seriously. As a major response, the Department of Communications (SADoC) has launched an important national Green/White Paper process on electronic commerce that will lead to specific national legislation by the third or fourth quarter of 2001 (SADoC 2000). This legislation is designed to build on the progress already made in restructuring the telecommunications policy, both in 1996 and again in 2001.

The process of developing and conducting these information and communications policies has been highly consultative. The government has tried to include the voices of as many relevant stakeholders as possible (Groenewald and Lehlokoe 1999). This section will briefly examine the policy perspectives that are emerging in South Africa's movement towards an e-commerce regime. Our primary data source for this section is the national Green Paper on Electronic Commerce, the background papers commissioned by SADoC, the papers of the working groups, other published government documents, academic literature and news accounts.

Of significant interest for our analysis is the fact that the Green Paper makes constant reference to the need to harmonise its emerging

national e-commerce regime with the growing global consensus and in line with its extant commitments to the WTO. 'In embarking on a national policy development initiative on e-commerce it is imperative that SA take cognizance of its WTO commitments, firstly, to ensure that such policy is compatible with the relevant WTO rules and regulations, and secondly, to determine the impact of e-commerce on those commitments' (SADoC 2000: 48).

The WTO has worked to review the impact of e-commerce on its structure and planning. At its last ministerial meeting, held in Seattle, Washington, the US and other developed countries wanted to explore the possibilities of a more comprehensive involvement for the WTO in e-commerce issues. 'In the Seattle Ministerial Conference, South Africa, together with the Southern African Development Community (SADC), supported the extension of the moratorium until the next Ministerial Conference when it would be reviewed' (SADoC 2000: 49). The current policy perspective recognises that 'any regulatory regime that South Africa adopts must be consistent and compatible with international frameworks' (SADoC 2000: 18).

General principles on electronic commerce

Consensus on general principles around issues of international import are a key indicator of the emergence of a new regime. In terms of the e-commerce policy formulation process, South Africa's approach is based on eight key principles, which are: (1) quality of life; (2) international benchmarking; (3) consultative process; (4) flexibility; (5) technology neutrality; (6) supporting private-sector-led and technology-based solutions and initiatives; (7) establishing and supporting public–private partnerships, and (8) supporting small, medium and micro-sized enterprises (SMMEs) (SADoC 2000: 18).

In terms of the substantive principles, South Africa believes the following:

1. The recognition that there is a need for legislation to support the national implementation of e-commerce transactions, within a framework of international standards;
2. That commercial transactions should be able to be effected through both paper and electronic means, without creating uncertainty about the latter;
3. Promoting a framework that increases the efficiency of South African commercial transactions, without being overly cumbersome;
4. The framework should be technology neutral;

5. To develop a uniform commercial framework that conforms to international standards;
6. That South Africa should build on the work of others and not reinvent the wheel; and that
7. South Africa should strive to maintain its sovereignty and independence, and meet its strategic national socio-economic development objectives (SADoC 2000).

Telecommunications and information infrastructure

Without increased access to information and communications infrastructure, e-commerce will not be able to meet its full potential (SADoC 2000). Since the restructuring of the telecommunications sector in South Africa in 1996, there have been a number of information infrastructure initiatives in the country (Cogburn 1998). SADoC has been at the forefront of this effort, particularly with its *Info.Com 2025* strategy, public information terminals (PITs), 'Public Key Infrastructure Pilot', and numerous other e-commerce and e-government initiatives. As these infrastructure initiatives unfold, the strategy should be to develop an infrastructure that is capable of handling a wide variety of applications and services. From the South African policy perspective, 'the challenge confronting South Africa is to create an ideal market structure for e-commerce that will stimulate and modernise network development and infrastructure; accelerate universal access; support affordable access; encourage investment and innovation' (SADoC 2000: 82). There is a realisation in the Green Paper that the infrastructure for e-commerce will consist of a range of networks, including 'backbone networks, end-user equipment and access services':

> The success of e-commerce will depend on the available of speedy access infrastructure; high quality of service within the backbone networks; and affordable prices. Access will not only be through fixed networks (terrestrial, wireline and cable TV) but also through wireless networks (cellular, satellite, and digital broadcast spectrum). (SADoC 2000: 83)

Perhaps one of the most important emerging regime principles is the importance of liberalisation, privatisation and a pro-competitive environment for telecommunications and information infrastructure. South Africa is proudly a founding member of the WTO, and has been working actively to promote the multilateral trading system (Manuel 2000).

At the moment, Telkom, the commercialised public telecommunications operator (PTO), has a monopoly on the provision of basic fixed telephony services. While the government chose to adopt this strategic equity partnership (SBC and Telkom Malaysia) for Telkom, the Green Paper recognises that 'Telkom's efforts alone are not sufficient to achieve all of the infrastructure needs for e-commerce [in South Africa]' (SADoC 2000: 85). As such, South Africa submitted an accepted offer in the WTO's ABT, and is now bound by the terms of that agreement to liberalise and privatise its telecommunications sector by 2002 (WTO 1997). However, at present, South Africa has not yet signed the WTO Information Technology Agreement (ITA), which would bring tariffs on a wide range of information and communications technologies down to zero by 2001.

Universal service/access

As stated above, there is a significant recognition that all of the potential benefits of global electronic commerce for South Africa will not be realised without sufficient attention to increased access to information and communications technologies for a wider portion of South African society. Often characterised as the 'digital divide', this disparity of access both within countries and between them is one of the most potentially limiting factors for global e-commerce.

In order to combat the digital divide and try to meet its universal service goals, SADoC has promoted a number of public access initiatives such as the development of multi-purpose community information centres (MPCICs), the Universal Service Agency (USA), and PITs to help South Africa to provide access for larger numbers of its citizens to the benefits and opportunities of global electronic commerce.

Customs/taxation

South Africa recognises that the transition to a digital economy engenders new ways of doing business, and new products and services. Many of these products and services are presenting tremendous challenges to the taxation regimes of governments around the world. 'There is a legitimate concern by certain governments that the development of the Internet may have the effect of shrinking the tax base and hence reducing fiscal revenue' (SADoC 2000: 36). In addition, South Africa recognises that there are significant difficulties in defining jurisdiction in electronic commerce, and to administer and enforce any kind of taxation scheme.

The South African Revenue Service (SARS) believes that the global consensus that is emerging around taxation principles, being led by the

OECD, does not conflict with its views. The important basic principles of this emerging regime are: (1) neutrality; (2) efficiency; (3) certainty and simplicity; and (4) flexibility. Of particular interest, there is apparently no opposition in the South African approach to the idea of 'no need for a special new tax' such as a 'flat rate' or a 'bit' tax, and that the Internet and e-commerce should continue to be a 'tax free' zone (SADoC 2000: 37).

However, South Africa wants to promote the idea of 'indirect taxes', being at the place of consumption. 'Indirect taxes should apply where consumption takes place, and an international consensus should be sought on the identification of the place of consumption. Consensus is important to avoid double taxation or unintentional non-taxation' (SADoC 2000: 40).

There is concern in South Africa that the development of electronic money that is 'unaccounted', and 'network' or 'outside' money, will lead to additional challenges in terms of tax monitoring, collection and enforcement. However, it believes that there is significant cultural conservatism that will limit the impact of these new forms of money. In order to promote compliance, South Africa believes that it should require that certain information should be a part of South African e-commerce:

> The following information should be furnished on any commercial website owned by a South African resident, company, close corporation or trust: trading name of the business; the physical as well as the postal address for the business; and e-mail address; telephone or other contact information and statutory registration number in respect of companies, close corporations and trusts. (SADoC 2000: 44)

The emerging tax perspective recognises that there are additional complications that reduce storage and transmission costs, and that storing information overseas is becoming easier and cheaper. As a result, South Africa believes that there is the need for a 'greater degree of international co-operation in revenue collection than currently exists' (SADoC 2000: 45). It appears that South Africa supports the role of the OECD, as a leader for this aspect of the regime, especially with its model tax conventions.

Electronic payment systems

The emerging policy perspective in South Africa is that multiple options should continue to emerge (both inside and outside money) that are interoperable and could allow for anonymous, pseudonymous and traceable methods. There is particular concern about the 'threat of cybercash'

and the impact of unaccounted money on the South African economy (both in the form of network-based money and stored value cards). Both of these methods have the potential to exchange value without identifying the user and without linking to specific bank accounts (SADoC 2000: 99). South Africa sees this as a 'make-or-break' issue for electronic commerce in South Africa. Another major challenge for South Africa, given its history of racial oppression and segregation, is the ability for the 'unbanked' have access to electronic payment systems.

South Africa has a well-developed financial system, and the South African Reserve Bank (SARB) has taken the lead on these e-payment issues. In 1998, it developed the South African Multiple Option Settlement (SAMOS) system that allows real-time settlement between banks. The SARB has also published a position paper on e-money in April 1999. The SARB is pushing hard for the principle that 'only banks would be allowed to issue electronic money', although there is the recognition that 'the issuance of electronic money may fall outside the definition of [the] business of a bank', as defined in the Banks Act 94 of 1990 (SADoC 2000: 102). The goal is to protect users, who the SARB feels may find themselves 'unprotected', in the event that the issuers of electronic money remain unregulated. The SARB feels strongly that 'primary and intermediary issuers of electronic value will therefore be subject to regulation and supervision by the South African Reserve Bank' (SADoC 2000: 102).

Global commercial code

South Africa recognises that global electronic commerce is posing a challenge to its national legal systems that support commercial transactions. The current legal framework in South Africa, like in most countries, was developed for an era of paper-based commerce, and thus contains words such as: 'document', 'writing', ' signature', 'original', 'copy', 'stamp', 'seal', 'register', 'file', 'deliver', etc. (SADoC 2000: 28). The South African Law Commission found that the Computer Evidence Act 57 of 1983 was insufficient to address the admissibility of 'computer evidence' in civil proceedings, and this will have to be addressed in an emerging e-commerce regime.

Also important is the ability to determine the attribution of electronic documents. Given the existing law in South Africa, this issue has to be addressed:

> However, in terms of the doctrine of 'estoppel' in South African law, a purported originator who never sent nor authorized a communication

to be sent, may nevertheless be held bound in law if his negligent conduct, whether by action or commission, induced a reasonable belief of authenticity in the mind of the addressee, which caused the latter to act thereon to his/her peril. (SADoC 2000: 32)

Additionally, it is important to ascertain the time and place of an e-commerce contract, in order to determine whether or not South African courts have 'jurisdiction to adjudicate a dispute involving both local and foreign nationals and, if so, which country's laws or courts would apply' (SADoC 2000: 32). How to effect a signature in cyberspace is another important issue for the South African policy environment. A framework for understanding electronic signatures (and the more specific subset 'digital signatures') must be put into place, and a common global commercial code should emerge to provide for the global rule of law and protection for contracts and private property. As the leading regime component in this area, South Africa strongly supports the United Nations Conference on International Trade Law (UNCITRAL) and its 'Model Law on Electronic Commerce'.

Intellectual property protection

The South African policy approach recognises that the transition to a digital economy presents new challenges for intellectual property protection. Digital goods can be copied and distributed around the world with relative ease, putting additional pressure on the system of intellectual property protection in South Africa, and countries around the world. Intellectual property regulation needs to be revised to reflect the realities of the digital economy, while still providing an incentive for the production of information goods, and thus balancing the needs of the individual with the needs of society.

'South African intellectual property law is not fully equipped to deal with the implications of the Internet, convergence, multimedia, digital technology and hence e-commerce. The advent of the Internet has changed the underlying assumptions of the original copyright laws entailed in the Copyrights Act 98 of 1978' (SADoC 2000: 57). South Africa has already made an attempt to comply with the WTO's Agreement on the Trade-Related Aspects of Intellectual Property (TRIPS) by amending its Intellectual Property Laws Amendment Act (Act 38 of 1997).

In order to try to help move forward the development of a global e-commerce regime, WIPO has developed its 'digital agenda' to guide its work in this area over the course of the next two years. The South African Department of Trade and Industry (DTI) convened a consultative

meeting in South Africa to discuss accession to these WIPO treaties and processes. 'The majority of stakeholders cautioned that before acceding to them, South Africa should analyse the benefits which accrue to small and medium enterprises' (SADoC 2000: 60).

Domain names

Currently, there are no direct linkages between domain names and trademark holders. This area, perhaps better than any other, highlights the significant contradictions that are at play in the development of global electronic commerce, in an environment of national-based legislation. As the South African Green Paper argues: 'Trademarks are territorial in nature, i.e. their registration applies to a particular country or jurisdiction. There is a general discrepancy between the national scope of trademark and the international nature of electronic commerce, particularly since e-commerce is borderless and instantaneous in nature' (SADoC 2000: 63).

South Africa recognises that domain names are an important and contested commercial asset, and famous marks should be protected while not allowing them to abuse smaller enterprises. There is some concern that the ICANN has not yet achieved complete legitimacy as the body charged with the responsibility to deal with domain name issues. South Africa is questioning whether or not it should support these structures, as well as structures such as AfriNIC, which has been formed to try to better represent the interests of Africa within ICANN (SADoC 2000: 97).

South Africa does, however, support the role of WIPO in its dispute resolution activities. It also supports the idea that in an information economy, the so-called country code top level domains (ccTLDs) should be managed by national governments as a national asset (SADoC 2000: 94). SADoC has proposed the creation of an independent Domain Name Authority (DNA) to represent all relevant stakeholders (private sector, public sector and civil society) and to manage the domain name issues for South Africa.

Personal data and consumer protection

In order to enhance trust in the digital economy, South Africa recognises that personal data should be protected. The challenge is to what degree the South African policy perspective will allow for legitimate corporate uses of data mining and profiling, targeted advertising and the use of other customer relationship management (CRM) tools. As fundamental principles, South Africa believes that consumers should be protected

against the following dangers:

- Unsolicited goods and communication;
- Illegal or harmful goods, services and content (e.g. pornographic material);
- Dangers resulting from the ease and convenience of buying on-line;
- Insufficient information about goods or about their supplier, since the buyer is not in a position to physically examine the goods offered;
- The abundantly accessible nature of a website;
- The dangers of invasion of privacy;
- The risk of being deprived of protection through the unfamiliar, inadequate or conflicting law of a foreign country being applicable to the contract, and finally
- Cyber fraud (SADoC 2000).

South Africa also recognises that when moving into electronic commerce, suppliers also face new dangers, especially in exposing themselves to new liabilities. The South African policy process would like to ensure that South African digital enterprises are an attractive competitor in the cyber world. SADoC sees this as 'an opportunity [for South African businesses] to establish a reputation for sound e-commercial practices, not only locally or within the SADC but also worldwide' (SADoC 2000: 78).

Of particular importance to South Africa is the impact that its privacy and consumer protection policies may have on its relationships with its trading partners, especially the European Union which has a very stringent privacy policy and consumer protection perspectives. There is a recommendation in the Green Paper that 'a combined government and industry database be set up to enable South African businesses to establish practices in any EU member country from which they may acquire personal data, for example, to establish profiles of their customers in that country' (SADoC 2000: 80).

Security, encryption and trust

South Africa believes that 'security measures used in conventional commerce may not be adequate to provide trust in the electronic economy' (SADoC 2000: 68). At the same time, it is important that national and personal security concerns are balanced with personal privacy concerns.   Four key elements are seen as crucial to ensuring that transactions in the digital economy can take place securely. These elements are: (1) authentication; (2) confidentiality; (3) integrity; and

(4) non-repudiation. From South Africa's perspective, achieving this level of security for the digital economy 'requires active partnership between government and the private sector' (SADoC 2000: 66).

These technologies are seen as critical to promoting trust in the digital economy, among both consumers and producers. It appears that South Africa is comfortable with the leading role being played by the OECD in promoting a regime consensus in this area.

Awareness

In South Africa, as in many other parts of the world, low levels of awareness about the potential benefits and opportunities in electronic commerce are a limiting factor for its growth. South Africa is developing a strategy to promote these opportunities, both to consumers and among the SMME sector:

> Central to this issue is educating the wider population about both the opportunities and potential threats of e-commerce. Coupled with that is the need to popularize or publicise an e-commerce policy process so as to invite participation. The creation of awareness and other related initiatives by government and its partners from the academic and business sectors to promote technological development should be done on an integrated approach. We need to build a new e-community that can take effective advantage of the e-commerce opportunities. (SADoC 2000: 112)

Within the South African public, private and civil society sectors, there are many bodies working to promote this level of awareness. Within the government, the Department of Communications is playing a leading role. Numerous private sector enterprises and bodies such as the Electronic Commerce Association of South Africa (ECASA) and the African Connection are also contributing in this area. In civil society, the Learning, Information, Networks and Knowledge (LINK) Centre at the University of the Witwatersrand is engaged in promoting an enhanced intellectual understanding of these issues, and the Internet Society of South Africa is building technical and user awareness.

Technical standards

The emerging South African perspective on technical standards is that they are of critical importance to the development and proper functioning of the Internet and global e-commerce. 'Standards are rules, and serve as a basis for comparison and a form of order. The major objective

for standardization is to achieve interoperability between networks and services and ensure compatibility' (SADoC 2000: 91).

'Standards are needed for long-term commercial success of the internet since they can allow products, services and applications from different firms to work hand in hand. Standards encourage competition and reduce stress or uncertainty in the market place' (SADoC 2000: 91). However, there is also recognition that 'Standards can also be employed as de-facto non-tariff trade barriers to "lockout" non-indigenous business from a particular national market' (SADoC 2000: 92).

Further, there are also the tremendous challenges of developing standards in 'an environment in which technology is developing rapidly may be counter productive at this stage of e-commerce' (SADoC 2000: 92). There is the recognition that these standards should be technology neutral and industry driven to the fullest extent possible.

South Africa supports the international organisations playing the leading role in developing this component of the global e-commerce regime, especially the role of the International Standards Organisation (ISO) and the ITU (SADoC 2000: 92).

Local content

There are numerous possibilities for promoting local content in the digital economy. In South Africa, there is a growing recognition that perhaps the primary source of this local content will be the growth and development of the SMMEs sector. SMMEs will be looked to increasingly to create employment opportunities for South Africa.

Several international organisations both governmental and non-governmental, including UNCTAD, WIPO, the International Chambers of Commerce (ICC) and others, are working to promote the impact of both developing countries and SMMEs on the digital economy.

Labour and society

As South Africa moves towards a digital economy, it is important to work to minimise the negative impact of e-commerce, while harnessing its potential. It is clear that both of these aspects are real possibilities in South Africa. On the one hand, new growth and new types of employment are indeed possible, while on the other hand, 'many workers could become displaced, temporarily or permanently as a result of this transformation' (SADoC 2000: 112). 'Clearly there is need for research in this area to evaluate the nature and number of jobs that could be created by e-commerce and lost or displaced due to efficiencies brought about by new ways of doing business and consumers, a new breed of

e-commerce firm "the infomediary" is being created to exploit the Internet' (SADoC 2000: 112).

Globally, many of the high-technology workers that have sought fame and fortune in the digital economy are now becoming highly disillusioned (see Lessard and Baldwin 1999). Recently, high-technology workers at one of the most widely known e-commerce companies, amazon.com, have attempted to unionise in the Washington Area Technology Workers (WashTech), a union structure within the Communications Workers of America. Currently, the ILO is reasserting itself as an important player in the international regime formation process for e-commerce, with a focus on understanding the impact on labour issues.

Human resources and capacity

While the shortage of human resources with the requisite skills in information and communications technologies requires immediate global attention, this situation is particularly problematic in South Africa. In South Africa, the Human Science Research Council states that 'there is a chronic shortage of highly skilled human resources in various segments of the market. The scarcity of technical expertise and skills, in the country is further exacerbated by the "brain drain" ' (SADoC 2000: 111).

South Africa further recognises that human development must occur on at least five different levels: (1) skills and human resources; (2) digital literacy; (3) digital skills for all South Africans; (4) skills for business; and (5) skills for the future (SADoC 2000: 111). Distance education and virtual campuses are seen as important elements of this strategy, and should be supported and developed in South Africa. Examples of the possibilities for human capacity development can be seen through field studies of geographically distributed collaborative learning (Cogburn forthcoming).

Implications of regime transformation for Africa and the developing world

As we can see from this case study of South Africa, this newly emerging information society regime will be wide ranging, and have a tremendous impact on nearly every area of how we 'live, work and play', as the evolving mantra goes. If this is so, it means that this regime involves perhaps the most important set of principles, norms and values that we have seen in an international regime.

In our initial discussion of international regime theory, we saw three possible alternative hypotheses for understanding the processes of regime formation, which were: (1) multi-stakeholder participation and

cooperation: (2) power; and (3) knowledge and epistemic communities. While this analysis is still very preliminary, we find that there are elements of all three of these at play in regime formation for the information society. For example, WSIS was an explicit multi-stakeholder process, attempting to involve civil society and the private sector along with governments in the negotiation process. However, numerous accounts of both phases of the WSIS process (Geneva and Tunis) point to the relative lack of civil society influence relative to the two other sectors (Cogburn 2004; Klein 2004). Governments continue to exercise primary power in these negotiations, frequently excluding the private sector and civil society from key meetings and negotiations. These non-state actors were also limited in their participation during the meetings to deliver prepared remarks for the first five minutes of plenary sessions, and then were forced to remain silent, while governments interjected for as long, and as frequently, as they desired. The highly organised civil society sector was able to develop numerous important position papers as input into the WSIS decision-making processes. However, the vast majority of those contributions were not included in any of the final documents laying the foundation for the emergent regime, such as the *WSIS Declaration of Principles* or the *Tunis Commitment*. So while multi-stakeholder participation was an important part of the WSIS processes, it was not decisive in predicting the outcomes, as least with respect to civil society.

From the regime theory perspective focusing on power, we see that the US government proved to be extremely influential, particularly in the final negotiations around Internet governance. So much so that the remainder of the Western and developed world (led by the Canadian government and the EU) opposed the US position to maintain unilateral control over the Internet domain-naming and IP-addressing system. However, several developing countries did play an important and influential role, especially the Republic of South Africa. Lyndal Shope-Mafole, the chair of the Information Society Commission in South Africa, played one of the most visible leadership roles in both phases of the WSIS (including chairing the so-called Subcommittee B, addressing nearly all of the information policy issues except for Internet governance). Along with South Africa, other important developing countries involved in the WSIS negotiations included Brazil, Iran, China and Cuba.

Finally, the international regime theory approach that favours knowledge and epistemic communities also finds some resonance in the WSIS processes. There is limited evidence that key transnational networks of scholars, scientists and research institutions were able to influence the framing of the WSIS agenda items.

3.7 Conclusions and future research

What can be done to influence the direction of the emerging regime so that it might be more just and equitable for a wider grouping of the world's citizens? This new regime requires countries, organisations and individuals to engage in strategic policy initiatives designed to stimulate and harness the full potential of their research capacity (including, public, private and academic sector resources). Developing countries need to work towards 'effective access' to the mechanisms and levers of regime formation. By effective access, I mean the ability to maximise the 'seat at the table' within the organisations of power and decision-making for information and communications policy.

Globalisation is a reality that is helping to fuel the development of an information society. Efforts at global regime formation in this area are taking place in both developed and developing countries. Interestingly, there is a significant level of information society activity in the African region and other parts of the developing world. However, the existing infrastructure gap in Africa between urban and rural areas, and further between the developed and developing countries, may hinder their ability to harness the potential of the information society. Additional research should focus on the strategies of other countries to respond to these global pressures and attempts to influence the development of an emerging regime for information and communications policy that benefits the majority of humankind.

Note

Earlier versions of this chapter were presented at the 2001 Telecommunications Policy Research Conference (TPRC) and the New Economy and Development Conference organised by UNU-WIDER, and appeared in *Telecommunications Policy*. This research was supported in part by grants from the University of Michigan School of Information, Center for Afroamerican and African Studies, W. K. Kellogg Foundation, the Alliance for Community Technology, and UNU-WIDER.

References

Axelrod, R. (1985) *The Evolution of Cooperation*, New York: Basic Books.
Cogburn, D. L. (1998) 'Globalization and State Autonomy in the Information Age: Telecommunications Sector Restructuring in South Africa', *Journal of International Affairs*, 51 (2): 583–604.
Cogburn, D. L. (2004) *Diversity Matters: Information Technology and International Development*, Cambridge, Mass.: MIT Press.

Cogburn, D. L. (forthcoming) 'Globalization and Human Capacity in the Knowledge Economy: Understanding Geographically Distributed Collaborative Learning between Developed and Developing Countries', in D. Mulenga, *Globalization and Lifelong Learning: Critical Perspectives*, Mahwah, NJ: Lawrence Erlbaum Associates.

Cowhey, P. (1990) 'The International Telecommunications Regime: the Political Roots of Regimes for High Technology', *International Organization*, 45 (2): 169–99.

Freiden, R. (1996) *International Telecommunications Handbook*, Boston: Artech House.

Groenewald, M. and D. Lehlokoe (1999) 'Towards an Electronic Commerce Policy for South Africa', proceedings of the INET'99, Annual Meeting of the Internet Society, http://www.isoc.org/inet99/1g/1g_4.htm

International Organization (1982) 'Special Issue: International Regimes', *International Organization*, 36 (2): 185–510. Includes: S. D. Krasner, 'Structural Causes and Regime Consequences: Regimes as Intervening Variables', pp. 185–205; S. Strange, 'Cave! Hic Dragones: a Critique of Regime Analysis', pp. 479–96.

Krasner, S. (1983) *International Regimes*, Ithaca: Cornell University Press.

Keohane R. O. (1984) *After Hegemony*, Princeton: Princeton University Press.

Keohane R. O. and J. S. Nye (1989) *Power and Interdependence*, Boston: Addison-Wesley.

Klein, H. (2004) *Understanding WSIS: an Institutional Perspective*, Cambridge, Mass.: MIT Press, ITID.

Lessard, B. and S. Baldwin (1999) *Net Slaves: True Tales of Working the Web*, New York: McGraw-Hill.

Manuel, T. (2000) 'Concluding Remarks by the Chairman, Hon. Trevor Manuel, Governor of the Fund and Bank for South Africa, at the Closing Joint Session', Prague, Czech Republic, 2000 Annual Meetings of the IMF and World Bank Group, http://www.imf.org/external/am/2000/speeches/pr68e.pdf

South African Department of Communications (SADoC) (2000) *Green Paper on Electronic Commerce for South Africa*, Pretoria: SADoC.

WTO (1997) 'South Africa, Schedule of Specific Commitments', Geneva: Committee on Trade in Services – Telecommunications, 11 April.

4
The Internet and Economic Growth in LDCs: a Case of Managing Expectations?

Charles Kenny

4.1   Introduction

The hope is widespread that the Internet will provide a powerful new tool in the battle against global poverty. These sentiments were echoed in the G8's recent Charter on the Global Information Society that declared:

> Information and Communications Technology (IT) is one of the most potent forces in shaping the twenty-first century.... IT is fast becoming a vital engine of growth for the world economy.... Enormous opportunities are there to be seized and shared by us all. (G8 2000)

To back these claims, there is mounting anecdotal, econometric and the-oretical support for the role of information technology in growth and development. This chapter does not dispute such evidence. Because of the scale of the improvement over previous communications tools, the invention of the Internet might lead to a significant impact on growth through better functioning of markets and firms. Added to such effects are those working within the sector itself – in particular the impact of network externalities, whereby the value of a connection to a network such as the telephone or Internet rises as others join the network. Beyond the theoretical, the increasing power for a given cost of com-puters has shown up significantly in US productivity figures. Businesses and jobs have been created, economies have gained, schools have acquired new pedagogical tools, NGOs and pressure groups have

exploited the technology to further agendas. And it is likely that this impact will grow worldwide.

This chapter does take a slightly more sceptical look at the likely impact of the Internet on long-term economic growth rates in developing countries, however. It is, of course, too early for there to be any firm answers about the relationship between the Internet and economic development in LDCs, but this chapter attempts to suggest likely orders of magnitude for such an impact. The results of such an exercise are perhaps worrying for those pinning LDC growth prospects on ICT roll-out.

The chapter is divided as follows: a brief review of some of the literature that posits significant gains from expansion of the Internet; a discussion of the theoretical role of technology in growth and the theoretical case for the Internet as a growth-inducing technology; evidence of the Internet's impact on growth rates in the US and OECD; the appropriateness of the Internet as a growth-promoting technology for LDCs; and estimates of future impacts in LDCs and a look at the past impact of individual communications technologies on worldwide growth rates.

In short, the chapter suggests that the evidence to date from the US and OECD is of widespread adoption and investment returns, but not supranormal returns outside production. The environment present in developing economies suggests that returns may be lower in these countries – they have smaller production sectors, higher costs of technology adoption, lower levels of education and a weaker institutional environment. Opportunities presented by the so-called 'death of distance' are not that large. Given all of this, it is not surprising that sober evaluations of the impact of the Internet are small in scale compared to the 'development gap'.

4.2   The Internet as a potent engine of development

A number of papers have suggested that the Internet might have a significant impact on the growth prospects of developing countries (see Madon 2000, for an early review and Pohjola 2001 for a longer discussion). There are also a few cross-country studies suggesting a considerable impact. Altig and Rupert (1999) try a novel approach, estimating the impact of 1999 Internet users as a percentage of population on GDP growth between 1974 and 1992 controlling for 1950 income per capita (from this, they estimate that 100 per cent Internet usage would be associated with about 4 per cent per annum additional economic growth). A study where causality issues are not so large involves trade,

where Freund and Weinhold (2002) find that greater Internet penetration may be associated with larger trade flows holding a number of controls constant. Even prior to the results of such papers, the development community was embracing the Internet as a tool in the fight against global poverty, not least through the G8's Digital Opportunity Taskforce (DOT force) created in the wake of their Okinawa meetings, and the ongoing WSIS organised by the UN. This chapter questions the scale of such early optimism, while not denying that the Internet is a useful tool for development.

4.3 Theories of economic growth: does technology cause growth? Is the Internet a likely candidate?

The Internet is a highly efficient tool for transferring information – e-mail, for example, is cheaper than a telephone call, leaves an electronic record and can be 'broadcast' simultaneously to many recipients. Further, the Internet is a technology which benefits from network externalities – my use of the system increases its value to others, by providing another partner in the web information transfer.

The Internet appears a good candidate as a technology that causes growth, then. And given that most recent theories of economic growth suggest a significant role for technological change (differing rates of broad technological adaptation are, for example, the driving force behind divergence in Romer's 1990 popular model), the impact of the Internet on growth might be substantial.

The definition of 'technology' used by Romer or by growth accountants in general spreads far beyond 'physical things that are invented', however. This is because, especially in most empirical discussions of economic growth, the impact of 'technology' is measured through estimates of total factor productivity (TFP). Growth accounting procedures measure increases in stocks of physical capital (the quantity of assets such as factories and roads measured by their dollar value), of human capital (the education stock, usually measured by average years of schooling) and of labour (measured in numbers of people of working age). The procedures then estimate how much output growth can be 'expected' from such increases in capital and labour stocks. TFP is defined as the actual measured growth of output minus the growth rate expected from increases in capital and labour stocks. As a measure of the efficiency with which capital and labour are combined to produce output, TFP is calculated as the residual from a growth accounting exercise.[1]

As such, as well as new inventions, 'technology' as defined by growth accountants includes 'business technology' (management techniques and systems), 'political technology' (forms of government and institutions) and 'social technology' (modes of human interaction) – indeed, it includes everything that might affect output which is not physical (and sometimes educational) capital or labour, including factors such as market power, increasing returns, technical complementarities, excess capacity, unmeasured fluctuations in work effort and hours and other errors in measurement.

Because 'technology' as defined by TFP equations is very broad, including far more than technology 'embodied' in physical capital, it might be that the effect of each individual technological advance is small and/or that other types of technology are more important for sustained growth than 'formally' invented, embodied (physical), technologies such as the Internet. Indeed, Paul Romer argues that 'technologies' such as Wal-Mart's management of inventory data – not invented under an R&D programme – are probably more significant than inventions such as the transistor (Perkins and Perkins 1999). The Internet might also have less impact than the invention of 'just-in-time' management, for example.[2]

Thus, technology 'broadly defined' as it is in TFP calculations covers a multitude of factors beyond 'inventions', such as the Internet – policies, institutions, social relationships – and these other factors might be more important in determining growth than all inventions, let alone the impact of just one such as the Internet. This chapter now turns to evidence from the US and the OECD regarding the impact of computers in general and the Internet in particular on economic growth to see if this evidence fits the idea of the invented technology of networked computing being vital to growth.

4.4   Evidence on computers, the Internet and economic growth in the US and OECD

This section will briefly review the evidence linking a small increase in TFP in the US in the last few years to the expansion in computer use and utility and evaluate the likely future productivity impact of the Internet. Looking at the US and OECD provides us with longer-term and better-quality evidence on the impact of networked computing than looking at developing countries alone because the 'Internet revolution' is further advanced in these countries and there are considerably more data with which to measure its impact. The section concludes that there

is evidence for a link, but not for significant spillovers (TFP increases outside the computer manufacturing sector) necessary for computers to have a major impact on long-term growth rates.

At the micro level, Lehr and Lichtenberg (1999) claim there have been excess returns to investments in computers across a range of industries compared to other types of capital (in the US), especially in the presence of skilled labour. Further, some argue that the impact of the IT revolution is at last beginning to be felt at the macro level. A recent 'survey of surveys' (Pohjola 1998) concluded that in the 1980s and the early 1990s, the consistent finding was that there was a broadly negative correlation between IT investment and economy-wide productivity in the US. A few studies in the late 1990s began to reverse this conclusion. Some of the more optimistic studies looking at the 1996–99 period suggest that computer hardware is responsible for between 0.49 and 0.82 per cent of US output growth in that period, and a significant percentage of productivity improvements (see Yusuf 2000).

This evidence has been disputed, however. 'Excess' micro-level returns apparently disappear when other factors, including company reorganisation, are taken into account (David 2000).[3] Gordon (2000) presents macro evidence that computers and the Internet do not represent a dramatic leap forward in productivity outside the durables manufacturing sector. He disaggregates the recent upsurge of 1.35 per cent in US TFP growth into 0.54 per cent of cyclical effects and 0.81 per cent of trend growth accounted for by the durable manufacturing sector – including computers, peripherals and telecommunications.[4] In the 88 per cent of the private economy outside of durables, TFP growth has actually *decelerated* – suggesting that there is no evidence of a spillover effect from computers.

Looking at labour productivity over a slightly longer span, IT-intensive industries outside the IT sector itself are some of the worst performing.[5] America's TFP change has averaged around 4 per cent in mining over the 1987–97 period, compared to close to minus 4 per cent per year in the banking sector – this despite the fact that IT spending as a percentage of output was highest in banking among the industries covered and second lowest (after construction) in mining (*The Economist* 23 September 2000).[6] This all suggests the 'Solow Paradox' – widespread evidence of computer use, little evidence of (widespread) productivity growth – continues, at least in modified form.

It should also be a concern that the share of ICTs in capital stock is fairly significant in a number of other OECD countries, and yet they have seen no increase in productivity. Broadly, the evidence from a recent study of OECD countries by Schreyer (2000) finds that, as with

the US, ICT capital goods have seen rapid improvements in the ratio of price to performance and as a result there has been a significant substitution of ICT capital for other types of capital and labour inputs. ICT's share of nominal productive capital stock increased from 2.4 to 3.2 per cent in France, 1.2 to 2.3 per cent in Japan and 3.6 to 5.2 per cent in the UK in the period 1985–96 (compared to 6.2 to 7.4 in the US). However, there is no evidence that in the period 1985–96 there was the increase in TFP growth that would be expected in OECD countries if there were spillovers from ICT investment. The UK, with the second largest share of ICT in total capital stock behind the US, has actually seen a productivity *slowdown* in the last few years (Bank of England 1999).

Regarding the Internet in particular, the timing of the small increase in US productivity was too early to be accounted for by e-commerce (contra Nezu 2000). In 1995, one estimate (from NUA, www.nua.ie) suggests that sales generated by the World Wide Web in that year were but $436 million. Even in 1998, e-transactions were only worth $43 billion (*The Economist* 24 July 1999), or equivalent to 0.5 per cent of US GDP.[7]

Again, because of the broad definition of TFP, a number of other factors could be behind the recent improvement in economic performance and what limited increase in TFP outside the durable manufacturing sector there might have been. Perhaps it is the result of the strong dollar, unrecorded increased labour, better monetary and fiscal policies, cheap commodities, the strength of Wall Street, low pressure on non-wage labour costs, the Asian crisis, or unsustainable corporate and consumer borrowing.

Looking forward, there have been many bold predictions. As a result of developing Internet-based applications for company procedures, Oracle planned to cut $2 billion out of $7 billion of global corporate expenses, for example (*The Economist* 11 November 2000). The empirical evidence to date has been less reassuring, however. Roberti (2001) notes that savings from companies that have moved earlier and more aggressively to the web have been smaller than expected. IBM, for example, bought $27.7 billion worth of goods electronically in the first three quarters of 2000 and saved but $247 million (or a little under 1 per cent) by doing so. On the sales side, 66 million customer service transactions were handled via IBM.com, but the headcount in call centres has remained exactly the same.

More sober evaluations of the real potential gains to e-commerce might account for the collapse in e-commerce growth – between 1998 and the end of 2000, the FEI/Duke Corporate Outlook Survey (www.duke.edu/~jgraham) suggests that the percentage of sales made online by surveyed companies remained unchanged at 5 per cent.

All of this evidence suggests that the impact of the Internet to date at the micro level has been marginal. A specific example of a widely used technology over which the Internet is but a marginal, evolutionary, advance is electronic data interchange (EDI). EDI systems use proprietary software to connect purchasers' and suppliers' computers to automate transaction and processing exchange. Such systems are already estimated to support about $3 trillion in economic activity in the US alone. While Internet-based systems are estimated to have operating costs of about 1 per cent of EDI systems, the cost of conversion to Internet-based systems is itself high enough to have discouraged the bulk of EDI users from so far switching to the Internet (World Bank 2000a). This suggests that the marginal improvement of using the Internet over EDI is in fact not that large.[8]

At the macro level, returns might be even lower than company level returns because of two negative externalities linked to e-commerce sites. First, the Internet allows businesses to force other companies and individuals to perform part of the service previously provided by the newly networked business. For example, expedia.com encourages the customer to search for cheaper flights through the air ticket database rather than its travel agents. This leads to savings for expedia.com, but does not necessarily increase economic efficiency.

Second, and perhaps of greater concern to LDC companies with less access to the new technologies, micro studies might find supranormal returns to investment absent in macro studies because Internet investment (by, for example, borders.com) involves defending market share (against amazon.com) – so that social returns to this investment are lower than private returns.[9]

The above discussion suggests at least two concerns for LDCs. First, if there is limited evidence of a past spillover impact of investment in computers and the Internet on economic growth in the US, and the case for a dramatic increase in productivity in the future is at least mixed, this suggests any benefits from the Internet in LDCs are likely to be greatly delayed and comparatively small. As we shall see, access to the capital required to use the Internet is very limited in LDCs, present use is a fraction of that in the developed world, and this is a state of affairs unlikely to change significantly in the near term. In other words, the present level of usage in the US is not promoting extraordinary growth, and this level of usage is already far higher than can be expected in developing countries for many years to come.

A second reason for concern is that the discussion above suggests that, in the US, moving online *has* become important to protect market share.

If this becomes true on a global level, those companies least equipped to move online are likely to lose market share to those better-placed. It is likely that the least-equipped companies will be concentrated in the developing world.

4.5　The Internet in LDCs

Turning back to the production of IT, as we have noted, this is the one sector of the US economy that has seen undoubted productivity gains. However, it is not a sector that is prevalent in many developing countries. That the picture is not totally bleak is proven by the fact that high-technology exports account for 28 per cent of East Asia's manufacturing exports. There is also the example of India's thriving IT export industry, where exports of software and services amounted to over $12 billion in 2003–4 – up from less than $1 billion in the mid 1990s – and employed about 800,000 people (Kumar and Joseph 2005). But India is very much the exception, and most LDCs import far more high-technology equipment and services than they export. The ITU estimates that exports of telecommunications equipment are only worth 8 per cent of imports of such equipment in low-income and 40 per cent of imports in middle-income countries, for example (ITU 2000). Overall, low-income countries are responsible for but 0.3 per cent of the world's high-technology exports. Furthermore, even in India, estimates suggest that TFP growth in the ICT-producing sector added as little as 0.05 percentage points to the country's growth in the second half of the 1990s (Qiang and Pitt 2003) – the sector, while apparently large in absolute numbers, remains small compared to the huge size of the overall economy.

A related phenomenon is that LDCs have far lower expenditures on developing new technologies. Expenditure on R&D in low-income countries combined totalled approximately US$5 billion in 1999, compared to the figure for the US alone of US$234 billion. Not surprisingly, this translates into OECD dominance of world patent applications; 1,114,408 patent applications were filed in low-income countries in 1998. Fewer than 10,000 of these applications – or under 1 per cent – were filed by residents. In turn, royalty and licence fee payments by low-income countries were nine times royalty receipts, whereas in the US, royalty receipts were 2.7 times payments (calculated from World Bank 2001).

These are significant figures because it appears that the major profits in the IT sector are made by patent owners rather than licensees (suggested by the fact that US companies produce 56 per cent of the

revenues yet garner 96 per cent of the profits from the global IT industry (Heeks and Kenny 2001)). Perhaps because of this, evidence from LDCs with significant IT industries does not suggest a productivity impact from that industry of the kind seen in the US. East Asia, the developing region with the largest IT industry, suggests no correlation between the proportion of high-tech exports in total exports and productivity growth (APEC 2001). Overall, LDCs are largely importing goods in the IT sectors, not inventing or even producing them. Given this is where the profits and productivity increases of the Internet revolution appear to be concentrated, this is a significant problem.

Turning to the potential spillover effects and wider productivity gains from use that proponents suggest will provide the more significant long-term impact of the Internet, LDCs appear in a weaker position to garner these benefits as well. First is the simple question of access to the network. Most producers and consumers in the US had telephone and computer access prior to the expansion of the Internet, making the cost of connectivity, the purchase of a modem and an ISP account, marginal. In LDCs, the picture is markedly different. Telephone lines per capita average 2.6 per 100 people in low-income countries as compared to 66.4 in the US. Albouy (1999) estimates that about 2 billion people, the vast majority in LDCs, lack access to electricity (in rural Tanzania, it is 99.2 per cent of the population). Computer ownership is 4.4 per thousand people in low-income economies compared to 511 per thousand in the US (calculated from World Bank 2001).

Further, while technological change is making both network and computer access cheaper, serving LDC populations will remain more expensive than serving OECD populations. Fifty-nine per cent of the population in low- and middle-income countries is rural, compared to 24 per cent in high-income economies. It is more expensive to provide networked services such as electricity and telephony to rural areas because the amount of infrastructure required per customer is higher than in urban areas. The physical costs of computer and telephone access are unlikely to drop below US$1000 even in relatively population-dense rural areas with electricity access (Kenny 2002). In low-density areas without networked services, costs of Internet infrastructure can rise as high as US$20,000 per computer.[10] Not only is this more than 38 times the average income per capita of low-income countries, it also suggests that Internet infrastructure investments in LDCs will generate lower returns in terms of network access than they do in the OECD (where costs are far less). In turn, this might suggest lower returns to investment in terms of economic impact as well.

Physical access, however, is but the first, and perhaps least significant barrier to exploitation of the new technology. This is suggested by low Internet usage rates even where access is available in developing countries. For example, Pigato (2001) finds in a survey of Tanzanian firms that computer usage remains very low even in firms that own a computer (only about 20 per cent had actually computerised basic business functions such as invoicing). Internet use was also low: among the 30 per cent who had access, less than half used it frequently and only 13 per cent rated it as an effective product promotion tool. Even in wealthier countries in East Asia, while over 90 per cent of the populations of Korea, Singapore and Hong Kong know where to access the Internet if they choose to, only one-third to one-half of the populations of these countries actually use the technology (calculated from Rose 2001).[11]

The non-physical costs of Internet use might help to explain these numbers. David (2000) estimates that, in the US, only 10 per cent of the cost of computer ownership to a company is accounted for by the purchase of the physical equipment itself – the other 90 per cent is made up of factors such as training and support. Where human capital is rare, these non-physical costs are likely to be an even more significant barrier to use. General education, specific technical and language skills and the broader institutional environment are all factors that might explain low usage rates.

Turning first to education, evidence from both the US and India suggests that those benefiting most from IT investments are the better educated and more highly skilled – who are being hired in greater numbers and increasing their pay differentials over unskilled, less educated colleagues (Autor *et al.* 1998; Lal 1996). And the great majority of users in the developing world are from the most educated sector of the population (in Ethiopia, 98 per cent of Internet users had a university degree in 1998 (CABECA 1998)). Yet, the stock of 'tertiary human capital' in LDCs, on average and as a percentage of US stocks, is about as small as the stock of physical capital (Heeks and Kenny 2001). Advanced education, of the greatest value in a 'global knowledge economy' is rare in LDCs. Indeed, approximately one-third of adults in low-income countries cannot even read – a vital skill for meaningful use of the Internet.

Looking more specifically at skills related to the Internet, the technical skills gap is frequently highlighted as at least as serious a barrier to Internet use as lack of access to the Internet itself (G8 2000). The extent to which basic computer skills are lacking in LDCs is suggested by a report from Wa in northern Ghana that locals trained in computer skills

and management could fetch $6000 per year – this in a country with an average GNP per capita of $390 (Hirsch 1998). Further, these skills gaps are likely to remain in the population at large – not least because, with per-student discretionary expenditures in secondary schools running as low as 12 dollars a year, the majority of schools in developing countries could not afford to install IT labs (Grace and Kenny 2001).

As important, there is a significant language skills gap, with perhaps one-half of the populations of the LDCs not speaking an official language of their own country – let alone English, the predominant language of the Internet. Language remains a significant barrier to use, as is suggested by a study of users in Slovenia, which found that 75 per cent of those who considered themselves fluent in English used the Internet compared to 1 per cent of non-English speakers (Kenny 2002). More generally, Guillen and Suarez (2001) find that, across country and allowing for a range of other factors, countries where English is the official or most widely spoken language see significantly higher Internet users per capita. This is hardly surprising given the quality and quantity of non-English web material. In 1999, 72 per cent of websites were in English. Conversely, the number of sites that can be found in languages such as Quecha (spoken by 10 million people in Bolivia, Ecuador and Peru) or Ibo (spoken by 15 million in Nigeria) can be counted on the fingers of one hand – and none of them offer interactive features (Kenny 2002).

Beyond the scarcity of physical and human capital needed to benefit from the development of the Internet, the institutional environment in LDCs is not conducive to rapid and successful exploitation of the technology. Mirroring microeconomic results, weak institutional capacity has been found to correlate across countries with lower access to networks and lower host site development (Kenny 2001; Oxley and Yeung 2000).[12] Weak institutions also lower consumer trust in e-commerce, perhaps the most important factor in determining willingness to purchase online.[13]

Poorly developed financial systems in particular, especially when combined with poor physical communications infrastructure, can significantly reduce the potential for e-commerce in LDCs. For example, a recent survey of business trust in the postal service (Kirkman *et al.* 2002) found that willingness to entrust the postal network with a package worth $100 was strongly correlated with GNP per capita, with Finland, Japan and Switzerland at the top and Venezuela, Honduras and Nigeria at the bottom. Regarding credit cards, results from Latin America suggest that only 28 per cent of online transactions in the region use credit cards, compared to 54 per cent using cash – and this is more a result of

lack of trust in, than lack of access to, the credit card system (Hilbert 2001). Miller (2001) argues that such weaknesses account for the fact that only 2.2 per cent of India's Internet subscribers have engaged in e-commerce activities.

The importance of strong educational and institutional capacity to more advanced uses of the Internet suggests 'leapfrogging' will be a difficult trick for developing countries. Indeed, the combination of low network roll-out, low skills and a poor institutional environment, when combined with the feature of network externalities, might leave LDCs stuck in a low-use low-utility trap regarding the Internet. With few employers, customers or suppliers with skills access, with little relevant (or comprehensible) content, firms and individuals will have little incentive to make use of the technology. With few firms and individuals induced to move online, the utility of the Internet will remain low.

There is some evidence that this Internet trap exists in LDCs. Pigato (2001) argues that the low IT usage she found in the Tanzania survey was due in part to entrepreneurs simply not knowing how to make use of it, but also because of scale effects – suggested by the fact that use was much higher among tourism enterprises, the one sector where a considerable part of the customer base was likely to be online. Furthermore, of 110,498 secure servers worldwide that use encryption technologies in Internet transactions (commonly used for e-commerce), only 224, or 0.2 per cent, are in low-income countries.

Turning to the upside potential for LDCs to trade more and different products due to 'the death of distance', Venables (2001) suggests that these opportunities are much overrated. Many 'knowledge goods' remain embodied in human or physical capital, that is still expensive (and difficult) to transport across international boundaries. Venables also notes that as goods become weightless, they also tend to be subject to dramatic productivity increases and price reductions. Taking the example of airline ticketing, he notes that the major impact of ICT has been to replace labour by computer equipment – and only secondarily to allow remaining workers to be employed in remote locations.

Looking at the type of 'low-tech' service jobs that are now exportable, it is doubtful that there are enough to make a significant difference to LDCs as a whole. Data entry (the low-skills end of the information processing sector) is a $US800 million industry in the US. Imagine (generously) that the US only has its share in global GDP of the data entry market (about 27 per cent of the world total) – so that, worldwide, the industry is worth approximately $3 billion. This is equal to a little less than the yearly exports of Estonia (Schware and Hume 1996;

World Bank 2000b). More generously, the ILO (2001) reports that perhaps 5 per cent of all service sector jobs in industrial countries are 'contestable' by LDCs – nonetheless, this totals but 12 million jobs, or 0.24 per cent of the population of the developing world (World Bank 2001).

There is even the potential for the Internet to act as a tool for divergence in incomes between rich and poor. The fact that general technologies are important for growth, and that rich countries today are by and large the countries that were rich 50 or 100 years ago (see Kenny 1999), suggests that 'the average' technology probably has a larger impact on growth prospects in wealthy countries than in poor countries (Heeks and Kenny 2001). Venables (2001) also suggests that innovations in communications technologies in the past have further concentrated income in a few geographic areas.

A number of studies based on the US and Europe also suggest that backward companies and regions are benefiting less from the Internet as well, as would be expected if network externalities and low-utility traps were at work. Indeed, the firms that are benefiting most from the introduction of IT are those that were already thriving in the 'old economy' (World Bank 2000a; Doms *et al.* 1997; Greenan *et al.* 2001). At the regional level, advanced regions in Europe have also benefited more from the roll-out of communications infrastructure than backward regions (Cornford 2001).[14] Looking at production of high-value-added 'knowledge goods' in particular, this has remained concentrated in wealthier regions in the UK, for example, despite falling communications costs (Cornford 2001). Finally, there is global evidence that 'dot.com' firms are also highly concentrated, and concentrated in regions that were wealthy prior to their creation (Gillespie *et al.* 2001).

LDCs face high costs to access ICTs, a number of barriers to exploit that access, limited opportunities if those barriers are overcome, and some threat that wider access to ICTs might actually speed divergence, then. It is perhaps for such reasons that even studies that find a historical link between IT investment and growth in developed countries fail to find such a link in LDCs (see Pohjola 2001 and Mayer 2000).[15]

4.6 Estimates of the future impact of the Internet on economic growth

We have seen that a range of businesses and economists are predicting significant savings and productivity increases from moving processes online. We have also seen early evidence that there is a risk that much of these savings might be swallowed up by competing for market share,

with little impact on the strength of the national economy. This chapter has presented a range of further arguments for caution in predicting a significant positive impact of the Internet on LDC economies. Nonetheless, this section suggests that even the more optimistic voices on the economic effects of the Internet lay out a scenario of comparatively little impact on the course of divergence, and that evidence from past 'revolutions' in transactions costs reductions supports this conclusion.

A range of estimates for OECD countries suggest an impact of e-business on growth as small as perhaps one-third of 1 per cent in 2005. Taking the US alone, one more generous estimate by Goldman Sachs is perhaps 5 per cent by 2010 (*The Economist* 1 April 2000).[16] More optimistic still, it has become common to assume that investments in telecommunications and IT, which account for the same proportion of today's capital stock as railways did in the late nineteenth century (a little over 10 per cent), will have a similar impact on US economic growth as is generously estimated for the railways – around 10 per cent (although Fogle (1964) would estimate one-third of that impact for railways). If this were gained over the next 20 years, it would be at a rate of a little under 0.5 per cent per year.

However, even assuming such a generous growth impact in the US, there are good reasons to believe that the impact of the Internet on growth in LDCs will be much less significant. Indeed, it is widely accepted even by Internet optimists that the impact of the Internet on developing countries at least over the near term is likely to be smaller than that in developed countries – and this chapter presents a range of evidence suggesting that the impact will remain muted. The consulting firm e-Marketer estimated that e-commerce revenues of 'the rest of the world' (RoW – outside North America, Europe and East Asia) would be 2 per cent of the global total in 2003 – which equals US$29 billion. Assuming that 10 per cent of revenues add to gross product, this suggests that e-commerce will add the equivalent of Guyana's GDP (a poor country with a population of a little under 1 million) to total RoW GDP in 2003.[17] One recent global estimate suggests that, over the longer term, 'effective' e-commerce policies could increase Latin America's GDP by about $45 billion – or about 2 per cent. However, the same source provides other estimates that are as low as 1.2 per cent for Latin America and 1 per cent for Asia (Mann *et al.* 2000).

These general estimates of the income impact of the Internet by ICT optimists are thus very small compared to the rich–poor gap. The GNP per capita of the US is about $30,000 compared to Sudan's GNP per capita of about $300, or about a 10,000 per cent difference (World Bank 2000b).

Compare this figure to the 10 per cent additional income that the Internet might most optimistically provide (World Bank 2000b, 2001).

Taking the past as prologue, these figures should, perhaps, not come as a surprise. Despite sharing the networking and transactions-reducing features of the Internet, and despite human and physical capital requirements far less demanding than the Internet, it appears that telecommunications has had a fairly limited growth impact as well.[18] Although there is some econometric evidence that increasing access to telephony has an impact on future growth rates, the size and geographical extent of that impact are arguable. Roller and Waverman (2000), Canning (1997) and Madden and Savage (1998) are three recent studies that find some sort of link (although Roller and Waverman only find that link in more advanced economies), Holtz-Eakin (1993, 1994) and Garcia-Mila and McGuire (1992) dispute it. Even if there is a link, the evidence suggests that it cannot be all that significant. Over the last 40 years – and particularly since the spread of mobile telephony – poor countries have seen a far more rapid growth in telephone networks than have developed countries. Nonetheless, there has been a divergence in income between rich and poor countries over the last 40 years, and LDC growth rates have slowed even as networks have expanded (calculated by the author from World Bank 2001).[19] As suggested at the start of this chapter, given the broad definition of technology, the impact on growth of one new invention, however impressive that invention, is likely to be small.

4.7   Conclusion

This chapter has taken a very narrow look at the likely impact of the Internet on development. And it should be remembered that even this narrow look suggests that there will be significant changes in the way business is done in LDCs – changes that have already begun. The same transactions savings that are available in developed counties from the Internet are available in LDCs – for example, Reliance Industries, a chemical firm in India, has linked its major customers through an Internet-based market exchange, reducing receivables delays by two-thirds and speeding order deliveries (Miller 2001). More broadly, the technology offers exciting possibilities in education delivery, for improving health services or the access of the poor to the tools of governance.

Also much of the analysis in the chapter has been 'static' – looking at the direct impact of the Internet on the costs of doing business, not the knock-on effects that the technology might have on creating new business models, or through its support for the development of a

better-educated workforce. Hence the Internet can be expected to be a powerful technology that will have a long-term impact on the quality of life in developing countries.

Having said that, our record in predicting the dynamic impact of technologies on development in the past has been very weak. To take three communications-related examples, the railway was predicted to spark the dictatorship of the proletariat, the telegraph was predicted to engender world peace and the television to revolutionise education. Broadly, it appears that even while the role of technology in economic growth cannot be questioned, the dynamic impact of a particular, invented technology is never very large. It looks increasingly as if the impact of the computer on US productivity will be a good example of this. The impact has been limited so far, and might not increase in the future.

Hard choices should be made based on an understanding of our comparative ignorance of the potential impact of the Internet. For example, if the Internet is considered necessary to ensure that businesses remain internationally competitive, does government policy focus on ensuring business access at the cost of equitable access? Similarly with education – if exploiting the Internet requires tertiary education, do governments rechannel resources from primary education for the many to university funding for the few? I would argue that, given the limited evidence of benefits, the great state of uncertainty and the immediate equity costs of such actions, the answer should be to support equitable access and primary education.

Overall, the largest determinant of the impact of the Internet in developing countries is likely to remain the broader environment outside the information infrastructure sector. This environment will also play by far the predominant role in determining the quality of life of LDC populations. For this reason, Microsoft Chairman Bill Gates's argument about the place of *direct* support to the Internet in development priorities might well be correct:

> I am suggesting that if somebody is interested in equity that you wouldn't spend more than 20 percent of your time talking about access to computers, that you'd get back to literacy and health and things like that. So the balance that makes sense is that more money should be spent on malaria. (Gates 2000)[20]

Notes

The views expressed in this chapter are the author's own, and do not necessarily represent the views of the World Bank, its executive directors, or the countries

that they represent. It was previously published as 'The Internet and Economic Growth in LDCs: a Case of Managing Expectations?' *Oxford Development Studies*, 31(1). Reprinted with permission.

1 'Technology' as defined by TFP is thus open to a wide range of assumptions about the importance of various factors to output that can dramatically alter its aggregate size. Calculating the scale of TFP growth is a process laden with more or less arbitrary decisions that can dramatically alter results. Depending what is defined as 'physical capital' (and what we define as the labour stock), how we measure the growth of the stock of capital, what we measure as 'human capital', whether we include measures of 'natural capital' or 'social capital', what (if any) allowances we make for technological change 'embodied' in capital investment, or market failures such as scale effects, whether we believe that capital can be substituted for labour one for one, what share we give to human over physical capital in output estimates and a range of other more or less arbitrary assumptions, we can come up with markedly different estimates for the residual from a growth accounting equation which is defined as 'TFP'. For example, one recent study looked at the impact of changing just two of these assumptions within reasonable bounds on long-term TFP growth in Korea, and produced estimates of annual growth 1960–97 that ranged between 3.0 per cent of GDP and minus 1.4 per cent (the two were assumptions about returns to scale and shares of physical and human capital) (Ghosh and Kraay 2000). This sensitivity of technology's estimated impact on growth to a range of more or less arbitrary assumptions is why, for example, the extent to which it has been important in practice in regions like East Asia remains hotly debated. Felipe (1999) concludes his survey of TFP growth and capital accumulation in East Asia by noting 'this work has become a war of figures .... It seems that re-working the data one can show almost anything.'

2 One reason to believe that technologies like the Internet that are traditionally 'researched and developed' cannot be a central cause of the process of economic growth is that the number of scientists and engineers employed in R&D in the US has increased fivefold 1950–90, while US growth rates have fallen over that period (Keely and Quah 1998).

3 Greenan *et al.* (2001) find no evidence of increasing computerisation and R&D over time having a significant impact on firm performance.

4 Even this small increase within the durable goods sector is in part the result of measurement bias (see Schreyer 2000).

5 Gross product originating per worker in IT-using goods and services fell an average of 0.1 per cent 1990–97, compared to a 1.1 per cent rise in non-IT intensive industries (Department of Commerce 1999). This all suggests the 'Solow Paradox' – widespread evidence of computer use, little evidence of productivity growth – continues.

6 See also Stiroh (1998) for a similar result.

7 The productivity impact was also surprisingly late to be credited to straightforward computer investments. Already, by 1990, 28 per cent of business expenditure on equipment was on hardware. Overall, corporations spent $1.1 trillion on computer hardware between 1990 and 1996, yet productivity grew by only 0.8 per cent per year (Perkins and Perkins 1999). The slowing of growth in the nominal share of computers in the economy suggests some macro evidence of a declining marginal return to computer ownership

coinciding with the expansion of the Internet. The nominal share of computer hardware in the economy rose rapidly *before* 1997. Growth since 1997 has continued the unit-elastic response to the decline in computer prices prevalent prior to 1995 – the share of nominal spending on computers has been stable since 1997 (Gordon 2000). (Recent figures suggest that growth might have slowed even below that.) Company IT budget growth in the US might slip below 5 per cent in 2001 from about 11 per cent in 2000 (*Financial Times* 4 January 2001).

8   To take an example on the B2C side, forecasters' estimates for B2C e-commerce growth suggest that it might reach 10 per cent of the total retail market by 2003 – this is still less than today's share of mail-order catalogues (Almasy and Wise 2000), which, for many, must be a reasonably good substitute.

9   Winners in the battle for market share become 'supersites', which dominate the web. This has already occurred in the case of news sites, for example, where the top three sites (MSNBC, CNN and the *New York Times*) account for 72 per cent of all news site visits on the web (*New York Times* 29 August 2001).

10   These are the costs reached in a rural access programme in Costa Rica discussed by Shakeel *et al.* (2001).

11   As a further example regarding more advanced use of the Internet, connectivity is already common in Argentine and Chilean firms – 60 per cent of (non-micro) enterprises in Chile are connected to the Internet as well as 87 per cent of Argentina's SMEs. Nonetheless, only 15 per cent of Chilean firms have their own website and only 20 per cent of Argentine firms have bought goods online (Hilbert 2001).

12   In a related finding, Guillen and Suarez (2001) find that a democracy index is significantly correlated with Internet users and hosts per capita after allowing for a range of other factors.

13   Jupiter Communications (online) found that four of the top five selection criteria for online purchases were connected with recognition, trust or experience of the retailer – in fourth place was 'I can find bargains'.

14   Greenan *et al.* (2001), for example, find that while there is no relationship between increasing expenditure on R&D and computerisation and French firm performance, firms that perform better tend to have higher R&D and computing expenditure.

15   Bedi's (1999) survey on this topic could find only one study with a significant result, which found a positive relationship that was likely to be plagued by an endogeneity bias.

16   Forestier *et al.*'s (2001) research predicts that, by 2003, e-business will reach $1.5 trillion, or equal to about 13 per cent of US GDP. If we assume the value added by this business being conducted online is 10 per cent, this would increase the country's GDP by 1.3 per cent (*The Economist* 30 October 1999). The OECD is less positive in its estimates. Its most generous forecast is that, for the whole of the OECD in 2005, e-commerce will equal $1 trillion (Nevens 1999). Again, assuming a 10 per cent impact on value added, this suggests that, by 2005, the OECD will have increased GDP thanks to e-commerce by about one-third of 1 per cent. See *The Economist* Survey: The New Economy, 23 September 2000 and World Bank (2000a).

17   A third study by Goldman Sachs (2000) estimates that online commerce outside North America, Europe and Asia will generate gross revenues of $59 billion by 2003, rising to $178 billion by 2005.

18 A similar story can be told for the railroad. Fogel's (1964) study of the impact of the railroad on the US economy estimates that the level of per capita income reached in the US on 1 January 1890, would have been reached by 31 March 1890 if railroads had never been invented. The problem here, as frequently noted, is that Fogel only looked at the static rather than the dynamic impact of the railroads on the US economy – and those dynamic impacts could have been large, even if they are hard to measure.

19 Regarding the role of reduced transactions costs in making LDCs more competitive in trade, evidence regarding progress in international trade talks suggests that this is not enough to spark LDC growth either. Assuming generously that the Internet might reduce transactions costs on goods and services by perhaps 10 per cent (see Goldman Sachs 2000), compare this marginal improvement to the scale of changes in 'institutional technology' over the past 40 years. Looking at the impact of the GATT and WTO trade rounds, for example, average tariffs in industrial countries fell from 40 per cent in 1947 to 5 per cent in 1988 – and have fallen further since (*Law Journal Extra* 1996). Falling transport costs and more rapid transport systems might have added a further 10 per cent cost reduction on top of this (Hummels 1999, 2001). Again, despite (or perhaps because of) such dramatic improvements, LDC income growth has fallen over that period, and fallen even further behind that of developing countries, suggesting that reduced transactions costs alone will not allow LDCs to 'close the gap'.

20 From within the development community, Amartya Sen notes similar scepticism regarding Bangalore's software export industry: 'even 100 Bangalores would not solve India's poverty and deep-seated inequality. For this to happen many more people must participate in growth. This will be difficult to achieve across the barriers of illiteracy, ill health and inequalities in social and economic opportunities' (quoted in Oxfam 2000).

References

Albouy, Y. (1999) 'Institutional Reform', in E. McCarthy and F. Martin, *Energy and Development Report, 1999: Energy after the Financial Crisis*, Washington, DC: World Bank.

Almasy, E. and R. Wise (2000) 'E-venge of the Incumbents: a Hybrid Model for the Internet Economy', *Ivey Business Journal*, 64 (5): 16–19.

Altig, D. and P. Rupert (1999) 'Growth and the Internet: Surfing to Prosperity?' Federal Reserve Bank of Cleveland *Economic Commentary*, September.

APEC (2001) *The New Economy and APEC*, Singapore: Asia-Pacific Economic Cooperation.

Autor, D., L. Katz and A. Kreuger (1998) 'Computing Inequality: Have Computers Changed the Labor Market?' *Quarterly Journal of Economics*, 113 (4): 1169–214.

Bank of England (1999) *Inflation Report: Summer*, London: Bank of England.

Bedi, A. (1999) 'The Role of Information and Communication Technologies in Economic Development: a Partial Survey', ZEF Discussion Papers on Development Policy 7, Bonn: ZEF.

CABECA (1998) (Menou, M. J.) 'Connectivity in Africa: Use, Benefits and Constraints of Electronic Communication – Synthesis Report – Part 2: Overview of the Findings of the Project' [Study carried out under the CABECA

project of Padis as part of the IDRC-sponsored research programme on the 'Impact of Information on Development']. Addis Ababa: UNECA/PADIS, May.

Canning, D. (1997) 'Does Infrastructure Cause Economic Growth? International Evidence for Infrastructure Bottlenecks', mimeo, Harvard Institute for International Development.

Cornford, J. (2001) 'The Evolution of the Information Society and Regional Development in Europe', mimeo, University of Newcastle.

David, P. (2000) 'Digital Technology and the Productivity Paradox: After Ten Years, What Has Been Learned', mimeo, Stanford University.

Department of Commerce (US) (1999) *The Emerging Digital Economy II*, Washington, DC: Department of Commerce.

Doms, M., T. Dunne and K. Troske (1997) 'Workers Wages and Technology', *Quarterly Journal of Economics*, 112 (1): 253–90.

Felipe, J. (1999) 'Total Factor Productivity in East Asia: a Critical Survey', *The Journal of Development Studies*, 35 (4).

Fogel, R. W. (1964) *Railroads and Economic Growth: Essays in Econometric History*, Baltimore: Johns Hopkins.

Forestier, E., J. Grace and C. Kenny (2001) 'Can Information and Telecommunications Technologies be Pro-Poor?', presented at World Bank Economists' Forum, 3–4 May.

Freund, C. and D. Weinhold (2002) 'Of the Effect of the Internet on International Trade', Federal Reserve International Finance Discussion Paper 693.

G8 (2000) Okinawa Charter on Global Information Society, http://www. oneworld.net/anydoc2.cgi?url=http%3A%2F%2Fwww%2Eg8kyushu% 2Dokinawa%2Ego%2Ejp%2Fe%2Fdocuments%2Fit1%2Ehtml

Garcia-Mila, T. and T. J. McGuire (1992) 'The Contribution of Publicly Provided Inputs to States' Economics', *Regional Science and Urban Economics*, 22: 229–41.

Gates, W. H. (2000) Speech given at the Digital Dividends conference in Seattle, 18 October. http://www.microsoft.com/billgates/speeches/2000/ 10-18digitaldividends.asp

Ghosh, S. and A. Kraay (2000) 'Measuring Growth in Total Factor Productivity', World Bank PREM Notes 42, September.

Gillespie, A., R. Richardson and J. Cornford (2001) 'Regional Development and the New Economy', EIB Papers 6, 1.

Goldman Sachs (2000) *B2B – Just How Big is the Opportunity*, http://www. gs.com/ hightech/research

Gordon, R. (2000) 'Does the New Economy Measure Up to the Great Inventions of the Past', *Journal of Economic Perspectives*, 14 (4).

Grace, J. and C. Kenny (2001) 'A Short Review of Information and Communications Technologies and Basic Education in LDCs', mimeo, Washington, DC: World Bank.

Greenan, N., J. Mairess and A. Topiol-Bensaid (2001) 'Information Technology and Research and Development Impacts on Productivity and Skills', in M. Pohjola (ed.) *Information Technology, Productivity and Economic Growth*, Oxford: Oxford University Press for UNU-WIDER.

Guillen, M. and S. Suarez (2001) 'Developing the Internet: Entrepreneurship and Public Policy in Ireland, Singapore, Argentina and Spain', *Telecommunications Policy*, 25: 349–71.

Heeks, R. and C. Kenny (2001) 'Is the Internet a Technology of Convergence of Divergence?', mimeo, Washington, DC: World Bank.

Hilbert, M. (2001) *Latin America on Its Path into the Digital Age: Where Are We?* Santiago, Chile: CEPAL/ECLAC.

Hirsch, A. (1998) 'Computer Training and Internet Access Issues in Wa, Upper West Province, Ghana', mimeo, Washington, DC: World Bank.

Holtz-Eakin, D. (1993) 'State-specific Estimates of State and Local Government Capital', *Regional Science and Urban Economics*, 23: 185–209.

Holtz-Eakin, D. (1994) 'Public-sector Capital and the Productivity Puzzle', *The Review of Economics and Statistics*, 76: 12–21.

Hummels, D. (1999) 'Have International Transportation Costs Declined?', mimeo, University of Chicago.

Hummels, D. (2001) 'Time as a Trade Barrier', mimeo, University of Chicago.

ILO (2001) *World Employment Report*, Geneva: International Labour Organisation.

ITU (2000) *World Telecommunications Indicators*, Geneva: International Telecommunications Union.

Keely, L. and D. Quah (1998) 'Technology and Economic Growth', mimeo, London: LSE.

Kenny, C. (1999) 'Why Aren't Countries Rich? Weak States and Bad Neighborhoods', *Journal of Development Studies*, 35 (5): 26–47.

Kenny, C. (2001) 'Prioritizing Countries for Assistance to Overcome the Digital Divide', *Communications and Strategies*, first quarter: 41.

Kenny, C. (2002) 'Information and Communications Technologies for Direct Poverty Relief: Costs and Benefits', *Development Policy Review*, 20 (2).

Kirkman, G., P. Cornelius, J. Sachs and K. Schwab (eds) (2002) *The Global Information Technology Report 2001–2002*, New York: Oxford University Press.

Kumar, N. and K. Joseph (2005) 'Export of Software and Business Process Outsourcing from Developing Countries: Lessons from the Indian Experience', *Asia-Pacific Trade and Investment Review*, 1 (1).

Lal, K. (1996) 'Information Technology, International Orientation and Performance: a Case Study of Electrical and Electronic Goods Manufacturing Firms in India', *Information Economics and Policy*, 8: 269–80.

Law Journal Extra (1996) 'A History of GATT and the Structure of the WTO', *International Contract Adviser*, II (1).

Lehr, B. and F. Lichtenberg (1999) 'Information Technology and its Impact on Productivity: Firm-level Evidence from Government and Private Data Sources, 1977–1993', *Canadian Journal of Economics*, 32 (2): 335–62.

Madden, G. and S. J. Savage (1998) 'CEE Telecommunications Investment and Economic Growth', *Information Economics and Policy*, 10: 173–95.

Madon, S. (2000) 'The Internet and Socioeconomic Development: Exploring the Interaction', *Information Technology and People*, 13 (2): 85–101.

Mann, C., S. Eckert and S. Knight (2000) *Global Electronic Commerce*, Washington, DC: International Institute for Economics.

Mayer, J. (2000) 'Globalization, Technology Transfer and Skill Accumulation in Low-Income Countries', Working Paper 150, Helsinki: UNU-WIDER.

Miller, R. (2001) 'Leapfrogging? India's Information Technology Industry and the Internet', IFC Discussion Paper 42.

Nevens, M. (1999) 'The Mouse that Roared', *The McKinsey Quarterly*, 1: 145–8.

Nezu, R. (2000) 'E-Commerce: a Revolution with Power', mimeo, Paris: OECD.

Oxfam (2000) *Education Now: Break the Cycle of Poverty*, Oxford: Oxfam, http://www.caa.org.au/oxfam/advocacy/education/report

Oxley, J. and B. Yeung (2000) 'E-commerce Readiness: Institutional Environment and International Competitiveness', mimeo, University of Michigan Business School.

Perkins, A. and M. Perkins (1999) 'Eyes Wide Shut', *Financial Planning*, 12/01.

Pigato, M. (2001) 'Information and Communication Technology, Poverty and Development in Sub-Saharan Africa and South Asia', mimeo, Washington, DC: World Bank.

Pohjola, M. (1998) 'Information Technology and Economic Development: an Introduction to the Research Issues', Working Paper 153, Helsinki: UNU-WIDER.

Pohjola, M. (2001) 'Introduction', in M. Pohjola (ed.) *Information Technology, Productivity and Economic Growth*, Oxford: Oxford University Press for UNU-WIDER.

Qiang, C. and A. Pitt (2003) 'Contribution of Information and Communication Technologies to Growth', Working Paper 24, Washington, DC: World Bank.

Roberti, M. (2001) 'General Electric's Spin Machine', *The Industry Standard*, 22–9 January.

Roller, L.-H. and L. Waverman (2000) 'Telecommunications Infrastructure and Economic Development: a Simultaneous Approach', CEPR Discussion Paper 2399, March.

Romer, P. (1990) 'Are Nonconvexivities Important for Understanding Growth?', NBER Working Paper 3271, Cambridge, Mass.: NBER.

Rose, R. (2001) 'Openness, Impersonal and Continuing Accountability: the Internet's Prospective Impact on East Asian Governance', background paper for S. Yusuf (ed.) *East Asia's Future Economy*, Washington, DC: World Bank.

Schreyer, P. (2000) 'The Contribution of Information and Communications Technology to Output Growth: a Study of the G7 Countries', OECD STI Working Paper DSTI/DOC(2000)2, Paris.

Schware, R. and S. Hume (1996) 'Prospects for Information Services Exports from the English-speaking Caribbean', mimeo, Washington, DC: World Bank.

Shakeel, H., M. Best, B. Miller and S. Weber (2001) 'Comparing Urban and Rural Telecenters' Cost', *The Electronic Journal on Information Systems in Developing Countries*, 4 (2): 1–13.

Stiroh, K. (1998) 'Computers, Productivity and Input Substitution', *Economic Enquiry*, 36 (2): 175–91.

Venables, A. (2001) 'Geography and International Inequalities: the Impact of New Technologies', mimeo, London School of Economics.

World Bank (2000a) *Global Economic Prospects*, Washington, DC: World Bank.

World Bank (2000b) *World Development Indicators*, Washington, DC: World Bank.

World Bank (2001) *World Development Indicators*, Washington, DC: World Bank.

Yusuf, S. (2000) 'East Asia's Future: a Project Outline', mimeo, Washington, DC: World Bank.

5
Can ICT Make a Difference in the Development of Transition Economies?

Marcin Piatkowski

5.1 Introduction

Since 1995, information and communication technologies (ICT) have contributed to faster GDP and labour productivity growth in a number of developed countries, particularly the US. This has been shown by numerous research studies on the impact of ICT on the macro, industrial and micro-level.[1] Despite the collapse of the 'Internet bubble' in 2001, fast growth in productivity spurred by ICT has not been arrested. Recent estimates of the US Department of Labor (2004) show that labour productivity growth in the US during 1995–2004 was more than twice the average of the previous two decades. Jorgenson *et al.* (2004) project that this high productivity growth will continue until 2010.

There is, however, hardly any research into the impact of ICT on developing and transition economies. While IMF (2001) and Lee and Khatri (2003) document the positive contribution of ICT production and capital to growth in South-east Asia in the late 1990s, there is a general paucity of studies on the contribution of ICT to economic development in transition economies.[2]

The purpose of this chapter is to fill this gap. It does so by extending the results of the previous papers by the same author (Piatkowski 2004; Van Ark and Piatkowski 2004) to ask whether ICT might accelerate the convergence of seven transition economies from Central and Eastern Europe and Russia (CEER) with the EU-15 and the US income levels.[3] The eight CEER countries are the only ones for which sufficient data were available.

The chapter investigates the question of ICT potential for faster productivity growth from both the macro and industry-level perspective. First, it argues that between 1995 and 2003 ICT contributed to accelerated productivity growth in four new EU member states (the case of technological leapfrogging) and thus to their faster convergence with the EU-15 (but not with the US). However, in Romania, Russia and, to a lesser extent, Bulgaria and Slovakia, the productivity gap widened, mainly owing to the lower quality of the economic and institutional environment, which inhibited the diffusion of ICT (a case of a growing digital divide). Second, based on the projection of the impact of ICT on GDP growth in Poland up to 2025, the chapter argues that ICT has a large long-term potential to accelerate the development of CEER countries. Third, the chapter shows that ICT use had an important role in stimulating productivity growth at the industry level in four CEE countries and that it offers significant potential for faster productivity growth in traditional, 'old economy' industries that do not currently use much ICT. If these industries were able to achieve the same rate of productivity growth as the ICT-using industries, then they would make a significant contribution to faster convergence. Realising this potential, however, will crucially depend on far-reaching structural reforms, business reorganisation, a larger investment in human capital, and a well-designed public 'push strategy'.

The chapter proceeds as follows. In section 5.2, it analyses the role of each of the three channels through which ICT contributes to productivity growth and convergence. It then analyses how the quality of the economic and institutional environment determines the diffusion and productive use of ICT. In section 5.3, the chapter speculates on the long-term contribution of ICT to GDP growth in Poland as a proxy for other advanced CEE countries. In section 5.4, the chapter adopts an industry-level perspective to show the divergence in labour productivity growth between ICT-using and non-ICT-using industries in CEE countries, the EU-15 and the US. Section 5.5 discusses the economic potential of a more intensive use of ICT in the non-ICT-using sector. Section 5.6 presents conclusions and policy recommendations.

5.2   The contribution of ICT to convergence and its determinants

The measurement of the contribution of ICT to labour productivity is based on the growth accounting methodology developed by Solow (1957) and later extended by Jorgenson and Griliches (1967).[4] According

to this methodology, ICT can affect economic growth through three channels:

1. Use of ICT capital as an input in the production of other goods and services;
2. Increase in total factor productivity (TFP) of production in the ICT sector, which contributes to aggregate TFP growth in an economy;
3. Contribution to economy-wide TFP from the increase in productivity in non-ICT-producing sectors induced by production and use of ICT (spillover effects).

As regards the contribution of the first channel to productivity in four CEE countries for which sufficient data are available, Figure 5.1 shows that in Hungary and Slovakia the ICT sector accelerated convergence, as its contribution to labour productivity growth was higher than in the EU-15.[5] However, it was not the case of Poland and – to a lesser extent – the Czech Republic, where the contribution of ICT production to productivity was lower than in both the EU-15 and the US. It mainly resulted from a slower productivity growth due to a lower share of high-value added products in total ICT production.[6] As argued by Piatkowski and Van Ark (2005), the divergence in the size of the ICT sector among four CEE countries was mostly driven by differences in the value of FDI flowing into the sector. This in turn depended on the degree of trade openness, basic rule of law, development of infrastructure, macroeconomic stability and privatisation policies.

A large ICT-producing sector is not, however, a prerequisite to benefiting from ICT to accelerate GDP growth and productivity (OECD 2004). This is so also because the evidence for positive spillover effects due to ICT production is scant.[7] What really matters is not production, but rather the use of ICT. This is particularly true in CEE countries, where because of the small size, the ICT-producing sector alone would not be sufficient to stimulate growth.[8] Hence, faster convergence with developed countries will have to rely on the use of ICT.

Fortunately, it turns out that the use of ICT may drive convergence. Figure 5.2 shows that between 1995 and 2003 the contribution of ICT investment to labour productivity growth in the Czech Republic, Hungary, Poland and Slovenia was higher than in the EU-15. Thus, these four countries managed to benefit from ICT more than the EU-15, due to faster growth rates and a higher return on ICT investment. This result is all the more noteworthy, as all four countries have considerably lower levels of GDP per capita (higher GDP per capita is usually closely related

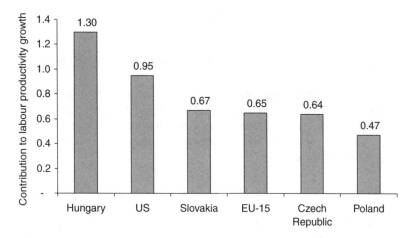

Figure 5.1 The contribution of the ICT-producing sector to labour productivity growth in four CEE countries, the EU-15 and US, 1995–2003 average, in percentage points

Source: Updated results from Van Ark and Piatkowski (2004)

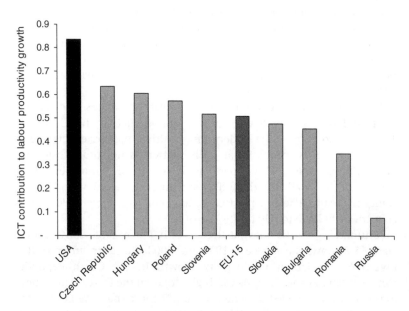

Figure 5.2 The contribution of ICT investment to labour productivity growth in CEER countries, EU-15 and the US, 1995–2003, in percentage points

Source: Van Ark and Piatkowski (2006). Updated results from Piatkowski (2004) for Russia

to the intensity of ICT investment). Nonetheless, the contribution of ICT investment to productivity growth was still lower than in the US. This lower contribution resulted from a lower level of ICT capital accumulated over time, as CEE countries started from a very low ICT capital base at the beginning of the post-communist transition. Worryingly, in the case of Romania, Russia and – to a lesser extent – Slovakia and Bulgaria, the contribution of ICT investment to productivity was below that of the EU-15 and the US. This was mostly due to a much slower growth in ICT investment (WITSA 2004). Thus, low ICT investment was one of the factors that slowed the closing of the income gap between these four countries and developed economies.

What explains such large differences in the intensity of ICT investment and its impact on productivity growth in transition economies? Van Ark and Piatkowski (2004) argue that this divergence seems to be primarily due to differences in the overall quality of the economic and institutional environment, including labour and product market flexibility, development of infrastructure, spending on innovation, quality of human capital, development of financial markets and macroeconomic stability.[9] Table 5.1 shows that in all of these economic and institutional dimensions, which Piatkowski (2002) combined in the *New Economy Indicator*, Slovakia, Russia, Bulgaria and Romania lag behind most other countries.[10] The World Bank (2005) and *Global Competitiveness Report* (2005–6) provide similar results. The strong relationship between the impact of ICT investment on productivity and the value of the New Economy Indicator underscores the importance of the appropriate economic and institutional environment for the diffusion and efficient use of ICT.

As opposed to the large impact of ICT investment on productivity, the contribution of ICT to growth through the two remaining channels, that is through the increase in TFP of ICT production and through spillover effects of ICT use, is not likely to be significant. This is due to the small size of the ICT sector and relatively low penetration of ICT networks, which limit spillover effects of ICT use (Piatkowski 2004).

5.3 The potential of ICT for long-term growth in transition economies

What are the prospects for the long-term role of ICT in growth? Can ICT drive convergence of not only the advanced CEE economies, but also of Bulgaria, Romania, Russia and possibly other transition and developing economies?

Table 5.1 The New Economy Indicator for CEER countries, EU-15 and the US, 1995–2003 average

Country	Rank	Value 1995–2003	Regulations and law enforcement	Infrastructure	Trade openness	Financial system	R&D spending	Human capital	Labour market flexibility	Product market flexibility	Openness to foreign investment	Macro-economic stability
United States	1	8.91	0.75	1.10	-1.60	2.87	1.23	1.49	2.16	1.03	-0.54	0.40
Sweden	2	8.45	0.84	1.76	-0.15	0.36	2.49	1.14	-0.04	0.69	0.88	0.47
Finland	3	6.91	1.09	1.15	-0.40	-0.38	1.71	2.26	-0.09	0.52	0.58	0.47
UK	4	6.88	1.01	0.71	-0.73	1.04	0.35	0.51	1.56	1.16	0.88	0.39
Ireland	5	6.60	0.83	0.38	2.06	0.41	-0.36	-0.40	0.51	0.90	2.02	0.24
Netherlands	6	6.24	1.05	0.76	0.91	0.96	0.47	0.04	-0.37	0.61	1.45	0.35
Denmark	7	6.24	0.95	1.42	-0.26	0.03	0.71	0.38	1.39	0.90	0.30	0.40
Belgium	8	5.79	0.35	0.17	1.81	0.06	0.50	0.37	1.23	0.51	0.34	0.45
Austria	9	3.15	0.90	0.44	0.19	0.55	0.38	0.08	0.13	0.60	-0.57	0.46
Germany	10	2.18	0.75	0.59	-0.66	0.83	0.96	-0.29	-0.70	0.53	-0.32	0.50
France	11	-0.17	0.22	0.36	-0.92	0.20	0.76	0.01	-1.30	0.12	-0.08	0.46
Portugal	12	-0.68	0.26	-0.19	-0.39	0.77	-0.89	-0.29	-0.86	0.35	0.26	0.30
Czech Republic	13	-1.73	-0.42	-0.58	0.91	-0.38	-0.44	-1.59	0.79	-0.14	-0.19	0.30
Spain	14	-1.79	0.23	-0.17	-0.78	0.34	-0.71	0.24	-1.30	0.24	-0.19	0.32
Hungary	15	-2.33	-0.28	-0.83	1.05	-0.94	-0.85	-1.00	0.29	-0.07	0.52	-0.23
Slovenia	16	-2.53	-0.46	-0.14	0.83	-0.83	-0.08	0.43	-1.19	-0.26	-0.73	-0.11
Italy	17	-3.23	-0.26	0.26	-0.89	-0.14	-0.53	-0.28	-0.81	-0.11	-0.84	0.37
Slovakia	18	-3.98	-1.04	-1.03	1.35	-0.53	-0.85	-1.64	0.18	0.07	-0.37	-0.11
Greece	19	-4.79	-0.38	-0.12	-0.93	-0.61	-1.03	0.37	-1.30	-0.09	-0.93	0.24
Poland	20	-6.12	-0.70	-1.36	-0.79	-1.01	-0.98	0.01	0.29	-1.13	-0.50	0.06
Bulgaria	21	-8.90	-1.38	-1.25	0.60	-1.06	-1.13	-0.83	-0.09	-2.15	-0.44	-1.17
Russia	22	-10.27	-2.56	-1.70	-0.72	-1.23	-0.54	0.91	0.68	-2.15	-0.82	-2.14
Romania	23	-14.82	-1.76	-1.73	-0.47	-1.32	-1.18	-1.92	-1.14	-2.15	-0.71	-2.44

Source: Van Ark and Piatkowski (2006).

Table 5.2 Projected ICT investment contribution to GDP growth in Poland during 2002–25, in % points

Real annual rate of growth in ICT investment (%)*	GDP	Total capital	Non-ICT capital	ICT capital	Labour force	TFP	Share of ICT in GDP growth (%)
5	3.76	1.94	1.59	0.35	0.32	1.50	9.3
10	4.01	2.19	1.59	0.60	0.32	1.50	15.0
15	4.26	2.43	1.59	0.85	0.32	1.50	20.0

* Before adjustment for changes in hedonic prices of ICT investment.

Source: Piatkowski (2004).

Based on the same growth accounting model, one can speculate about the long-term contribution of ICT to economic growth. The size of this contribution will mostly depend on the projected growth rate in ICT investment. The rate of growth, as argued in the previous section, will in turn be closely related to the pace of improvement in the overall business environment. Piatkowski (2004) shows that depending on the projected rate of growth in real ICT investment, ICT investment alone would contribute between 10 and 20 per cent of annual GDP growth in Poland between 2002 and 2025 (Table 5.2).[11] Given the similar levels of income per capita and ICT investment, the results for Poland could also be seen as representative for other advanced CEE economies.

The projected contribution of ICT investment to GDP growth in Poland is considerable. This projection, however, does not take into account the additional impact of ICT on growth through the increase in productivity (TFP) in the ICT-producing sector and spillover effects of ICT use. If these two channels were factored into the projection, the total contribution of ICT to GDP growth would most likely surpass 25 per cent.[12] Hence, provided that the growth in ICT investment continues, ICT could have a large contribution to the future development of Poland and – per proxy – other advanced transition economies. It could also benefit Bulgaria, Romania, Russia and other less developed transition economies as long as the institutional and economic environment improves sufficiently to stimulate faster growth in ICT investment and use.

The potential of ICT, however, does not stop here. It is because the impact of ICT on the pace of economic development could be

much larger than what is now possible to measure with traditional economic methods. It mostly concerns the non-linear effects of the spread of ICT networks, which can stimulate even higher productivity growth through:

(a) Facilitating faster production, diffusion, and sharing of knowledge which is likely to accelerate the pace of innovation;
(b) Stimulating changes in business models and investment in human capital;[13]
(c) Galvanising the development of yet unknown applications enhancing overall productivity growth, as did earlier technological revolutions based on general-purpose technologies such as electricity and the combustion engine.[14] In this sense, ICT investment is generally superior to investments in alternative assets (real estate, machinery, means of transport and so on) since the potential of the latter for stimulating new applications is most often dramatically smaller than that of ICT.

The ICT-driven boom in productivity will not happen, however, without substantial progress in the penetration of ICT networks in CEE countries, as the benefits of their use grow exponentially with every additional participant in the network. Alas, despite the extraordinary progress in recent years, ICT penetration in CEE countries is still much lower than in the EU-15 (Eurostat 2005). Consequently, until the CEE countries achieve higher ICT penetration, the network effects of ICT use are not likely to be significant.

The ICT-led productivity boom will not materialise immediately, either. This is because firms investing in ICT need time to learn to use it productively. It took the US economy more than 20 years to fully benefit from ICT investment started already in the early 1970s. Until the mid 1990s Solow's (1987) famous 'productivity paradox' still seemed to be valid.[15] It is only after 1995 that ICT started to drive the productivity boom. The adoption of electricity, another revolutionary general-purpose technology, exhibited a similar pattern: it was only in the 1920s – 40 years after the discovery of electricity – that more than half of US companies learned to use electricity in the production process (David 1990).

Therefore, it seems very likely that, in line with the growth in ICT penetration, a similar sequence of events could unfold in transition economies. This time, however, thanks to the much higher level of countries' openness and the development of the Internet, which immensely

facilitates the exchange and sharing of knowledge, the learning process of ICT use may be shorter than earlier. Given that investment in ICT in most CEE countries started in earnest only around 1995, ICT use should start to strongly feed into the productivity statistics around 2010.

Such a positive scenario, however, is by no means given. As argued by Piatkowski and Van Ark (2005), the economic potential of ICT in transition economies will hinge on a continued increase in ICT investment and – even more importantly – on the ability to incorporate ICT into business models, improve the quality of human capital and enhance managerial skills.

5.4   ICT use and convergence from a sectoral perspective

Aside from the macro perspective, it is also useful to look at the potential of ICT from an industry-level perspective. The first thing to note is that given the small size of the ICT-producing sector in CEE countries and the fact that the most straightforward transition growth reserves (i.e. those resulting from an almost completed privatisation, an advanced stage of institution building, macroeconomic stability, elimination of loss-making state-owned enterprises, and so on), have already been exhausted (although less so in Bulgaria, Romania and Russia), the sustained convergence with developed countries will have to rely on faster productivity growth in the non-ICT-producing sectors, particularly in services.

Van Ark and Piatkowski (2006) provide estimates of labour productivity growth rates in ICT-producing, ICT-using and non-ICT-using, 'old economy' industries in four CEE countries (the Czech Republic, Hungary, Poland and Slovakia), the only ones for which sufficient data are available, for the period 1995–2003.[16]

Table 5.3 shows that productivity growth rates in ICT-using manufacturing in four CEE countries were significantly higher than in non-ICT-using, traditional manufacturing. This suggests that ICT use on the industrial level has been an important source of productivity growth and thus of convergence.[17]

Productivity growth rates in ICT-using manufacturing in CEE countries are also substantially higher than in the EU-15 and in the US. Such a rapid productivity growth resulted mostly from the deep restructuring of ICT-using manufacturing industries driven by basic fundamental reforms allowing for inflows of FDI, product market liberalisation, an

Table 5.3   Labour productivity growth of ICT-producing, ICT-using and non-ICT-using industries, 1995–2003

	EU-15	US	Czech Republic	Hungary	Poland	Slovakia
Total economy	1.3	2.2	2.8	2.4	3.3	2.5
ICT-producing industries	7.2	9.6	13.0	7.8	5.8	8.5
ICT-producing manufacturing	11.9	23.0	15.4	7.5	8.1	7.1
ICT-producing services	5.5	1.8	12.9	8.6	4.6	9.2
ICT-using industries	1.6	4.6	4.4	1.0	4.8	1.8
ICT-using manufacturing	1.6	0.1	9.2	7.1	12.0	7.1
ICT-using services	1.5	5.4	2.3	−0.6	2.3	−1.1
Non-ICT-using industries	0.6	−0.2	1.3	2.3	2.4	2.4
Non-ICT-using manufacturing	1.3	0.2	5.3	2.6	4.6	3.4
Non-ICT-using services	0.2	−0.2	−1.5	2.1	1.9	4.1
Non-ICT-using other	1.9	0.7	2.3	2.6	1.3	−1.8

Note: Real estate has been excluded from both GDP and total persons engaged for all countries; for CEE countries the US ICT deflators exclude prices of computers and semiconductors. Productivity growth defined as GDP per person employed.

Source: Updated results from Van Ark and Piatkowski (2004).

increase in management skills, labour shedding and replacement of old equipment with new capital embedding modern technologies, particularly ICT. Due to high productivity growth, ICT-using manufacturing industries in CEE countries had a considerable contribution to total labour productivity growth (Table 5.4).

However, as opposed to ICT-using manufacturing, productivity growth in ICT-using services in CEE countries was much lower than in the US and in manufacturing (Figure 5.3). The difference in the productivity growth in the ICT-using services in favour of the US provides grounds for a hypothesis of a 'two-phase' convergence.[18] In the first phase, as argued by Van Ark and Piatkowski (2004), productivity growth is driven by the restructuring of ICT-using manufacturing based on a relatively simple replacement of old machinery with new equipment and growth in FDI-driven ICT production. Quite importantly, such a replacement does not require any major changes to enterprise organisation or large investments in human skills. In the second phase, however, economy-wide productivity growth needs to be driven by ICT use in the service and 'old economy', non-ICT-using sectors. This requires a more conducive business environment, the full opening of product markets to competition, more flexible labour markets, and reorganisation of

Table 5.4 Contributions to labour productivity growth of ICT-producing, ICT-using and non-ICT-using industries, 1995–2003

	EU-15	US	Czech Republic	Hungary	Poland	Slovakia
Total economy	1.34	2.19	2.83	2.41	3.33	2.5
ICT-producing industries	0.58	0.98	0.68	0.68	0.21	0.15
ICT-producing manufacturing	0.2	0.73	0.15	0.27	0.06	0.12
ICT-producing services	0.38	0.25	0.53	0.42	0.15	0.03
ICT-using industries	0.46	1.17	1.55	0.54	1.57	0.4
ICT-using manufacturing	−0.01	−0.12	0.67	0.46	0.65	0.98
ICT-using services	0.47	1.29	0.89	0.07	0.92	−0.58
Non-ICT-using industries	0.29	0.06	0.6	1.19	1.56	1.96
Non-ICT-using manufacturing	0.01	−0.18	0.94	0.31	0.66	1.84
Non-ICT-using services	0.3	0.1	−0.01	0.8	0.75	1.54
Non-ICT-using other	−0.01	0.14	−0.33	0.08	0.15	−1.43

Note: see Table 5.3.

Source: Updated results from Van Ark and Piatkowski (2004).

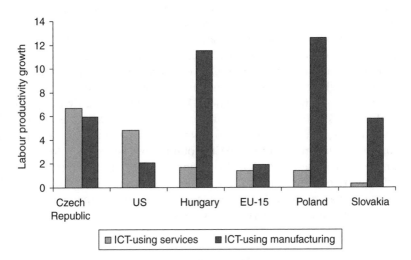

Figure 5.3 Labour productivity growth rates in ICT-using services and ICT-using manufacturing in CEE, the EU-15 and the US, 1995–2003 average

Note: Countries were ordered according to the size of labour productivity growth in ICT-using services

Source: Updated results from Van Ark and Piatowski (2004)

business processes around ICT rather than automation of the existing organisational structures, which yields only marginal benefits (OECD 2004; Davenport 1992; Brynjolfsson and Hitt 2000). It also requires larger investment in human and ICT skills and improvement in management practices. As for the latter, Dorgan and Dowdy (2004) show, on the basis of an enterprise survey in the US, UK, Germany and France, that productivity growth stemming from IT investment can be substantial only when it is supported by high-quality management practices. These seem to be indispensable to allow for the process innovation necessary to reap full benefits of ICT use.

Piatkowski and Van Ark (2005) argue that among the analysed group of CEE countries, EU-15 and the US, only the latter has succeeded in creating a sufficiently conducive business environment to move to the 'second phase' of the productive use of ICT as evidenced by much higher productivity growth rates in ICT-using services. OECD (2004), WEF (2005) and Timmer and Van Ark (2005) also point to the success of the Nordic countries and Australia in promoting the diffusion and productive use of ICT.

As for CEE economies, this means that to move to the 'second phase' of convergence they will have to implement far-reaching structural reforms largely modelled on either the US, Australian or Nordic economies. This, however, will not be easy, given the social sensitivity to enhancing labour market flexibility (including the ease of hiring and firing) and opening industries to full competition (particularly in telecommunications, postal services and utilities). Furthermore, given the lack of fiscal space for substantially higher public spending in most CEE countries (IMF 2005), it will be difficult to increase spending on R&D and innovation. Lastly, as argued by Piatkowski (2004), given that under the centrally planned economic system there were no incentives to innovate, because of the lack of a history of innovation, enterprises in CEE countries will be less likely to experiment than those in developed economies. All in all, if the structural reforms are not implemented, the ICT-led convergence may slow as the restructuring process in ICT-using manufacturing nears completion and further investment in ICT yields only diminishing returns.

5.5 The potential of ICT use in services and 'old economy' industries

Since ICT-using industries in CEE countries reported higher productivity growth than non-ICT-using services and 'old economy' industries, higher

investment in ICT business applications (enterprise resource planning (ERP), customer relationship management (CRM), online procurement, e-commerce and so on), coupled with organisational innovations and enhanced human skills, could contribute to faster productivity growth in 'old economy' industries and thus accelerate convergence with developed countries.

What would be the impact on a nationwide productivity growth if the non-ICT-using, 'old economy' industries increased their productivity growth thanks to a more intensive ICT use? Figure 5.4 shows that under the assumption that the 'old economy' manufacturing industries in CEE countries could achieve the same rate of productivity growth as in modern ICT-using manufacturing, the additional contribution to the economy-wide productivity growth would be substantial. In the case of Poland, the additional 1.01 percentage point contribution to labour productivity growth would allow it to catch up with the average EU-15 level of productivity six years earlier than in a baseline scenario, that is, in 2023 instead of 2029. The Czech Republic, Hungary and Slovakia would also catch up faster.

Is this projected acceleration in productivity growth in non-ICT-using, 'old economy' industries in CEE countries realistic? It seems so, given this existing considerable productivity gap. According to Havlik and

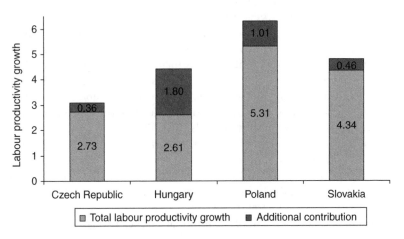

Figure 5.4 Additional contribution to aggregate labour productivity growth from ICT-led acceleration in productivity growth in the non-ICT-using, 'old economy' manufacturing in CEE countries, 1995–2003 average

Source: Author's own calculations based on updated results from Van Ark and Piatowski (2004)

Urban (2003), in the Czech Republic, Hungary and Poland the level of labour productivity in the 'old economy' industries of food processing, textiles, wood products, pulp, paper and publishing, chemicals and basic metals in 2002 did not exceed 40 per cent of the average EU-15 level. Hence, there is ample scope for ICT-driven productivity growth.

As argued by Piatkowski (2005a), similarly large economic benefits to the whole economy would ensue if the ICT-using services in CEE countries caught up with the labour productivity growth rate in the ICT-using service sector in the US.[19] However, as asserted in the previous section, such a sizeable productivity increase could not be achieved without a large increase in ICT investment, supported by macroeconomic stability and fully developed market institutions, complemented with improvements in business organisation, process innovation, human skills, management practices and in the quality of the business climate.

Apart from the private sector, ICT use can also stimulate productivity growth in the public sector (eGovernment Observatory 2005). Potential benefits from more intensive ICT use would be particularly large for transition economies, where the overall quality and efficiency of the public sector are low relative to developed countries (World Bank 2005). A more intensive use of ICT would increase the public sector's productivity, enhance the quality of spending, improve collection of tax revenue, and generate large savings in operating costs.[20] It would also boost productivity of the private sector through the reduction of red tape, a decrease in corruption, better quality of services, and easier access to information. These benefits could go a long way towards generating additional resources for funding additional investments in infrastructure, human capital and ICT.

A more intensive use of ICT in the public sector and active public ICT policies are also indispensable to promote the diffusion and use of ICT in the private sector, as shown by the Nordic countries, the US and Australia (OECD 2004). Public 'push strategy' is particularly important in the context of transition economies, where the market mechanisms do not yet work as efficiently as in developed countries and thus leave more scope for effective public intervention. A number of countries in the CEE region have demonstrated the benefits of active public ICT policies. This in particular concerns Estonia and Slovenia, the two regional leaders in ICT diffusion and development of the information society (Gáspár 2004).[21]

5.6   Conclusions

Between 1995 and 2003 ICT contributed to faster growth and accelerated convergence of the Czech Republic, Hungary, Poland and Slovenia with

the EU-15. However, Romania, Russia and – to a lesser extent – Slovakia and Bulgaria lagged behind. This was due to the lower quality of the economic and institutional environment, which stymied the diffusion and efficient use of ICT. The cross-country divergence in the economic impact of ICT investment indicates a close link between the diffusion of ICT and advancement of economic reforms. Given that Bulgaria and Romania will join the EU in 2007–8, which will strengthen their economic environment as well as provide each with substantial additional funds for investment in ICT, the role of ICT in the development of these two countries is likely to increase. Likewise, increased EU funding and an improved business climate should also spur ICT investment in Slovakia, already an EU member. However, this will not be the case for Russia and other transition economies not joining the EU. There is hence a risk that the divergence in the ICT contribution to growth between EU members and other transition countries will grow.

Far-reaching structural and institutional reforms modelled on best practices from the US, Australia and the Nordic countries are the main way to benefit from the large potential of ICT for faster economic development. The same reforms, however, will also be vital to stimulate overall growth not only through ICT, but also through the 'old economy', traditional sources of growth: more intensive innovation, higher physical investment, and enhanced quality of human capital. Nonetheless, ICT can be a potent source of growth on its own, as its production and use until 2025 are likely to accelerate economic growth in CEE countries by more than one-quarter.

At the sectoral level, since the ICT-producing sector in CEE countries is too small to be a main driver of growth and because the simple transition growth reserves have already been exhausted, sustained productivity growth and convergence with the EU-15 and the US will now have to rely on the productive use of ICT in the non-ICT-producing sector, in services and in the 'old economy' manufacturing industries. This chapter provides evidence that ICT use had an important role in stimulating productivity growth, as ICT-using industries reported much higher productivity growth rates than non-ICT-using industries.

If non-ICT-using industries, both in the service and 'old economy' manufacturing sector, were able to increase the intensity of ICT investment and thus achieve the same rate of productivity growth as the ICT-using industries, they would provide a considerable boost to the convergence with developed countries. Realising this potential, however, would require further structural reforms aimed at opening borders to trade, increasing inflows of foreign capital and spending on human

capital, improving effectiveness of law enforcement, enhancing macro-economic stability and – above all – promoting vigorous competition in the labour and product markets. At firm level, this would in turn require accelerating reorganisation of business processes around ICT, improving management practices, increasing spending on innovation and, finally, augmenting investment in human capital and ICT skills. These recommendations are valid for not only transition economies, but also for most advanced developing countries.

The public sector could also have a special role in driving ICT-led growth by stimulating a conducive business environment and promoting ICT use. The latter could be done primarily through full development of public e-services, including e-procurement. This would not only bring considerable savings in the public sector, decrease bureaucracy, reduce corruption and enhance the quality of the business climate, but would also stimulate the interest of enterprises in using more advanced ICT applications. Such a public 'push strategy' could then have sizeable spillover effects on the use of ICT in the whole economy.

Notes

This chapter should not be reported as representing the views of the International Monetary Fund. It has been printed with copyright permission from *Information Technologies and International Development*.

1 For macro research on the US see, for instance, Jorgenson *et al.* (2004); on the EU-15 see Timmer *et al.* (2003). On the industry level in the US and the EU: Stiroh (2002), Timmer and Van Ark (2005) and OECD (2003). On a micro-level in the US and the EU: Brynjolfsson and Hitt (1996, 2000) and OECD (2004, 2003). For an initially sceptical view of the ICT impact on the US economy, see Gordon (2000). Later, however, Gordon changed his mind (Gordon 2004).
2 See also a recent paper by Jorgenson and Vu (2005), which analyses the impact of ICT on growth in a large sample of developed, developing and transition economies. On a more general level, Kolodko (2000) provides an insightful analysis of the sources of growth in post-communist countries.
3 CEE includes Bulgaria, Czech Republic, Hungary, Poland, Romania, Slovakia and Slovenia.
4 In essence, the growth accounting methodology divides labour productivity growth into its sources in the change of physical capital available in an economy and in residual productivity that cannot be directly attributed to growth in either capital or labour (so-called TFP which can grow due to a more efficient use of the existing physical capital, rising quality of human capital, improvement in managerial skills, etc). For details on the methodology, refer to Van Ark and Piatkowski (2004).
5 There are not enough consistent data on the ICT-producing sector in other CEE countries and Russia. However, Gáspár (2004) provides some data on the share of the ICT sector in GDP in Slovenia, Bulgaria and Romania. In turn,

Perminov and Egorova (2005) estimate the contribution of the ICT-producing sector to growth in Russia. Alas, due to different methodologies, their results are not directly comparable with this chapter.

6   Higher productivity growth in the ICT-producing sector in the US was mostly due to rapid productivity growth in the production of semiconductors (Intel, AMD), which are not manufactured in CEE countries (Van Ark and Piatkowski 2004).

7   Trajtenberg (2005) provides a useful example. He argues that while since 1990 the ICT sector in Israel grew at a double-digit rate per year, at the same time the rest of the economy stagnated. Productivity in some non-ICT-producing sectors even declined. Thus, conversely to the argument of spillover effects, Trajtenberg asserts that the gap between the ICT sector and the rest of the economy actually increased socio-economic inequality in Israel and led to the emergence of a 'dual economy'. The latter may affect the growth potential of the Israeli economy by restricting the pool of skilled labour and creating tensions detrimental to growth.

8   Even if the share of the ICT sector in CEE countries grew to 10 per cent of GDP and its productivity growth increased to 10 per cent a year, its annual contribution to GDP growth would amount to only 1 percentage point. This is not enough, given that CEE countries need to grow at close to 4–5 per cent a year to continue to close the income divide with developed countries.

9   Other studies on the determinants of the productive use of ICT call attention to the same factors (Clarke 2003; OECD 2003, 2004; Muller and Salsas 2003, 2004). Vu (2004) adds to the list institutional quality and fluency in English. Alas, given the paucity of data and the small size of the sample, it is not possible to statistically test the relative importance of each of these determinants for transition economies.

10 The *New Economy Indicator* has been constructed to measure the institutional capability of transition economies to exploit the potential of ICT. The indicator combines ten variables based mostly on data from the World Bank's 'World Development Indicators' and OECD. The sample mean of values of all variables is subtracted from each number and then the result is divided by sample standard deviation. This implies a mean of zero and a standard deviation of one across countries in the sample. Hence, all results are comparable and can be aggregated. For a complete methodology of the *New Economy Indicator*, please refer to Piatkowski (2002) and Van Ark and Piatkowski (2004).

11 Piatkowski (2004) assumes that the quality-adjusted (so-called hedonic) prices of IT hardware, software and telecommunications equipment until 2025 will decrease at a rate equal to the 1990–2001 average for the US, that is, respectively, 20.7, 1.3 and 3.2 per cent annually.

12 Since projections on the future of the ICT industry in any country are burdened with a large risk, any long-term assumptions as to the size, TFP growth rate in the ICT sector and ICT spillover effects are purely speculative. Nonetheless, it is very likely that the ICT sector – in line with the increasing penetration of ICT – should be growing faster than the rest of CEE economies.

13 It is not possible to introduce, for instance, ICT-based 'just-in-time' procurement without substantial changes in enterprise organisation and additional

employee training. The introduction of ICT thus stimulates changes that are likely to enhance the productivity of the whole enterprise.

14   The history of the steam engine is a fitting example. The original purpose of steam engines was only to run pumps draining water from underground coal shafts. It was only much later that the potential of steam engines was fully realised in transport, manufacturing and almost every other aspect of economic and social life. ICT seems to have the same extraordinary potential, which is still far from being fully discovered.

15   Solow (1987) famously quipped that 'You can see the computer age everywhere but in the productivity statistics.'

16   ICT-producing industries include manufacturing of computer hardware, software and telecommunications equipment, and provision of computer and telecommunications services. ICT-using industries are those that intensively use ICT in their operations, as reflected in the high share of ICT capital in total assets. These industries include, *inter alia*, printing and publishing, mechanical engineering, aircraft building, wholesale and retail trade and financial intermediation. Non-ICT-using, 'old economy' industries include, among others, food, textiles, pulp and paper, basic metals, hotels and catering, transport, public administration, agriculture and utilities. For the complete list refer to Van Ark and Piatkowski (2004). For the methodology underlying the ICT classification, turn to O'Mahony and Van Ark (2003).

17   It has to be remembered, however, that these results do not prove the causality between ICT and productivity growth. It may be that either ICT use contributes to faster productivity growth or that industries with high productivity growth rates happen to use ICT intensively. However, given the available evidence from developed countries and CEE countries, the first proposition sounds more plausible.

18   It is worth noting, though, that the measurement of productivity growth in the service sector is plagued by a number of measurement problems. See, for instance, Triplett and Bosworth (2004).

19   Although the high productivity growth in the US service sector seems to have been at least partly driven by factors unique to the US, including economies of scale, stock market boom, and the 'Wal-Mart effect'. See, for instance, McKinsey (2001).

20   For instance, according to Poland's Ministry of Finance (2005), streamlining the existing more than 200 various IT tax systems and creating a single treasury management account could generate annual savings of up to 1.5 per cent of GDP.

21   Piatkowski (2005b) also recounts a story of a successful public push strategy in Poland. In 1999 the Polish Social Security Agency (ZUS) made it mandatory for all firms, large and small, to file social security documentation only in an electronic form. As a result, despite some early complaining, within a couple of years computer penetration in the business sector became practically universal.

References

Brynjolfsson, E. and L. Hitt (1996) 'Paradox Loss? Firm-level Evidence on the Returns to Information System Spending', *Management Science*, 42 (4): 541–58.

Brynjolfsson, E. and L. M. Hitt (2000) 'Beyond Computation: Information Technology, Organizational Transformation and Business Practices', *Journal of Economic Perspectives*, 14 (4): 23–48.

Clarke, G. R. (2003) 'Bridging the Digital Divide: How Enterprise Ownership and Foreign Competition Affect Internet Access in Eastern Europe and Central Asia', mimeo, Washington, DC: World Bank.

David, P. (1990) 'The Dynamo and the Computer: an Historical Perspective on the Modern Productivity Paradox', *American Economic Review*, 80 (2): 355–61.

Davenport, T. H. (1992) *Process Innovation: Reengineering Work through Information Technology*, Harvard Business School Press, pp. 1–352.

Dorgan, S. J and J. J. Dowdy (2004) 'When IT Lifts Productivity', *McKinsey Quarterly* 4, http://www.mckinseyquarterly.com/ab_g.aspx?ar=1477&L2=13&L3=11

eGovernment Observatory (2005) 'The Impact of e-Government and Competitiveness, Growth and Jobs', IDABC Background Research Paper, February, http://europa.eu.int/idabc/servlets/Doc?id=19230

Eurostat (2005) *New Cronos Database: Information Society Statistics*, http://epp.eurostat.cec.eu.int

Gáspár, P. (2004) 'Factors and Impacts in the Information Society: a Prospective Analysis in New Member States and Associated Candidate Countries in the EU – Synthesis Report', Sevilla: IPTS.

Global Competitiveness Report (2005–6) Geneva: World Economic Forum.

Gordon, R. (2000) 'Does the "New Economy" Measure up to the Great Inventions of the Past?', *Journal of Economic Perspectives*, 14 (4): 49–74.

Gordon, R. (2004) 'Why Was Europe Left at the Station when America's Productivity Locomotive Departed?', CEPR Discussion Paper 4416, London: CEPR.

Havlik, P. and W. Urban (2003) 'Industrial Development in the Accession Countries', *Structural Report 2003 on Central and Easter Europe*, Vol. 1, October, Vienna, pp. 27–68.

IMF (2001) *World Economic Outlook. The Information Technology Revolution*, Chapter III, Washington, DC: IMF, pp. 103–42.

IMF (2005) *World Economic Outlook. Building Institutions*, Washington, DC: IMF, pp. 1–294.

Jorgenson, D. W. and Z. Griliches (1967) 'The Explanation of Productivity Change', *The Review of Economic Studies*, 34 (99): 249–80.

Jorgenson, D. W., M. S. Ho and K. J. Stiroh (2004) 'Will the U.S. Productivity Resurgence Continue?', *Current Issues in Economics and Finance*, 10 (13): 1–7.

Jorgenson, D. W. and K. Vu (2005) 'Information Technology and the World Economy', *Scandinavian Journal of Economics*, 107 (4).

Kolodko, G. W. (2000) *From Shock to Therapy. The Political Economy of Post-socialist Transformation*, Oxford: Oxford University Press for UNU-WIDER.

Lee, Il-Houng and Y. Khatri (2003) 'Information Technology and Productivity Growth in Asia', IMF Working Paper 03/15, January, Washington, DC: IMF.

McKinsey (2001) *U.S. Productivity Growth, 1995–2000: Understanding the Importance of Information and Technology Relative to Other Factors*, Washington, DC: McKinsey Global Institute.

Muller, P. and P. Salsas (2003) 'Internet Use in Transition Countries Economic and Institutional Determinants', TIGER Working Paper Series 44, August, Warsaw.

Muller, P. and P. Salsas (2004) 'Internet Use by Businesses in Old and New EU Member Countries', TIGER Working Paper Series 63, September, Warsaw.

OECD (2003) *ICT and Economic Growth: Evidence from OECD Countries, Industries and Firms*, Paris: OECD.

OECD (2004) *The Economic Impact of ICT*, Paris: OECD.

O'Mahony, M. and B. Van Ark (eds) (2003) 'EU Productivity and Competitiveness: an Industry Perspective. Can Europe Resume the Catching-up Process?', Luxembourg: Office for Official Publications of the European Communities.

Perminov, S. and E. Egorova (2005) 'ICT Impact on Labor Productivity and Employment in Russia', TIGER Working Paper Series 73, February, Warsaw.

Piatkowski, M. (2002) 'The "New Economy" and Economic Growth in Transition Economies. The Relevance of Institutional Infrastructure', Discussion Paper 2002/62, Helsinki: UNU-WIDER.

Piatkowski, M. (2004) 'The Impact of ICT on Growth in Transition Economies', TIGER Working Paper Series 59, July, Warsaw.

Piatkowski, M. (2005a) *The Potential of ICT for the Development and Economic Restructuring of the New EU Member States and Candidate Countries*, IPTS Technical Report, February, Directorate-General Joint Research Center, European Commission.

Piatkowski, M. (2005b) *Information Society in Poland. A Prospective Analysis.* Warsaw: Leon Kozminski Academy Publishing House, pp. 1–206.

Piatkowski, M. and B. Van Ark (2005) 'ICT and Productivity Growth in Transition Economies: Two-Phase Convergence and Structural Reforms', TIGER Working Paper Series 72, January, Warsaw.

Poland's Ministry of Finance (2005) Information from www.mofnet.gov.pl

Solow, R. (1957) 'Technical Change and the Aggregate Production Function', *Review of Economics and Statistics*, 39 (3), August: 312–20.

Solow, R. (1987) 'We'd Better Watch Out', *New York Times* Book Review, 12 July: 26.

Stiroh, K. (2002) 'Information Technology and the U.S. Productivity Revival: a Review of the Evidence', *Business Economics*, XXXVII (1): 30–7.

Timmer, M. P. and B. van Ark (2005) 'Does Information and Communication Technology Drive Productivity Growth Differentials? A Comparison of the European Union Countries and the United States', *Oxford Economic Papers* (accepted).

Timmer, M. P., G. Ypma and B. van Ark (2003) 'IT in the European Union: Driving Productivity Divergence?', GGDC Research Memorandum GD-67, October, University of Groningen; Appendix Tables updated in the GGDC Total Economy Growth Accounting Database June 2005, http://www.ggdc.net

Trajtenberg, M. (2005) 'World Bank, Europe and Central Asia (ECA), Knowledge Economy Study, Part I: Public Support for Innovation', draft, Washington, DC: World Bank.

Triplett, J. E. and B. Bosworth (2004) *Productivity in the U.S. Services Sector. New Sources of Economic Growth*, Washington, DC: Brookings Institution Press.

US Department of Labor (2004) 'Productivity and Costs, Second Quarter 2004', USDL 04–1727, October, Bureau of Labor Statistics.

Van Ark, B. and M. Piatkowski (2004) 'Productivity, Innovation and ICT in Old and New Europe', Research Memorandum GD-69, March, Groningen Growth and Development Centre.

Van Ark, B. and M. Piatkowski (2006) 'Productivity, Innovation and ICT in Old and New Europe', in G. Cette, M. Fouquin and H. W. Sinn (eds) *Divergences in Productivity between Europe and the United States*, London: Edward Elgar.

Vu, K. M. (2004) 'Measuring the Impact of ICT on Economic Growth: an International Comparative Perspective', paper presented at the workshop on 'ICT as Drivers of Economic Development in Post-communist Countries', Conference Board, New York, 19–20 January.

WEF (2005) *Global Information Technology Report (2004–2005)*, Geneva: World Economic Forum.

WITSA (2004) *Digital Planet 2004: the Global Information Economy*, World Information Technology and Services Alliance.

World Bank (2005) *Doing Business. Removing Obstacles to Growth*, Washington, DC: World Bank.

6
ICT Initiatives in India: Lessons for Broad-based Development

P. D. Kaushik

6.1 Introduction

The success of India's export-oriented software industry is well known. But whether information and communication technology (ICT) can contribute to development beyond the obvious income effects generated by software exports depends on how pervasive ICT's impacts are on the economy, ranging from improving the efficiency of existing businesses to enabling the production of new kinds of goods and services. In a developing country such as India, it is of particular interest whether such benefits can reach the poor. For instance, transformation of public and private services into ICT-enabled services may be relatively more valuable for poor people who cannot afford to access such services via conventional means.

Poor infrastructural facilities dampen the potential of harnessing the full benefits of digital media. Pohjola (2000) among others observed that investments in ICTs have a strong influence on economic growth in OECD countries. But his observations confirm that requisite benefits have somehow eluded the developing countries as a result of the poor stock of physical infrastructure in these countries. However, the developing region can ill afford to delay transformation into an information society due to perennial infrastructural limitations. Prahalad (2005) highlighted the potential of ICTs at the bottom of the pyramid, which will considerably help in directly reducing the deprivations associated with poverty.

Technological transformation of a country hinges on its ability to unleash the creativity of its people, enabling them to understand and master technology, to innovate and to adapt technology to suit their

own needs and opportunities. In view of this, developing countries have been experimenting with ICTs for developing a broad-based development strategy. This chapter focuses on three such ongoing ICT-based initiatives in India. Understandably, the inherent infrastructural limitations do exist, but these ICT-based initiatives have made a significant contribution in improving people's quality of life.

6.2   ICT initiatives: Madhya Pradesh, Punjab and Haryana

ICTs have emerged as a strategic tool to overcome ills of poor governance. Some states, like Andhra Pradesh, Maharashtra, Karnataka and Tamil Nadu, have successfully attempted to improve accessibility and affordability for its citizens through proactive state government policies.[1] A few poor states like Madhya Pradesh and Rajasthan have introduced ICT-enabled processes in the government to reach the rural population.[2] The results may vary from region to region, however such isolated but successful experiments have paved the way for others to follow. Two progressive states in northern India, namely Punjab and Haryana, have attempted to replicate these experiments. It is a strange paradox that the two most progressive states of India tend to replicate the ICT initiatives developed by the laggard states in India.

6.2.1   Comparative scenario: Madhya Pradesh, Punjab and Haryana

Madhya Pradesh was the biggest state in the country in terms of area before a new state was carved out in 1999. It is a centrally located state bordering seven others, namely Uttar Pradesh, Bihar, Orissa, Andhra Pradesh, Maharashtra, Gujarat and Rajasthan. It is ranked quite low in terms of agricultural and industrial production and human development indicators as compared to Punjab and Haryana (see Table 6.1). In terms of ICT penetration, its performance is still worse. But in terms of governance, Madhya Pradesh is one of the first states in India which initiated complete devolution of power at village and district level.

Punjab is known as the 'granary of India' because it is the largest supplier of food grains to the central pool. Its average growth rate of 10 per cent is among the highest in the country. It has the highest per capita income in India. On the infrastructure front, the Centre for Monitoring the Indian Economy (CMIE) gives Punjab the highest rating in the country. It has a diverse manufacturing sector, comprising engineering goods, pharmaceuticals, leather goods, food products, textiles, electronic

Table 6.1   Madhya Pradesh, Punjab and Haryana at a glance: 2003–4

Items	Units	Madhya Pradesh	Punjab	Haryana
Geographical area	km^2	443,406	50,362	44,212
Population	100,000	604.8	243.59	217.45
Language	–	Hindi	Gurmukhi	Hindi
Per capita	Rs	5,926	15,880	14,757
Food grain production	100,000 t	15.50	226.91	123.29
Factories	No.	8,620	14,102	8,974
Districts	No.	48	17	19
Villages	No.	51,806	12,278	6,678
Roads	km	67,744	47,605	23,050
Per capita (power)	kWh	313	854	530
Literacy rate	%	63.7	69.7	67.9
No. of telephones	Per 1,000 people	7	44	24

goods, sugar, machine tools, hand tools, agricultural implements, sports goods, paper and paper packaging.

Haryana is a state that was carved out of Punjab after independence for administrative reasons. Not very far behind Punjab, Haryana is also a major agricultural producing state with an equal industrial base. Pucca (bitumen) roads and electricity connect all villages in Haryana and Punjab. Recent liberalisation of the Indian economy has brought Haryana into the global business mainstream due to its proximity to Delhi. One of the reasons for Haryana's fast-paced economic growth can be attributed to the ICT revolution in India. Haryana has emerged as the centre of business process outsourcing (BPO) in north India.

Madhya Pradesh is, compared with Punjab and Haryana, a relatively poor state. However, in terms of ICT-based government-to-citizen initiatives, Madhya Pradesh has left the other two better-developed states behind. The need to initiate the Gyandoot project, an ICT-based initiative, was primarily driven by an attempt at decentralisation by the government of Madhya Pradesh. A close examination of the ICT-based initiatives, namely Gyandoot in Madhya Pradesh, TARAhaat in Punjab and Drishtee in Haryana, provides general guidelines for developing an ICT-based strategy for broad-based development of rural India (see Table 6.2). These initiatives seek to mark a paradigm shift in government delivery systems by using ICT for rural people. The objectives of all three initiatives are similar: to improve affordability and accessibility of ICT-enabled services for the rural population. But there are stark differences in their product

Table 6.2 Product mix of Gyandoot, TARAhaat and Drishtee, and gaps

Service	Observations
E-mail	Functional in Gyandoot and Drishtee
Computer education	Functional in TARAhaat
Market prices of agricultural produce	Functional in Gyandoot and Drishtee
Government services	Functional in Gyandoot and Drishtee
Financial services	Non-functional
Medical services	Partially functional in Gyandoot
Public grievance redress	Functional in Gyandoot and Drishtee

Observations are based on the field survey at Dhar, Bathinda and Sirsa.

mix and characteristics of the main collaborator, which result in significant variation in end-users' response.

6.2.2 Basic framework of rural-based ICT initiatives

Rural-based ICT initiatives have three key stakeholders, namely official agencies, local entrepreneurs and NGOs. Official agencies comprise district administration and locally elected representatives. An entrepreneur is the front-end stakeholder, the contact point for the rural population. Civil society acts as a facilitator or promoter for the initiative. The business model is simple and pluralistic: the main collaborator at the district headquarters is connected to the multimedia kiosks or info-kiosks or *soochanalayas* spread over the entire district via a closed network (intranet). These kiosks are located at places where local people frequently visit or assemble, for instance village council offices, bazaars (markets), local shops, bus depots, etc. The *soochak* or the person operating the *soochanalaya* is an entrepreneur with limited numeric data-entry skills. Although the initiatives have slight variations in their business model, close inspection reveals that the common interface between service provider and citizen is the *soochanalaya*. The back-end activity rests with main collaborators, namely government and NGOs.

6.2.3 Brief profile of the ICT-based initiatives

Gyandoot

Gyandoot is a form of government-to-citizen (G2C) e-commerce activity via a closed network (intranet), which is giving the rural population, in the Dhar district of Madhya Pradesh, affordable access to various

government services and market information. Gyandoot, operational since January 2000, has 21 multimedia kiosks or cyber cafés spread over the entire district of Dhar. Each kiosk provides public services to 20–30 villages, almost 20,000–30,000 people. Gyandoot received international recognition when it was named as joint winner in the Public Services and Democracy category of the Stockholm Challenge Award in 2000.

The architecture of the Gyandoot project rests mainly with the district administration. The District Rural Development Agency (DRDA) acts as the main collaborator, with the village *panchayat* (council) as the local collaborator. The village *panchayat* recommends a local resident to the DRDA who review the applications and select the person to run the kiosk in the village. The DRDA assists the kiosk owner to obtain a bank loan for purchasing requisite hardware and the local *panchayat* covers the cost of the phone line. The NGOs in Dhar district have played an active role in raising the awareness of local residents about the services offered by the info-kiosks. The rural population use Gyandoot to keep track of market prices and accessing government services. The revenues from the kiosk are shared between kiosk owner and *panchayat*.

TARAhaat

The TARAhaat project was launched with financial assistance from its promoter Development Alternatives, an NGO focusing on sustainable rural development in India (Development Alternatives 2001). Technology and Action for Rural Advancement (TARA) is the marketing arm of Development Alternatives. TARAhaat uses a franchisee-based business model to bring computer and Internet technology to rural India. Its business model is based on B2B, B2C and C2C, which attempt to create revenue streams using ICT. It is a horizontal portal, but several domains such as medical services, commodity trade, distance education, etc., appear as strong vertical elements. The portal displays information in the local language. For the majority of the illiterate rural population, the portal uses animated pictures, self-explanatory diagrams and voice-over. The TARAhaat's central core is built around the information needs of the end-user. It has been operational in the Bathinda district of Punjab since January 2001.

TARAhaat has opened eight TARAkendras with assistance from DRDA, Bathinda. All franchisees are located at the focal points identified by the government of Punjab (1997, 2000) and have been operational since early 2001. The TARAkendras are currently linked to the Internet by dial-up connections. TARAhaat has segmented the rural market into five different habitats based on population size.[3] Each *kendra* has a catchment

area of 5 km radius, depending on habitat type. Rough estimates of TARAhaat reveal that each *kendra* serves the needs of 4–6 villages, a population of about 10,000–15,000. The TARAhaat plans to open 47,000 such *kendras* in the country by 2006.

Drishtee

Drishtee is a revenue-generating platform for rural networking and marketing services that enable e-governance, education and health services. It is a project replicated from the Gyandoot project in the form of a commercial initiative. Drishtee is currently associated with Digital Partners for logistic support. It has developed a software package which facilitates communication and information interchange within a localised intranet between village kiosks and the district centre. This initiative addresses the socio-economic developmental needs of the villagers through a G2C-based model.

Drishtee is currently installing low-cost, self-sustaining and community-owned rural intranet projects in the Sirsa district of Haryana. Information services are provided through the Drishtee's *soochanalaya* in a village (or a group of villages). These kiosks or *soochanalayas* provide user-charge-based services to rural people. Each kiosk is equipped with a computer wired through an intranet network connected with the district headquarters. These *soochanalayas* cater to 25–30 surrounding villages or 15 *gram panchayats*, providing information services to a population of 20,000–30,000. With the help from the local DRDA, *soochanalayas* are established in the buildings of *gram panchayats*, which are located either at block headquarters or at prominent bazaars (e.g. a weekly marketplace in tribal areas) or on major roads (e.g. main highways).

In their first phase of operational strategy, Gyandoot and Drishtee have focused on delivery of government services. TARAhaat, on the other hand, has focused on computer education services. Rural society has responded well to such initiatives, and related developmental benefits are evident in terms of response of end-users and the growing number of info-kiosks in the respective districts. However, there exist inherent weaknesses in the initiatives, which considerably affect respective revenue streams.

6.3 Performance appraisal of ICT initiatives

The three ongoing IT initiatives provide an interesting insight into the operational environment. The approach plans of Gyandoot, TARAhaat

Table 6.3 Performance appraisal of TARAhaat, Gyandoot and Drishtee (December 2001)

Indicators	TARAhaat	Gyandoot	Drishtee
Number of kiosks	8 TARAkendras	21 soochanalayas	27 kiosks
Investment required per kiosk	Rs 250,000–300,000 (US$6000–7000)	Rs 50,000–60,000 (US$1250–1500)	Rs 50,000–60,000 (US$1250–1500)
Population covered per kiosk	15,000–20,000	20,000–25,000	10,000–15,000
Services offered	Education services (three modules)	Public services (local services)	Public services (local services)
Unique selling proposition	Increase computer literacy through affordable computer education services	G2C (government-to-citizen)	G2C (government-to-citizen)
Connectivity status	All kendras connected to Internet	All kiosks are connected	Only 50% connected
Revenues per month*	Rs 3500–6000 (US$100–150)	Rs 3000–4000 (US$80–1000)	Rs 3000–4000 (US$80–100)
Franchisee's share	40% (later reduced to 25% for 2001–2)	20%	20%
Marketing strategy	Generate local support through increased public awareness	Delivery of services by reducing opportunity costs	Delivery of services by reducing opportunity costs
Support to kiosk from actors	Visit by TARAhaat local officials, other HRD-related support absent, no formal maintenance support	Gyandoot operations are overseen by DRDA and AMC provided	One-week training, periodic meetings of kiosk owners, government and Drishtee officials
Market response	Lukewarm with seasonal fluctuations	Gradually gaining acceptance	Gradually gaining acceptance

Government response	Infrastructural support from government and *panchayat* but active participation absent	Active participation of *gram panchayats*, periodic meeting with DC, credence given to electronic applications	Active participation of *gram panchayats*, periodic meetings, with DC, credence given to electronic applications
Future plan of action	No new kiosks launched, review of partnership with existing kiosks in April 2002 for fresh franchisee lease	Gyandoot experiment is being replicated in other backward districts of MP	22 new kiosks opened in six months by Drishtee. Further additional 10 kiosks per month planned for other locations

* The revenues are calculated exclusively on the basis of services offered by main franchisees.

HRD = human resource development; AMC = Municipal Corporation of Ahmedabad; DC = district commissioner; MP = Madhya Pradesh.

and Drishtee exhibit striking commonality in terms of fundamental principles of ICT penetration in rural society. But during the implementation of the plan the initiatives underwent a distinct change in their functioning and systemic architecture (see Table 6.3). Their timing of entry into the respective districts coincided, in 2000–1. Thus, a comparison between the three initiatives has not been influenced in terms of period of operation but their success entirely depended on marketing strategy and product mix offered. Examination of these initiatives reveals a very positive picture of the socio-economic development of rural society in terms of benefits, like improved market accessibility, employment opportunities, raising income levels, and altering the caste-based power structure.

An approach strategy is the path adopted to penetrate a new market, which builds on exclusivity and ease of operation.[4] TARAhaat based its approach strategy on TARAgyan, a computer education module, to improve computer literacy in the rural environs of Bathinda. Gyandoot and Drishtee based their approach strategy on ease of operation by bringing people near to the government (e-governance). The different strategies exhibit both exclusivity and ease of operation, but complexity of operation acted as a major impediment. For instance, TARAgyan required basic info-communication infrastructure to impart affordable computer education to the rural masses without depending on systemic arrangements. Delivery of public services lacked ease of operation because of multi-modal and multi-layered systemic architecture. Thus, the complexities associated with e-governance depended more on extraneous factors than internal ones, evolving high risk in its operation; failure of one link in the system may adversely affect the initiative.[5]

A sound performance appraisal must include qualitative and quantitative indicators, like the number of kiosks, start-up investment, unique selling proposition, overall marketing strategy, support systems, etc. Observations made on various indicators during the field survey at the respective districts are as follows.

6.3.1   ICT initiatives: lessons learnt

6.3.1.1   Start-up cost

An investment of Rs 250,000–300,000 (US\$6000–7000) is beyond the reach of many prospective rural entrepreneurs. Thus, bank finance became an essential requirement for start-up operations.[6] For such loans, the seed capital or margin money limit is a major limitation. But the official formalities of seeking a bank loan are far too numerous. The formality of producing collateral security for obtaining a bank loan is

one such real dampener. As a result, kiosk ownership is usually restricted to a higher-income group among the rural population. Start-up costs of less than Rs 100,000 (US$2500) are more suitable for rural society because any educated youth is eligible for a government loan of Rs 100,000 under the Prime Minister's Rozgar Yojana (PMRY) for self-employment purposes.[7] In addition, another advantage of this amount is the waiver on collateral security requirement under PMRY. Low start-up cost is a major advantage for educated unemployed rural youth to start an enterprise. Low-cost benefits are in terms of equitable distribution of opportunities for the low-income group and economically weaker sections of society. In the selection criteria for a PMRY loan, due representation is given to women, backward castes, low-income groups, the disabled etc., as per government norms. Low investment means low interest liabilities,[8] thus lowering the overall operation cost for kiosk owners.

6.3.1.2 Product mix

The range of services offered has a major impact on the market and revenues. Computer education as a first step to educate the rural population is a broad-based strategy to improve computer awareness and literacy. But an ICT initiative cannot depend solely on a single service. For instance, the target market segment for TARAgyan was designed to suit student needs. As a result, the TARAgyan experienced seasonal fluctuations – a high turnout of students during holidays and low during working days. Thus, seasonal fluctuations influenced TARAhaat's revenue pattern. A broad range of product mix may compensate kiosk owners for seasonal fluctuations in the market. If the product mix constitutes delivery of a single service, like computer education, the service could be designed to suit a broader market segment in order to gain wider acceptability and broader utility.[9] Public services have a wider market. Although public services are targeted at the entire rural market, the range of services offered are targeted at the lower end of the market segment, like filing below poverty line (BPL) applications, registration of birth and death certificates, etc. (see Box 6.1)

The Gyandoot and Drishtee initiatives focused on the delivery of government services.[10] It may prove to be a good marketing strategy in terms of a wider market segment, but it is hamstrung in terms of revenue collection. Since the target market is the weaker sections of society, user charges are kept low relative to opportunity costs. Thus, such service offerings may not make the IT initiative sustainable in the long run. Moreover, the internal dynamics of back-end activity highlighted that

---

Box 6.1   Ellenabad *soochanalaya* (Sirsa) – details of activities (November–December 2001)

15–20 requests	Registration of vehicles
15–20 requests	Driving licence application
35 requests	Complaints
115 requests	Application for BPL/OAP

Note: Certificates for below poverty line (BPL) and old age pension (OAP).

---

the end-user has the facility of registering their request electronically but the respective government department takes its own time for application processing. But such services keep the urban population away because these government schemes are targeted at the rural population. The urban population seeks other types of public services like municipal corporation clearances, property tax, driving licence, electricity and water bills, etc. Thus, the product mix is a critical element for long-term sustenance. An ICT-based initiative must have a broad range of information services available to suit the requirements of the major cross-section of population for a continuous stream of revenue.

6.3.1.3   Market size

An optimal market size for an info-kiosk is an important issue for a sustainable revenue stream. However, the market size envisaged for the info-kiosk is almost the same in all the initiatives. But in areas where the number of info-kiosks increased, the market size of the info-kiosk shrank considerably.[11] In areas where there was stagnation, the existing kiosks catered to a slightly bigger market by default.[12] Indeed it is difficult to establish an optimal market size for an info-kiosk; estimates of the ICT initiatives suggested that 10–15 villages, or 10,000–15,000 population, is a relatively optimal market size. In fact, lessons from the ongoing initiatives suggested that financial liability and the range of product mix are critical elements in ascertaining optimal market size. If the financial liability is higher, the kiosk needs to generate more revenue from the existing product mix by trying to cater to the needs of more villages.[13] On the other hand, if the range of product mix is wide, a relatively smaller market may be sufficient to generate adequate revenue for the kiosk owner. Thus, an optimal market size is dependent on other extraneous factors than headcounting.[14]

6.3.1.4 Unique selling proposition and marketing strategy

The unique selling proposition (USP) is the core competence of any business, which forms the very basis of marketing strategy. Language of communication is definitely a USP, but all three initiatives used the local language as a means of communication. The three ICT-based initiatives have exhibited distinct USPs in terms of service offerings; for instance, TARAgyan is the USP for the TARAhaat initiative in Bathinda. Education is a primary need of rural society and quality education is matter of concern for many. Thus, any initiative with core competence in education services evidently has a large market in rural society. Field surveys revealed that TARAkendras used ingenious methods of advertising their USP by making announcements on gurdwara (place of worship) loudspeakers.[15] Similarly Gyandoot and Drishtee's USP was seen as a strategic delivery channel of public services. These initiatives focused on reducing the distance between government and people. But government in this initiative became a dominant stakeholder, riddled with inherent operational inefficiencies. Therefore, the USP of the e-governance initiative rested on reducing opportunity costs for the villagers and not in improved efficiency in the delivery of public services.[16] All three initiatives based their USPs on market needs. But each initiative was deficient in terms of integrating its USP with a strong and aggressive marketing strategy because the main collaborator left the kiosk owners to devise their own marketing strategy in the field.

6.3.1.5 Support system

Another aspect of marketing strategy is a strong support system. It was observed that Drishtee's support system had followed an aggressive line to instil efficiency, both in the government systems as well as the info-kiosks. First, Drishtee used its local partner to act as a central node, connected to all info-kiosks via an intranet. Thus, more people were available to provide necessary support to the kiosk owners. Second, it provided a platform for periodic interaction with kiosk owners to understand location-specific problems and identify solutions. Third, it arranged periodic meetings of the kiosk owners with the administration for speedy redress of government-related problems. Finally, the CEO of Drishtee visited Sirsa for all such periodic meetings to remain in touch with the kiosk owners and apprise them of the new services that Drishtee planned to launch in the near future. This form of support system became an integral part of instilling confidence in the kiosk owners. Though the Gyandoot model was replicated in the form of Drishtee, being an initiative launched by the government of Madhya Pradesh it

lacked in terms of support system because of bureaucratic inefficiencies. On the other hand, TARAhaat failed to cultivate a proper support system resulting in the alienation of kiosk owners. Thus, an ICT-based initiative must cultivate a proper support system involving active participation of all the stakeholders.

6.3.1.6 Revenues

Sustainability of an initiative depends primarily on the revenue stream. Each initiative offered limited information services. Thus, revenues were limited. Field surveys revealed that initiatives based on delivery of public services (Gyandoot and Drishtee) usually earned between Rs 3500 and 5000 (US$100) per month per kiosk. The major partner Drishtee took a share of 20 per cent in the total receipts from the kiosk. In real terms, the approximate earning of a kiosk came to around Rs 3000–4500 (US$87). On the other hand, the education-based initiative TARAgyan was not able to maintain its revenue stream on a constant basis; a few kiosks earned approximately Rs 4000–6000 (US$120) per month, but mostly info-kiosks in Bathinda failed to achieve break-even. The interest liability for many kiosks ranged between Rs 5000 and 6000 (US$120–150) per month per kiosk. Although the main collaborator, TARAhaat, failed to broaden its product mix, the info-kiosks started delivering other types of services such as cookery classes, English speaking classes, etc. to meet the monthly expenses. In addition, the district administration assisted TARAkendras in launching computer courses recognised by the Punjab Technical University. Thus, it was evident that there was a constant flow of revenue: broader product mix offerings lead to better earnings. The info-kiosk owners suggested a few services that can significantly improve revenues, like keeping land records, electronic railway ticket reservation, primary health care facilities, etc.

6.3.1.7 External response

This is a key indicator of the future prospects of such initiatives, especially the response from the government and market. Increased transparency in the government and direct market access may be advantageous for many, but it may transgress others' interests. The official agencies and markets both responded positively to these initiatives. Markets usually respond to change, which TARAhaat, Gyandoot and Drishtee persistently ignored. Markets also responded well to these initiatives. For instance, Gyandoot entered into strategic partnership with various *mandis* (village markets) in the district. Any inquiry about the market prices of farm input or outputs reserved the right of the information seeker to

purchase or sell at the rates exhibited on the portal. The info-kiosk issued a receipt to verify the bona fides of the information seeker and the agreed rate, so that in the physical transaction in the *mandi*, the price remained stable.

6.3.1.8   Other lessons

Gyandoot and Drishtee depended on the inefficiencies of the channels of communications between the government and citizens. The initiative was directed at improving G2C contact, which received a positive response from both. The weaker sections of rural society responded positively to this initiative because of considerable reduction in opportunity costs and harassment. The middle and higher sections also attempted to patronise this channel of communication in a limited manner. All three initiatives experienced stagnation in terms of services as no new service was added to the product mix. Although the DRDA announced introduction of new services like online retrieval of land records, payment of electricity bills, railway reservations, etc. nothing took off during the period of field surveys. Moreover, the urban population remained alienated from these initiatives because of the type of the product mix available. E-governance initiatives proved to be a risky proposition as they depended heavily on the support of the district administration. Too many complaints or clashes of interest between the officials (i.e. legislative body *panchayat* and DRDA) marred the future prospects of the initiative. It was evident that government officials recognised their central role in the Gyandoot and Drishtee initiatives and government functionaries used their clout as a lever against the kiosk owners for achieving their objectives.[17]

Thus, the lessons from respective ICT-based initiatives converge on general guiding principles for developing a sustainable ICT initiative for a rural environment. First, the initiative must ensure low start-up cost. The product mix should be designed to target a wider market segment. Stagnation in the services offered result in the erosion of the exclusivity criterion in the initiative. Thus, the initiative must have the flexibility to respond to market needs and changing consumer tastes and preferences. The changing demand pattern of rural society needs a wide range of services. Since market size is a factor in financial liability and product mix, the initiative should not allow mushrooming of info-kiosks unnecessarily for reasons of competition. The marketing strategy should integrate all the actors, especially the info-kiosk, and operational strategy should be designed to target exclusive market segments. The performance appraisal revealed limited coverage of rural needs. An attempt is made to

map the informational needs of rural society to highlight exclusion of the majority of rural needs by the respective ICT initiatives. It is imperative to highlight the commonality between the nature of information services offered and rural needs.

6.4   Rural needs and the Triad Model

Indian rural society is riddled with a wide variety of deprivations; for instance, almost half of the population lives below the poverty line, the majority of the population is deprived of basic civic amenities like primary health care, drinking water facilities, housing and education, etc. An ICT-based strategy for economic development of rural society is bound to confront all such barriers. But the essential aspect of the ICT-based developmental strategy is understanding the information-related needs of the rural population.

6.4.1   Rural needs

Rural society comprises a poor, landless and vulnerable population at the base, a mid-section constituting low-income earners and small land-holders, comprising a mix of both higher and lower castes, and an apex constituting a population with large landholdings and high income. The lower and middle segments of the income pyramid are usually deprived of access to basic services like education, health care, etc. (see Figure 6.1).

All government-sponsored anti-poverty measures are targeted at the lower segment, which require efficient and effective delivery of public services, for example subsidised food, free education, health-care facilities, etc. In the mid-section, the small-entrepreneurial class, especially, further widens the need requirements to government finances and market prices. All segments exhibit their need for private economic benefits, intermediate services, final consumption services, etc., but government services become an essential requirement. Even the influential class of large landholders have need of government loans, market prices of farm inputs and produce, entertainment, quality education and health-care facilities, etc. (see Table 6.4).

Illiteracy and other forms of deprivation make the poor dependent on the influential and educated class, which considerably increase their opportunity cost for consuming government services. To obtain anti-poverty benefit, lack of information paves the way for rent seeking. The higher class is more politically and economically active and therefore has easy access to information, law enforcement and other official

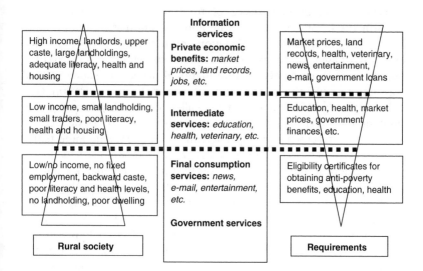

Figure 6.1 Rural society, informational services and requirements

Table 6.4 Information-related services

Private economic benefits	Intermediate services	Final consumption services	E-governance
Market prices	Education	E-mail	Eligibility certificates
Employment	Health	Entertainment	Licences
Government benefits	Veterinary	News	Complaints
Land records	Training	Weather forecast	Law and order
Railway booking	Child care	Horoscope	Empowerment

agencies. The middle and lower segments confront barriers in accessing government benefits and other forms of public services due to lack of physical or monetary clout. Thus, these segments are likely to shift to ICT for accessing government services. The product mix offered by ICT initiatives must include such services for a sustainable revenue generation stream.

Private material economic benefits are concerned with information related to enhancing income opportunities and other benefits. It may include market-related information on the prices of farm produce or inputs, employment opportunities in the lean seasons, etc. In terms of rural needs, market information is critical for income generation among small farmers and traders. Similarly, intermediate services like education

and health are primary needs of rural society. Increase in public investments in primary health care and education is becoming more and more difficult. Distance education and telemedicine have emerged as an ICT-based alternative to reach out to remotely located rural populations. Other aspects of informational needs are related to final consumption, like news, entertainment, personal communication, etc.

The respective ICT initiatives have failed considerably to respond to rural needs. Except for the front-end activity, the back-end activity remained a single owned and operated initiative. The Gyandoot initiative remains essentially a government initiative without any participation of private enterprise and NGOs. The TARAhaat initiative remained purely a private initiative without any active participation of the government. The Drishtee initiative, which displayed an effective public–private partnership, continues to focus on a product mix that essentially reflects government as the key player. Thus, respective ICT initiatives could not form a strong public–private partnership, which restricted broadening of the product mix to suit the requirements of rural needs. This is quite evident in the performance appraisal. Each initiative tends to focus on the delivery of a single form of informational services, resulting in the exclusion of the other needs of rural society. In other words, no initiative can become sustainable on the basis of a single market segment. The triad concept is an attempt to build strategic partnership between the main actors.

6.4.2   Triad Model: a conceptual framework

The Triad Model is a conceptual model for establishing a strategic partnership between rural institutions. Since the objective is to establish the shortest and most efficient link between stakeholders and the market, it is pertinent to shift the focus on to civil society. It is an established fact that civil society is nearest to rural society in the formation of a strong coalition, while official agencies are supposedly the furthest. Information as an important resource clearly portrays an antithesis. The official agencies are nearest to information, and civil society and the people are furthest from it. Thus, there is an urgent need to formulate a strategy to reverse the current practice by bringing civil society closer to the informational base. Moreover, NGOs are adequately placed to build strong community linkages for active popular participation. The official agencies could use such coalitions to design and formulate suitable ICT initiatives. The Triad Model (see Figure 6.2) attempts to build a strategic partnership between three stakeholders: official agencies, civil society and the market.

It was observed that a major cross-section of the rural population require government services, therefore the Triad Model e-governance is

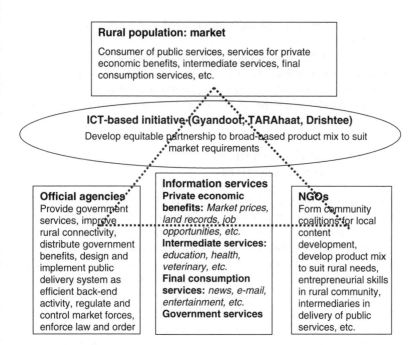

Figure 6.2   The Triad Model: a concept for sustainable ICT initiative

an integral aspect of the ICT initiative. However, the role of government is essentially transformed into a back-end activity, especially in providing connectivity and computerisation of government departments. Civil society or private initiative is responsible for taking the front role in managing the information. With equal participation from government in extending credit facilities, civil society's role becomes more of a facilitator, providing logistical support. Its main function is not limited to overseeing the initiative but to build confidence in the market by building a strong coalition in the rural community.

Civil society must take the responsibility for content development by involving the community, especially in primary education, health care, veterinary services, news, etc., to suit the needs of rural society. Since the NGOs have direct communication linkage with the rural population they are better placed to understand rural needs. Ultimately, the third but major stakeholder is the market or consumer (rural population). Thus, the Triad Model envisages equity in terms of functionaries and roles, as well as delivery of informational services. If all the stakeholders in the Triad Model successfully play their roles in the

initiative, evidently the product mix offered will cover a major section of rural needs.

In fact, very little work has been done to coordinate the efforts of rural institutions and this leaves scope to explore the linkages between them. The primary aim of ICT is connecting people and sharing information. The Triad Model links the main actors with a definitive role in the ICT-based initiative.

6.5   Impact of ICT initiatives on developmental objectives

Today, the major dilemma is whether ICT is a vehicle for growth only for the privileged classes or if it has a spillover effect on the deprived ones as well. Some argue that technology is a reward of development, making it inevitable that the digital divide follows the income divide. But on the contrary, empirical findings have shown that ICT has enabled people to increase their income, enjoy a better standard of living, improve their quality of life by greater transparency in governance and build communities for creative participation (UNDP 2001).

A perception of ICT as a fundamental developmental tool rests on certain assumptions. At the macro-level, the introduction and use of ICT will improve the efficiency of rural infrastructure, enhance economic performance and strengthen competitive capacities in the market (Braga 1996; Kenney 1995). At the level of human development, ICT contributes to the improvements in provision of basic social services, helps to disseminate valuable information on production and conservation, improves the efficiency of governments, and enhances the provision of education and health services (World Bank 1996). In other words, global networks have reorganised production and channels of distribution. Networks have reduced the distance to markets and considerably influenced markets themselves. A concept of good governance has emerged, which provides greater transparency in government distributive channels. Thus, the role of ICT in economic development is gaining more visibility in the present context and contributing towards strengthening democracy, increasing social participation and removing barriers to modernisation. The following conclusions are drawn from field studies of the respective ICT-based initiatives.

6.5.1   Income generation

Exploitative market forces prevailing in rural society are a major impediment for income generation. By lowering transaction costs, ICT may

enhance economic efficiency in developing countries (Norton 1992). Furthermore, empirical work has suggested that the spreading of markets and reduction of information monopolies provide impetus for institutional change. The *World Development Report* (World Bank 1998) points out that in rural Costa Rica, small farmers use ICT to obtain information on international coffee and cocoa prices from the city. Similar experiences are shared for Sri Lanka, Mexico, Bangladesh, etc. Field surveys in Madhya Pradesh, Punjab and Haryana revealed that market intermediaries tend to push prices down while procuring directly from the farmers and inflate transaction costs considerably to charge better prices in the market.[18] In the entire market procurement and delivery system, producers remain ignorant of the prevailing prices of produce in the market as well as of the price of inputs. Market negotiation depends primarily on the opportunity cost for the commission agent and the search cost for the producer. Use of ICT considerably lowers search and opportunity costs. In the event of reduction in opportunity and search costs, market information improves the producer's capabilities in obtaining a significant share of the savings on mutually agreed terms. Thus, market information has a considerable influence on income opportunities for rural society.

6.5.2   Human development and entertainment

Education, health care, access to basic amenities, etc., remain the weakest links for human development in developing countries. Distance education programmes have emerged as a major benefit of ICT in the present context. Communication networks have shown great potential in taking education to communities for whom access to quality education is difficult. Educational content developed and put in one place is made accessible to all locations without physical travel and is the concept behind distance education. Innovations in multimedia have paved the way for distance education learning, especially primary and secondary education.[19] The TARAgyan module is providing such services in rural Punjab. Multimedia are also good for reference works like encyclopaedias and dictionaries. Such intermediate services open newer opportunities for educated youth in developing and providing relevant educational content for rural society.

Likewise, ICT has a similar role to play in the delivery of health and veterinary services to remote locations.[20] Field surveys revealed that rural society is now using the telephone, health-based portals of academic institutes and other means of communications to access information and services of medical practitioners. In addition, the concept of

telemedicine has also given a boost to 'barefoot technicians'.[21] There is ample evidence of the use of the telephone by barefoot technicians in providing basic health and veterinary services in rural areas.

Personal communication via e-mail is an important service for rural society. There are reported instances of labourers sending e-mails to their families at a nominal fee from the info-kiosks in Punjab.[22] Similar experiences have also been reported from urban centres like Mumbai. Frequent use of e-mail facilities by taxi drivers hailing from Uttar Pradesh and Bihar working in Mumbai have further broadened the scope of ICT in rural society. In addition, ICT provides a novel method of leisure and entertainment. In the absence of cinemas and other means of entertainment in rural areas, a multimedia kit provides an efficient medium of entertainment, like computer games for children, movies, etc.[23] Another aspect of consumption services are horoscopes. Though horoscopes are usually treated like any other use of computers in Western societies, they play an important role in Indian society; whether it is matchmaking for marriage, birth of a child, opening a business establishment or buying a house, horoscopes and the placement of the stars are deeply etched in the Indian psyche, be it urban or rural.

6.5.3   Good governance

No one can ignore government, whether for any benefit or maintaining law and order. Such experiments if looked at from the supply side shift the focus on to another benefit of ICT, commonly known as e-governance. E-governance is not only about bringing transparency and accountability into government but is also about efficient delivery of government services.[24] Empirical analysis and other related works validate that breakdown in the communication process results in poor governance and ineffective implementation (Gaiha *et al.* 2000). For instance, the land records of a village may be kept by the village *patwari* (government official who maintains land records), but maintenance and updating of the records are done manually. This method, though time-consuming, less accurate and discretionary, is important for rural society because land revenue is fixed on the basis of ownership of agricultural land.[25] There are other forms of information needed to plan and implement economic development plans and anti-poverty measures. Population size, demographic data and human development indicators are a few among others, which could be essential for planning and implementation.[26] In fact, information on disbursement of benefits is an essential requirement to control and monitor all government-sponsored programmes, like identifying people BPL, beneficiaries for OAP, etc.

In addition, there are scores of other services provided by government departments like issuing driving licences, bona fide resident certificates, issuing passports, etc. Likewise, supply of essential commodities through the public distribution system (PDS) is another type of benefit for rural communities. E-governance is all about efficient delivery of services, but these services cannot be delivered efficiently without proper collection, collation and validation of information. Introduction of ICT at governmental level paves the way for smart governance.

6.5.4   Empowerment

The Bangladesh Grameen Mobile Phone Experiment has further strengthened the role of communication systems in empowerment of the poor because it was observed that mobile phones not only brought them nearer to the markets but telephone connectivity brought them nearer to government administration (UNDP 1998).[27] It is already established that info-communications have closed the knowledge gap. Literacy is critical in helping the poor to absorb and diffuse knowledge within the community. But information is important for giving a voice to the poor. In the main, past experience has emphasised that the poor have no voice in the actual decision-making of the implementing organisations. As awareness increases among the poor about their own circumstances and comparison is made with possible alternatives, they are bound to make a choice; it benefits them in terms of discovering possible ways to overcome the obstacles they face.

Increased awareness generates the ability to voice concerns, desires, suggestions and complaints. Ultimately, it leads to an expressing of a voice among the poor. This inference strengthens the rationale for public action to ensure that the poor have access to education and information. The net impact of info-communications on social inequalities is positive. Access to IT strengthens the voice of the poor, whether in terms of marketing their goods or in advocating policies that address their needs. It brings with it an increase in communication across the country, and will help to narrow differences on grounds of region, caste and worship. Increasing accessibility into remote rural and backward areas with the help of a computer and a telephone line could be used to promote education and bring these areas closer to the urban, more prosperous areas of the country. The causes of ethnic differences largely lie in ignorance and lack of information. A well-informed and educated society could not be easily misled by individual interests. Most ethnic differences emerge from illiteracy and ignorance.

6.5.5   Employment generation

It is difficult to estimate the impact of ICT initiatives on employment generation in rural areas, but the respective ICT initiatives do provide self-employment opportunities to unemployed educated rural youth. The proportion of beneficiaries under the initiatives may be a small fraction, but indirectly these initiatives inform and train people in improving their job prospects. TARAgyan delivers computer education to the rural population, resulting in the upgrading of skills of rural youth thus improving their job prospects. Moreover, Gyandoot and Drishtee inform people about the various government schemes for self-employment. These initiatives improve job prospects for rural youth. For instance, the Gyandoot portal displays the details of public works being carried out at various places in the district. Also, it displays the requirements for gaining employment under PMRY, the employment guarantee scheme, etc. Information such as this contributes to improving job prospects.

Although no empirical evidence is available on the number of beneficiaries from these initiatives, they are surely instrumental in changing the employment pattern in rural society. For instance, the Drishtee initiative has opened up new opportunities in content development. People with adequate computer skills in the Sirsa district are hired on a piecemeal basis to develop content for the local population. The TARAgyan initiative launched a scheme to 'learn and earn', which allows students on advanced computer courses to teach in computer familiarisation courses. These students are compensated with significant discounts in fees.

6.6   Conclusion

The three initiatives, Gyandoot, TARAhaat and Drishtee, provide an important insight into the dynamics of rural society. Understandably, Madhya Pradesh, which significantly lacked development in the post-independence period, was one of the first states in India to adopt ICT as an integral part of its development strategy, focusing especially on improving the quality of life in rural areas. Rural society in the respective districts is beginning to appreciate the benefits of the initiatives.

Each initiative has highlighted certain critical elements for success, especially validating the successful attempt at building public–private partnership. The Triad Model attempts to include all the critical elements of success and defines the roles of the main collaborators in the ICT-based initiative. It is vital in designing the architecture, selecting

a good product mix, integrating interest between strategic partners, making a concrete marketing strategy in line with rural needs and establishing optimal market size for each info-kiosk. Alone, government or private initiative is not capable of catering to local requirements. A balanced product mix comprising primary needs like education, health care, etc., along with public services like land records, various types of eligibility certificates, etc., is a must for broadening the impact of the initiative on the life of the people. The weaker sections of society do not have adequate facilities to avail themselves of the opportunities presented by ICT. Moreover, their role is marginal in influencing the relevant market forces and structure. The role of government also becomes vitally important in reaching people, especially the last person in the row for the disbursement of benefits that they are entitled to receive.

Thus, the government needs to focus its attention on integrating info-communications within the operational framework at the grass roots level to effectively implement smart or e-governance. The impact of respective ICT initiatives is direct in some cases, but a major impact is observed as part of the spin-off benefits. ICT initiatives have a direct influence on income generation, human development and good governance. But their impact is more profound indirectly, in changing employment patterns and implementing anti-poverty measures. Some immediate measures could be adopted on the following lines:

(a) Increase the knowledge base of the poor through the digital medium, especially about their rights and available alternatives.
(b) Communicate with the deprived to understand their real needs.
(c) Expand income generation capabilities, with a primary focus on women's participation.
(d) Coordinate the efforts of the rural institutions, especially by bringing NGOs near to the information.
(e) Develop an info-communication infrastructure with the primary aim of increasing the penetration ratio in the rural sector.

Such measures facilitate the dissemination of information to a larger section of the deprived population. Information inculcates transparency in the system, expedites decision-making, optimises the utilisation of benefits, and establishes better monitoring and evaluation. Most problems are linked to gaps in knowledge and imperfections in information. Rural institutions are the key actors to raise the general awareness of the rural poor. Appropriate partnership between these institutions and the main collaborators provides a strong base for creating an information society in the rural environs of India.

Notes

1　Andhra Pradesh and Karnataka have put their district centres online. Maharashtra is currently connecting via networks all sales tax circles at the district level. The telecentre experiment in Tamil Nadu has connected most villages at the district level.

2　The Gyandoot project by the government of Madhya Pradesh in the Dhar district has emerged as an economically viable form of G2C activity, which has further expanded into e-commerce. This project gives the rural community affordable access to government services and market information.

3　These habitats are cities (population below 500,000), block towns [within administrative units set up for development planning] (15,000–50,000), large villages (5000–15,000), medium villages (2000–5000) and small villages (<2000).

4　Exclusivity is the uniqueness of product mix that no other institution can offer within the region.

5　Such a high-risk embodied approach strategy is not usually preferable, especially while penetrating new markets because of high costs of penetration and end-users' (market) confidence.

6　Start-up cost for TARAhaat is approximately Rs 250,000–300,000.

7　PMRY is a centrally sponsored scheme directed at generating self-employment for the educated rural youth at nominal interest.

8　Under normal circumstances, a bank loan of Rs 150,000 for a three-year period may involve a monthly liability of Rs 5000–6000 in interest.

9　Sukhchain Singh, a farmer, enrolled at the TARAhaat kiosk at Leheran Mohabbat to gain information on the latest agricultural techniques and weather reports. He purchased a PC after joining a computer familiarisation course for personal messages with his relatives abroad. As the need arose, he used the Internet for communicating his farm-related queries to Punjab Agricultural University.

10　At the time of writing, Drishtee has still to broaden its service offerings to computer education and e-commerce. The Drishtee portal currently targets a rural segment, especially weaker sections of society. Field interviews revealed a low user turnout at the info-kiosk at Sirsa town, highlighting the limitation of product mix.

11　Gyandoot *soochanalaya* in Dhar and Drishtee *soochanalaya* in Sirsa.

12　TARAkendra in Bathinda.

13　In real terms, the earnings from TARAgyan at Bathinda may not be able to repay the monthly interest payments of the info-kiosks.

14　The info-kiosks at Sirsa were not burdened by monthly interest payments. With the current revenue stream these kiosks were able to break even.

15　A kiosk owner in Chak Fateh Singh Wala used the gurdwara premises for a live Internet demonstration.

16　For instance, once a villager files an application for registration for BPL electronically the respective government department carries out the verification and registration in due process, taking its own time. Therefore, the benefit of electronic filing of an application is seen only in terms of opportunity cost and not in efficiency.

17　For instance, state roadways staff allegedly misbehaved with some girl students at Ellenabad. The student community and other locals resorted to a *dharna* and

chakka jaam (a strike and closure of the main road) to draw the attention of the district administration to take appropriate action. The kiosk owner was one of protesters, and the local officials reported his participation to higher authorities. The assistant commissioner threatened Drishtee officials, to warn the kiosk owner about abstaining from such activities or the kiosk would be closed down.

18 For instance, Bathinda is a major farm produce market in the north, but farmers tend to sell their entire produce to commission agents, who sell the produce in the market. There is no physical exchange of money between the intermediary and the farmer: the intermediary's outlets take care of all the farmer's material needs. For diesel, the intermediary issues a receipt to the farmer for a particular diesel depot, who exchanges the diesel for the receipt. The intermediary makes payment directly to the depot and deducts the amount from the farmer's account.

19 The Open University in the UK has a new course (THD204) for students stationed at remote locations such as oil rigs, on active military service, etc., through which lessons and the students' library are sent on CD-ROM, replacing the earlier practice of sending printed materials by post.

20 For example, telemedicine services are provided using teleconferencing and other forms of advisory services via computer networks. For a pilot project in Tamil Nadu, a local veterinary institute and logistic support from Cornell University (US) is providing services in rural parts of the state.

21 'Barefoot technician' is a novel concept in rural India, where NGOs train an educated youth in the villages to supply basic health care and veterinary services. In event of an emergency they are trained to provide immediate relief to allow the patient to reach the nearest government hospital for specialised treatment.

22 Large numbers of the economically active population migrate from Bihar and Uttar Pradesh for gainful employment in richer regions like Punjab and Haryana during the harvesting season. These agricultural/menial labourers are away from their homes for long periods and letters are the only means of personal communications. Private courier service is almost unaffordable and the public postal service is highly unreliable. E-mail has emerged as a boon to this community, being reliable and fast. It is reported during another field survey that labourers from Uttar Pradesh and Bihar send their e-mail messages at charges varying between Rs 7 and 10 each in Hindi fonts to an e-mail address of the public info-kiosk in their region. The recipient kiosk owner then takes a printout and delivers it to their residence, or family members collect the printout from the kiosk themselves at a nominal fee of Rs 2.

23 Due to militancy in Kashmir, all cinema halls have closed down. Schools and other educational establishments have started using multimedia to show popular films to students.

24 For instance, if a person from the village needs a BPL certificate to get government-sponsored anti-poverty benefit, the option available is to travel from their village to the district centre to file the application. This is a costly and time-consuming process. The use of ICT for filing such applications, at a nominal cost, at the village info-kiosk saves time and results in a considerable reduction of opportunity costs. In another instance, people are rarely aware of the respective official dealing with BPL certificates; identification of the right person is difficult under the existing governmental system. This results in intermediaries/touts, which increases opportunity costs considerably, because of ignorance.

25   For example, the agricultural land may have a small section of rocky land or a pond, which is not used for agriculture. If the *patwari* has omitted to record such observations in the land record, the revenue assessment will be made for use of the full area of land, thus the farmer pays more than required to the government.

26   The government of Madhya Pradesh released the Madhya Pradesh Human Development Report 1999. This further strengthens the argument that relevant information exists at various levels; it is a question of maintaining and updating a database.

27   Also, the Director-General of Police (DGP) in Uttar Pradesh launched his personal website for receiving complaints about erring police officials in the state. In the first month of its operation the DGP received a variety of complaints against his department relating to corruption, extortion, harassment, refusal to file reports by the police station in charge, etc. This experiment assisted the DGP in streamlining the functioning of his department. (As narrated by the DGP Uttar Pradesh at the 2–4 December 1999 meeting on Equity, Diversity and Information Technology.)

References

Braga, C. (1996) 'The Impact of Internationalisation of Services on Developing Countries', *Finance and Development*, March, Washington, DC: IMF.

Development Alternatives (2001) 'TARAgyan: Empowerment through Education', *Newsletter*, 11 (7).

Gaiha, R., P. D. Kaushik and V. Kulkarni (2000) 'Participation or Empowerment? The Case of Panchayats in India', in M. Unnithan-Kumar and V. Damodaran (eds), *The State Development and Participation*, New Delhi: Manohar Publications.

Government of Punjab (1997) *Punjab: Rural Industrial Focal Points – Special Package of Incentives*, Chandigarh: Directorate of Industries, Government of Punjab Publication.

Government of Punjab (2000) *Punjab: Information Technology Industry – Special Package of Incentives*, Chandigarh: Directorate of Industries, Government of Punjab Publication.

Kenney, G. I. (1995) 'The Missing Link – Information', *Information Technology for Development*, 6 (1).

Norton, S. (1992) 'Transaction Cost, Telecommunications, and the Microeconomics of Macroeconomic Growth', *Economic Development and Cultural Change*, 41.

Pohjola, M. (2000) 'Information Technology and Economic Growth: Cross-Country Analysis', in M. Pohjola (ed.), *Information Technology, Productivity, and Economic Growth*, New York: Oxford University Press for UNU-WIDER.

Prahalad, C. K. (2005) *The Fortune at the Bottom of the Pyramid*, New Delhi: Pearson Education.

UNDP (1998) *Human Development Report 1998*, New York: Oxford University Press.

UNDP (2001) *Human Development Report 2001*, New York: Oxford University Press.

World Bank (1996) 'Harnessing Information for Development', a Proposal for a World Bank Group Strategy, Washington, DC: World Bank.

World Bank (1998) *World Development Report 1998–99: Knowledge for Development*, New York: Oxford University Press for the World Bank.

7
The Software and Information Services Sector in Argentina: the Pros and Cons of an Inward-oriented Development Strategy

Daniel Chudnovsky and Andrés López

7.1 Introduction

The software and information services (SIS) sector has been growing rapidly in recent decades. Developed countries are both the main producers and consumers of SIS.[1] Several large firms based in these countries have consolidated dominant positions at the world level in different segments of the SIS sector (Windows, Oracle, SAP and Symantec are some of the most obvious examples in this regard). Nonetheless, there is room for firms from developing countries to enter and grow in this sector, as proven by the experience of India, Brazil, Singapore, Taiwan, Korea, Costa Rica and others.

SIS technologies, markets, products and business strategies are constantly evolving (see OECD 2002, for an overview of the trends in the software sector). In this scenario, some firms from the 'three I' countries (India, Israel, Ireland) have managed to compete in export markets through truly innovative products aimed at certain niches. However, most firms located in what Carmel (2003) defines as 'new software exporting nations' compete via costs (low wages) selling information services. In fact, there are several strategies available for firms from developing countries in the SIS sector, each requiring specific endowments and capabilities and having different consequences for the dynamics of the sector (Heeks 1999).

The objective of this chapter is to analyse the strengths, weaknesses and prospects of the Argentine SIS sector revealed in a survey conducted

in 2000–1. The main interest of this case study is to learn about the impacts – 'pros' and 'cons' – derived from following an 'inward-oriented' strategy in the SIS sector (that is, selling almost exclusively in the domestic market), as that traditionally followed by Argentina's SIS firms. The strengths and weaknesses of the SIS sector in Argentina will be examined in the light of the model proposed by Heeks (1999) to analyse the conditions that allow developing countries to perform successfully in this industry.

SIS activities began in Argentina in the 1970s and the sector developed until very recently without any government support, following the ups and downs of the domestic economy. Most producers are locally owned young small and medium-size enterprises (SMEs) supplying the domestic market, but there are also many large firms accounting for the lion's share of that market.

Though they had good performance in the 1990s, due to the growth of the domestic market in a context of trade liberalisation and privatisation of almost all state firms,[2] so far most of Argentina's SIS firms have not been able to make significant inroads into foreign markets and break away from an inward-oriented strategy.

Note must be taken that since the large peso devaluation of early 2002, the scenario for the development of the SIS sector in Argentina has begun to change. The combination of the big depression in 2001–2 and the new (and more favourable) foreign exchange rate made firms more prone to export. At the same time, a law was passed in 2004 granting fiscal incentives for SIS firms, and a sectoral forum – in which public authorities, the SIS industry associations, private firms and experts from universities and research centres have participated – was created with the aim of debating a long-term development strategy for the sector. Hence, prospects for the expansion of the SIS sector in Argentina have improved rather substantially. This is reflected not only in the fact that many firms have been increasing their exports but also in the interest shown by large foreign firms to invest in Argentina to develop software and provide different kinds of information services.

Unfortunately, there are not enough data available to make a rigorous analysis of the new trends and prospects of the SIS sector in Argentina. This chapter is based on a survey made in 2000–1, and is aimed at exploring the inward-oriented strategy followed by the sector until very recently. Hence, it shows the strengths and weaknesses of the SIS sector before the peso devaluation and the recent adoption of fiscal incentives.

Although our analysis will emphasise the shortcomings of the inward-oriented strategy, which are a sort of negative legacy that the

sector has to overcome even in the new more favourable scenario,[3] the original motivation of our research was the conviction that there were potential competitive advantages that could allow for a successful penetration of Argentinean SIS firms in foreign markets.

First, the country has a relative abundance of well-trained professionals in areas related to SIS activities. Second, it preserves at least some of its old cultural influence on the rest of the Spanish-speaking Latin America, a factor that could help Argentine firms penetrate those markets, taking advantage not only of the geographical but also of the cultural proximity to them. Third, compared with other developing countries, Argentina has a sizeable domestic market, which could be a relevant 'learning base' for local firms. Finally, the SIS sector was able to meet – without any kind of public support – the increased domestic demand for updated products and services in the 1990s, which led to the accumulation of capabilities and competences that may obviously be helpful when trying to penetrate foreign markets.

Our main argument is that the inward-oriented strategy adopted by SIS firms in Argentina has so far hampered their ability to profit from the advantages mentioned above. Since they enjoyed a sort of 'natural protection' in Argentina's market that allowed them to survive and expand by exploiting their knowledge about domestic legislation and business culture and their capability to adapt to changes in those areas, SIS firms have not paid enough attention to some key issues necessary for success in export markets. This lack of attention was aggravated by the absence of public support for the sector and a domestic environment that lacked cheap and easy access to investment and working capital and other key elements for competitiveness in SIS activities.

Section 7.2 briefly reviews the experience of the SIS sector in the 'three I's' and in some developing countries, and presents the conditions suggested by Heeks (1999) as necessary for successful performance in this activity. Section 7.3 presents the main results of the survey. Section 7.4 discusses the impact of some key institutional and macroeconomic variables on the evolution of the SIS sector in Argentina. The main conclusions and policy suggestions are presented in section 7.5.

7.2   SIS in developing and the 'three I' countries: a brief review

According to Heeks (1999), firms in developing countries usually face the following main limitations when trying to make progress in

the SIS sector:

- The physical and communications infrastructure of their home countries is weak.
- Their domestic home markets are usually small (and often supplied by illegal copies), which hinders the chances of recovering the costs involved in the development of innovative products.
- Access to finance is seldom easy and interest rates are often high, while mechanisms such as venture capital are almost unknown.
- Local firms rarely have strong marketing capabilities.
- The diffusion of stringent quality standards is usually very limited.

Furthermore, when trying to enter into foreign markets, firms from developing countries must face additional obstacles such as:

- Uncertainty about the compliance with quality standards and schedules and lack of confidence about their technical capabilities.
- The lack of detailed knowledge about foreign customers' requirements.
- Linguistic and cultural barriers and little knowledge of the business culture and norms in foreign markets.

Firms wishing to prosper in this sector must adopt strategies that fit with their endogenous capabilities and the endowments and assets of their home country. At the same time, they must try to circumvent the limitations posed both by their own history and the lack of certain skills. The government may help this process through different measures, both by trying to strengthen local technological and innovative capabilities and infrastructure, as well as by contributing to solving some market failures that constrain the development of the SIS sector.

In fact, there have been successful experiences of firms from developing countries in this sector. Firms from Asia, Latin America and Eastern Europe have acquired dominant positions in their home countries and entered developed countries' markets. Some large American and European SIS firms have made foreign direct investments in some developing countries to adapt their products and services to the cultural, linguistic and institutional features of the regional markets.

Different entry strategies may be observed. A first dividing line separates those countries whose firms have mainly followed 'inward-oriented' strategies (for example, Brazil and South Korea) from those where 'export-oriented' strategies have been dominant (for example, India,

Ireland and Israel).[4] The second dividing line depends on whether local firms or foreign corporations' affiliates have played a dominant role in the development of the SIS sector.

Among 'export-oriented' strategies there are different modes of competition. While Indian firms have mainly competed on the basis of low wages and the provision of information services (including the so-called 'body-shopping' activities), Israel's firms have developed significant innovative capabilities in some niche areas such as anti-virus, software security and protection and encryption technologies. Several large American and European firms have chosen Ireland as a base for serving European markets.

Though SIS firms in developing countries and the 'three I's' have been largely oriented towards the export of services, there are cases where the export of software products has played a larger role. These exports may take place through different channels. While in Ireland they mostly involve adapting and 'localising' American software products to the needs of different European markets, in Israel local firms export locally developed products. India has experienced an upsurge of 'offshore' software development activities.

While in Ireland foreign corporations are clearly dominant, in Israel or India they are not. However, in the latter countries local firms have different kinds of ties with their counterparts in industrialised countries that include subcontracting arrangements, joint ventures and strategic alliances.

Different strategies require different conditions, different assets, or both in order to be implemented successfully. For instance, in the case of Ireland, having an English-speaking population played a major role in the decision of American software companies to install affiliates in that country, but the public policies aimed at attracting FDI through tax incentives were also a major driver for those decisions. Neither factor in isolation would have led to the observed massive arrival of foreign investments in the SIS sector.

While counting on a relatively abundant endowment of skilled personnel with low wages has been a clear precondition for the success of the Indian strategy, strategies such as those followed by Israel's firms require high-skilled personnel, domestic research capabilities, and sophisticated local customers (in the case of Israel, notably the military).

Table 7.1 summarises the main features of the different strategies followed by the 'three I' countries in the SIS sector, including also information about Brazil and Argentina. Each of the 'three I' countries have followed a strategy well suited to take advantage of their respective key

Table 7.1 National strategies in the SIS sector

Country	Market orientation	Nature of SIS provided	Type of firms	Key assets
India	Export-oriented	Services (body-shopping–outsourcing)	Domestic and foreign	Low wages English-speaking professionals
Ireland	Export-oriented	Products (adaptation–localisation)	Mostly foreign	Access to the European market English-speaking professionals Public policies
Israel	Export-oriented	Products (innovative)	Mostly domestic	High-skilled professionals R&D capabilities Demand from the military
Brazil	Inward-oriented	Products and services	Mostly domestic	Large domestic market
Argentina	Inward-oriented	Products and services	Mostly domestic	See below

assets. Although Brazil's objective of making a significant inroad in world markets was not attained, the large dimension of its domestic market allowed for the development of a large SIS sector.

Heeks (1999) also identifies some key general factors beyond the kind of strategy adopted for developing countries' firms to be competitive in the SIS sector. They include microeconomic or enterprise elements such as:

- Identification of demand-growth markets and synergies.
- Ability to compete via costs or service innovation.
- Good marketing.
- Access to investment and working capital.
- Access to programming, analysis and management skills.
- Access to information technology.
- Networking mechanisms, both intra-firm as well as with other software firms, potential or actual clients, and so on.

At the same time, public policies play a key role in areas such as:

- Finance (access to working and venture capital and tax incentives).
- Education and training.[5]
- Research and development.
- Intellectual property rights protection.

- State procurement.
- Infrastructure (telecommunications, Internet).

Last, but not least, a 'national vision' is also needed (that is, of the desirable specialisation and competitive pattern for the SIS sector in each country), which should aim not only at fulfilling the general basic conditions for successful performance but also at taking advantage of the specific assets and endowments possessed by each country.

In the next sections we will show that Argentina followed an inward-oriented strategy that limited the SIS sector's ability to expand, and that the basic conditions that Heeks deems necessary to be successful in this sector are largely absent so far. However, in our judgement, the country has potential and mostly unexploited key assets that may allow for a more vigorous development of its SIS sector. At the end of the chapter we will suggest what these key assets may be and what kind of strategy could be based on them in order to foster the SIS sector in Argentina.

7.3 The SIS sector in Argentina

During the import substitution industrialisation process in the 1970s, there was already an incipient activity in the SIS sector in Argentina. The first study on this sector was undertaken in the mid 1980s (SECYT 1987). At that time, nearly 70 per cent of the domestic market was supplied by imported software, but about 300 local firms engaged in the provision of SIS. Access to skilled human resources and knowledge about specific features of the local fiscal and accountancy regulations were the main advantages of local firms. Their main limitations lay in the relatively small size of the domestic market, the lack of R&D and marketing capabilities, and the obstacles to accessing financial support (see also Correa 1990).

Some years later the situation had not changed much. When the economically turbulent 'lost decade' ended in the early 1990s, about 300 SIS firms were in business, employing nearly 4500 people. Two-thirds of the local market was supplied by imports, and exports were negligible (Correa 1996).

The significant structural reforms that took place in Argentina in the early 1990s (such as trade liberalisation and privatisation) led to a sharp increase in imports of goods and services, a boom in FDI inflows, and rapid economic growth between 1991 and 1998. Under these circumstances one might expect that a more vibrant SIS sector would have emerged. The analysis presented in the next sections will shed light on the extent to which this transformation has taken place.

7.3.1　Methodology

The data presented in these sections are based on an e-mail survey of 510 firms conducted in 2000–1. Ninety-eight responses (19.2 per cent) were obtained. To reach as many SIS firms as possible, we sent the questionnaire to all members of the country's sectoral associations. We also made a search through the Internet and other media to identify SIS firms not affiliated with any association.

We discussed the contents of the questionnaire with the main sectoral chambers and sectoral experts. To ensure that our survey would yield results that could be compared with previous work, we also examined surveys conducted among SIS firms in other countries – especially Brazil – and surveys previously undertaken in Argentina. The questionnaire included 30 questions aimed at learning about issues such as: size and patterns of corporate ownership of SIS firms, sales, exports and employment, clients' profiles, programming tools, hardware platforms, marketing channels, types of products and services offered, specialisation areas, intellectual property concerns, innovative activities, quality systems, linkages with universities and suppliers, favourable and unfavourable competitiveness factors and public policies' impacts.

7.3.2　The Argentinean SIS sector: size and profile

According to our estimates, based on the survey, the SIS sector's sales grew 40 per cent, and employment levels increased by 43 per cent between 1998 and 2000, a recessive period in the Argentine economy. This growth was due to growing local demand for SIS and efforts to address the 'Y2K' problem.

By 2000, the surveyed firms employed about 6400 people and had US$630 million in sales. By making certain assumptions about the market structure of the sector, we estimate that the annual turnover of the nearly 500 firms in the Argentine SIS sector reached around US$2000 million (0.7 per cent of GDP) and that these firms employed approximately 15,000 people (Table 7.2). Sectoral experts confirmed the plausibility of these estimates.

The SIS firms employ highly skilled personnel: 45 per cent of the employees of the surveyed firms were university graduates, while 37 per cent were technicians and university students. Nearly 70 per cent of those employees with graduate and postgraduate degrees studied informatics-related careers. Nonetheless, the proportion of employees with postgraduate studies was very small (4 per cent, half of which corresponded to informatics careers).[6] In comparison, Brazilian firms have on average three employees with postgraduate degrees, a figure that more than doubles that of Argentina (Weber *et al.* 2000).

Table 7.2 The SIS sector in Argentina, 2000 (US$ million and %)

Activity	Surveyed firms (US$ million)	Sectoral turnover (US$ million)	Relative share (%)
Software products	323.2	973	49
– local products	109.9	346	17
– foreign products	199.3	627	32
Information services	323.4	1,017	51
Total sales	*632.6*	*1,990*	*100*
Employment	6,400	15,000	–
Exports	14.4	35	–

Software products constituted nearly half of the surveyed firms' sales, and service activities made up the rest. Local products represented about 36 per cent of software products' sales. The share of imported software (more than 60 per cent) in the domestic market was not very different from what had been observed in previous (above-mentioned) studies.

The Argentine SIS sector is still strongly inward-oriented. In 2000 exporting was carried out by a small number of firms and constituted a negligible share of the sector's revenue.[7] Only six of the few (20) firms that exported in 2000 had an exports/sales ratio above 10 per cent; only three enterprises exported more than US$1 million. The low level of exports was due to microeconomic factors (for example, the type of products and services offered by local firms and poor quality control and marketing capabilities) and elements related to the environment in which the firms operated (for example, high labour costs fuelled by an overvalued exchange rate, lack of access to finance, and the absence of public policies supporting SIS exports). More is said about these issues in the following sections.

How did the Argentine SIS sector compare with those of other countries? Table 7.3 (which includes data for 2000–1) shows that in sales and export performance, Argentina was well behind India, Israel, Ireland, Singapore, and even its smaller neighbour, Uruguay. While exports were also very low in Brazil and Korea,[8] their domestic sales were much higher than Argentina's, partially compensating for the absence of exports.

7.3.3 Age, size, nationality and recent performance of SIS firms

Most Argentine SIS firms are young. The surveyed firms were, on average, 11 years old. Sixty five per cent were established after 1990, and very few were created before 1980. The latter often provide hardware

Table 7.3 The SIS sector: an international comparison, latest available year (US$ million)*

	Turnover	Exports	Exports/ turnover ratio (%)	Employment	Number of firms
India	10,200	7,800	76	400,000	6,000
Ireland	10,000	8,500	85	30,000	900
Israel	4,100	3,000	73	15,000	400
Brazil	3,300	80	< 3	130,000	3,500
Uruguay	240	80	33	2,500–3,000	250
Argentina	*415*	*70*	*17*	*14,500*	*500*
Costa Rica	n.a.	50	n.a.	3,500–4,000	150
Chile	200	15	8	2,000	200
Singapore	1,660	476	29	n.a.	n.a.
China	9,600	700	7	290,000	5,000
Korea	7,700	240	< 3	63,000	4,900

* The estimates of this table include the provision of information services and the sales of local software. We have tried to exclude, as far as possible using the available data, the sales of foreign software. Nonetheless, given the heterogeneity of the sources, it is possible that the definition of the SIS sector in each country may differ slightly, a fact that may hinder, to some extent, the comparability of the figures.

Sources: Instituto de Estudos Economicos en Software y Ministerio de Ciencia y Tecnología for Brazil, NASSCOM for India, Enterprise Ireland's National Informatics Directory for Ireland, Israel Association of Software Houses for Israel, Computerworld Chile (1999) and Comité pro-Industria de Software (2000) for Chile, MIEM (1999) and Stolovich *et al.* (2001) for Uruguay, Caprosoft for Costa Rica, Coe (1999) for Singapore, China Software Industry Association for China, Lee *et al.* (2001) and Ministry of Information and Communication for Korea and our own estimates for Argentina.

and telecommunications equipment and associated information services. In spite of being a minority within the sector, the firms that were established before 1990 accounted for more than two-thirds of the SIS sales in 2000.

The structure of the sector is very heterogeneous, with a small group of large, and mostly foreign-owned firms having the lion's share of the local market. Although most firms sold less than US$2 million in 2000, foreign firms accounted for 66 per cent and firms with more than 50 employees had 86 per cent of the sales of the SIS sector (Tables 7.4 and 7.5). At the same time, 80 per cent of the firms that responded to our survey were SMEs, and 85 per cent were locally owned.

Firms whose main activity is the provision of information services account for nearly half of the sector sales and employment levels

Table 7.4 Sales, employment and exports of the surveyed firms, 2000 (US$ million, number of employees and %)

By origin of capital	Sales		Employment		Exports	
	US$ million	Share (%)	Number of employees	Share (%)	US$ million	Share (%)
Foreign firms	415.1	66	2,702	42	10.5	73
Local firms	217.4	34	3,697	58	3.9	27
Total	632.6	100	6,399	100	14.4	100
By size						
Large[a]	544.2	86	4,598	72	10.1	70
Medium[b]	74.5	12	1,340	21	3.9	27
Small[c]	13.9	2	461	7	0.4	3
Total	632.6	100	6,399	100	14.4	100
By main activity						
Local products[d]	112.3	18	2,082	33	10.8	75
Foreign products[e]	231.9	37	1,164	18	0	0
Information services[f]	288.3	46	3,153	49	3.6	25
Total	632.6	100	6,399	100	14.4	100

[a] 50 employees or more.
[b] Between 10 and 50 employees.
[c] 10 employees or less.
[d] Local and foreign firms whose main activity in the SIS sector is the development of software products in Argentina.
[e] Local and foreign firms whose main activity in the SIS sector is the commercialisation of foreign software products in Argentina.
[f] Local and foreign firms whose main activity in the SIS sector is the provision of information services (customised software, implementation of software packages and consultancy).

Table 7.5   Turnover levels of the SIS firms in Argentina (%)

	Share (%)
Less than US$1 million a year	46
Between US$1 and 2 million a year	22
Between US$2 and 5 million a year	13
Between US$5 and 15 million a year	10
More than US$15 million a year	9

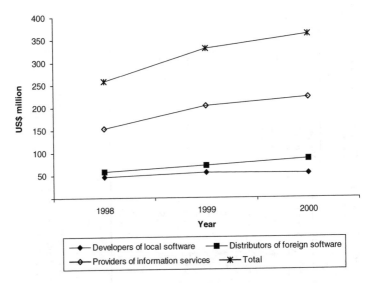

Figure 7.1   Total turnover by type of firms, 1998–2000

(Table 7.4).[9] A small group of firms that sell foreign packaged software products contribute with 37 per cent of the sector's sales. Several companies that are mainly dedicated to developing software products account for 18 per cent of the sales and 33 per cent of the sector's employment.

Different types of firms performed differently. Firms selling foreign software products or providing information services increased sales the most. The largest firms grew more than the SMEs, and foreign firms grew more than local ones (Figures 7.1, 7.2 and 7.3).

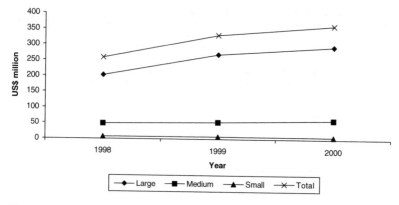

Figure 7.2   Total turnover by size of firms, 1998–2000

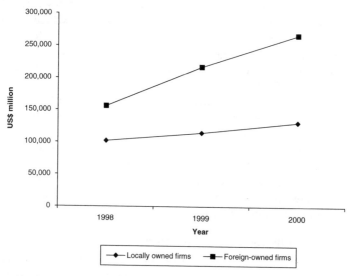

Figure 7.3   Total turnover by origin of firms, 1998–2000

7.3.4 Customers' profile

The main customers of the Argentine SIS sector are large firms, which account for two-thirds of the sector's sales (Table 7.6). Large firms and the government sector contribute more than 80 per cent of the sales of large and medium SIS firms.[10] These customers acquire mostly foreign

Table 7.6   Turnover structure by type of user (%)

				Type of SIS firms			
	Total	Local products	Foreign products	Information services	Big firms	Medium-size firms	Small firms
Home users	1	0	6	0	1	0	10
SMEs	16	29	37	3	15	17	55
Large firms	66	55	50	77	66	74	32
Government	16	16	7	19	18	7	2
Others	1	0	1	1	0	2	0
Total	100	100	100	100	100	100	100

software products and information services related to the implementation and customisation of complex software packages.

Home users are not too relevant as customers for the SIS sector.[11] The government is a large buyer of SIS but purchases almost exclusively from medium and large firms. Many SMEs have reported difficulties in becoming suppliers of the government. Often tenders for the provision of SIS to the public sector are open only to a 'short list' composed exclusively of foreign firms.

In contrast, the main customers of the small SIS firms are SMEs, which account for 50 per cent of the sales of that group of firms. Given the fact that SMEs in Argentina have been deeply affected by the recession that began in 1998, it is not surprising to find that small SIS firms' performance was worse than that of medium and large firms between 1998 and 2000. While SMEs' customers are key for those firms that sell packaged products, large customers are more relevant for those companies specialising in professional services.

7.3.5   Programming tools and platforms

Visual Basic is the most used programming language, used by nearly two-thirds of the firms surveyed. HTML and Java, which are mostly oriented towards Internet applications, are used by 58 and 48 per cent of the surveyed firms, respectively. Among object-oriented languages, Java is widely used, while a few use Smalltalk. C++ is used by 38 per cent of the firms. The largest SIS firms use the most modern languages, presumably because they have access to a larger pool of skilled personnel.

Almost all firms develop software products for personal computers, and many of them only offer software products for PCs. The Windows environment is dominant. Eighty-eight per cent of the firms developed

products for Windows NT, a fact that is consistent with the finding that most SIS firms are oriented towards business customers (see below). Not surprisingly, large and medium-sized firms are the main providers of SIS for mainframes, AS/400 and workstations. Few firms are oriented towards less conventional platforms such as industrial equipment and consumer devices. On the other hand, nearly half of the surveyed firms develop software products for UNIX-type operating systems, particularly Linux, Solaris and HP-UX.

7.3.6 Quality standards and marketing capabilities

Large firms tend to adopt better quality standards than SMEs. Nearly 60 per cent of the large firms surveyed make strategic plans that are periodically updated, set quality goals and measure quality indicators in a systematic way. In contrast, only around 30 per cent of SMEs undertake those practices regularly.

Only 16 per cent of the firms surveyed have earned quality certifications, a very low percentage in comparison with other developing countries. For instance, a survey of Brazilian firms in 1999 showed that 26 per cent of them had a quality certification in 1999 (Weber *et al.* 2000). As expected, due to the high costs involved, quality certifications are more common in large firms than in SMEs.

Though most firms employ two or more marketing channels, they prefer direct contact with customers. Consultancy activities are a means of getting new contracts. In turn, subcontracting is almost non-existent. The key role played by direct contact with the customers is consistent with the highly inward-oriented strategies of local SIS firms. Nonetheless, some firms have opened commercial offices abroad, trying to reproduce the network of contacts they have developed locally.

7.3.7 Competitive advantages and disadvantages

The customers of the local software developers are mostly located in banking, retail and wholesale trade, health care, telecommunications and public administration. In all these sectors, firms developing software concentrate on making products for accountancy and enterprise management solutions. These products are oriented towards domestic SMEs that cannot afford to buy expensive software packages provided by large international software firms such as SAP, Peoplesoft and others. Moreover, there are highly country-specific features of local legislation in accountancy rules, fiscal and labour regulations and other laws that give an advantage to the domestic software providers. Though the software packages offered by large international providers may be adapted

to meet local requirements, the customisation costs are far beyond the budget of most domestic SMEs.

This advantage of the local software developers may become a constraint when they try to sell their products abroad. The same factors that hinder local customers from using foreign software packages hinder Argentine software developers from penetrating foreign markets. Furthermore, in foreign countries Argentine firms lack the knowledge about the 'business culture' and the personal contacts that are key advantages in the domestic market.

When asked about their main strengths and weaknesses, most local firms answered that their main strength was their ability to adapt to the specific requirements of their customers. The lack of scale of their production and the inadequacy of their marketing channels were their primary weaknesses.

When asked, many local SIS firms declare that they are able to offer a highly diversified set of products and services. This may reflect great flexibility in meeting varied demands; on the other hand, it could suggest that the local market is too small to support a strategy of specialisation. The latter may be the case particularly for small SIS firms, which try to meet diversified demands in order to keep on the market. Nonetheless, this range of activities may retard future development of this sector, since these firms are losing the potential gains that may be derived from following business strategies that focus on developing 'core' specialisation areas.

Furthermore, the sort of 'natural protection' that local SIS firms used to enjoy due to the idiosyncrasies of the local market is gradually eroding because:

- Large international software providers are increasingly entering the 'top' of the SMEs market by offering less expensive packages suited to the needs of that kind of firm.
- Many foreign firms (especially from Spain) are competing via prices in the SMEs segment with packaged products.
- Technological changes such as software updates through Internet and technical support via call centres are eroding the localisation advantages enjoyed by local firms.
- Several local firms have been acquired by transnational corporations (TNCs), whose affiliates tend to prefer foreign software packages (see Stamm 2000).

The market for local SIS firms could eventually grow since most domestic SMEs need to upgrade their informatics structure. However, that

growth may have limits since SMEs have been going through a difficult restructuring process during the last decade and face severe economic and financial problems.

Given the limits faced by local SIS firms when trying to sell business software products abroad, we may conclude that specialisation in the SIS market does not look very promising for Argentine firms.

Even if previous studies have stated that Argentina has competitive advantages for developing SIS for certain market niches ('edutainment', applications for health-care systems, industrial automation, public administration and agricultural production),[12] our survey does not show any trend towards specialisation in any of these areas by local SIS firms.

Furthermore, local firms rarely make true 'innovations'; of the firms responding to the survey, only one built its market success on its innovation capability. They concentrate on improving and adapting their products to new technologies and platforms or on widening the range of application of their products. The lack of more ambitious research activities is the result of different factors: (i) the relatively small size of the domestic market poses an obstacle for making innovative activities, since their costs could be difficult to recover; (ii) local firms have very few linkages with R&D institutions, universities or consultancy firms; (iii) domestic demand, especially that of SMEs, does not seemingly induce SIS firms to significantly upgrade their innovative and learning capabilities.

7.4 The impact of the macroeconomic and institutional environment

According to the firms surveyed, the Argentine macroeconomic conditions and institutional environment have both positive and negative impacts on the development of the SIS sector.

The high quality of the domestic human resources is the advantage most mentioned by SIS firms surveyed. Moreover, the use of information technologies has substantially grown, in both the public and the private sector. However, even if Argentinean diffusion of ICT is above the Latin American average, other countries such as Uruguay, Brazil, Chile and Mexico show comparable or even better indicators.

On the other hand, labour costs were deemed relatively high. They were higher than those of some countries of the European periphery (Portugal, Greece, Ireland) that surpass Argentina as locations for developing export-oriented SIS activities since they are closer to the main markets and they belong to the EU. However, with the huge devaluation

of the peso in 2002, labour costs are now much lower than before and should help increase the price competitiveness of local SIS firms.

While Argentine graduates in informatics-related careers may be well trained, there are few university departments that have a staff of full-time professors and treat research on a par with teaching activities (Perazzo *et al.* 1999). Since wages are very low compared with those in the private sector, universities have difficulty attracting high-quality personnel. Furthermore, university careers do not seem to foster entrepreneurial attitudes among their students, a factor that may be hindering the upsurge of new firms.

There are very few postgraduate courses, and their quality is often assessed as mediocre. Since budget restrictions have for a long time prevented the creation of a wide programme of grants to fund studies abroad, it is no surprise that only about 30 people with doctoral degrees were working in Argentine SIS firms in 2001. The lack of postgraduate professionals is an obstacle for undertaking high-level consultancy or research activities.

The scarcity of high-level personnel is a major limitation to developing innovative activities and ensuring the quality of academic training. Moreover, as in recent years the local demand for SIS professionals continued to increase at fast speed, at present there is a shortage of personnel in this sector.

The telecommunications infrastructure presents additional problems; even if it has substantially improved over the last decade, local firms deemed telecommunication costs high. Though these costs were reduced with the peso devaluation, the quality of service may have declined due to the higher costs of importing components and equipment for telecom companies. These increasing costs may delay further technological modernisation of the communications infrastructure.

Another negative factor is the lack of access to finance. SIS firms, particularly SMEs, have difficulties accessing the formal financial system (since they are not only small, but are often young and produce intangible goods). They lack financing alternatives, since the stock market is weak and venture capital is almost unknown.[13] Public policies aimed at easing SMEs' access to credit have been in place for many years, but they have not addressed the specific needs of SIS firms mentioned above. The situation has worsened since 2001, given that the difficulties that arose in Argentina's financial sector after the foreign debt default and currency devaluation closed access to formal financial mechanisms.

Given the difficulties of credit access, some local firms wishing to expand their operations look for funds abroad.[14] At least two firms that

have taken this step ended up selling their majority stake to foreign owners. This is not necessarily bad news in so far as the management remains in local hands and domestic development activities are preserved.

Formal R&D activities by private firms are rare, while those undertaken by universities are weak and are not likely to have any commercial impact. The government created some initiatives in fostering R&D activities in private firms in the mid 1990s (Chudnovsky 1999), but they have had only a marginal effect. In this sense, SIS firms consider the domestic market too small to recover the high cost of undertaking innovative activities.

Which public policies do SIS firms think would help to foster the SIS sector most? Since firms state that the tax burden most hinders their operations, it comes as no surprise that fiscal incentives have been the policy measure they request most.

In contrast, the firms did not feel that policies aimed at facilitating access to foreign markets were effective. This may be evidence that SIS firms seem not to be worried about the inward orientation of the sector (though this attitude may have begun to change after the devaluation). Policies geared at fostering entrepreneurship, such as incubators, have also been judged as hardly relevant by the firms surveyed.

Finally, software piracy levels are above the Latin American average. This is more due to the low level of enforcement of the domestic laws, rather than to the absence of regulations about software piracy.[15] Firms that distribute foreign software products are the most worried about this situation.

7.5 Conclusions and policy suggestions

Our survey on the SIS sector in Argentina shows that there are a small number of large, and mostly foreign-owned firms that had performed very well during the 1990s. They sell foreign software products and provide information services to the public sector and large domestic customers. Compared with SMEs, these firms have better access to human resources and finance, have more advanced quality management systems, and use more sophisticated programming tools. However, they seldom undertake innovation activities and rarely export their products and services from Argentina.

On the other hand, small and medium SIS firms survive primarily through inward-oriented strategies, profiting from the 'localisation advantages' that come from their knowledge and ability to adapt to local regulations, customers' requirements and business culture.

Our findings show that the Argentine SIS sector lacks most of the conditions that Heeks (1999) considers key to successful performance. Table 7.7 summarises the comparison between Heeks's conditions and our findings about Argentina's case.

What lessons can be drawn from our study? Some authors have suggested that some countries that follow an export-oriented strategy may be locked into a low-innovation trajectory, that is, a trajectory where the firms find it difficult to jump from cost-based to innovation-based competition (see D'Costa 2000 and 2003, for the case of India). The case of Argentina shows that 'inward-oriented' strategies may also lead to the same type of 'lock-in'. The same factors that help SIS firms to survive in their local environment may prevent them from developing a learning process, which, in our view, is a precondition for a sustainable strategy of expansion in this sector. Inward-oriented strategies, at least in countries without huge and relatively sophisticated domestic markets, seemingly have more 'cons' than 'pros'.

The Argentine SIS sector may continue to grow in response to local demand, but it is highly improbable that it will turn into a dynamic and internationally competitive sector if it keeps attached to an inward-oriented strategy, since the domestic market has a small size and is not very challenging. Furthermore, the lack of access to finance, the absence of networking mechanisms, the weaknesses of the quality management, the poor marketing and R&D capabilities and the lack of personnel place limits on sectoral development that are not likely to be overcome in the near future.

Overcoming these limitations will require public policies in support of this sector and actions aimed at improving the SIS firms' capabilities and endowments. A consensus seems to be developing within the Argentine government on the importance of fostering this sector through different kinds of incentives (mainly tax deductions). There is an opportunity, then, to adopt policies aimed at restructuring the SIS sector in order to increment its capabilities in order to successfully compete in international markets.

Fortunately, Argentina's SIS firms seem to be aware of the need to redefine their business strategies and increase their presence in foreign markets. They know that although the peso devaluation may have temporarily improved their chances of competing via labour costs, such a strategy is not viable for a country like Argentina in the long term (since labour costs measured in US dollars are expected to grow in the medium term). Furthermore, it is not indeed a very promising strategy either (as it means keeping attached to low value-added activities).

Table 7.7 Does the SIS sector in Argentina fulfil Heeks's conditions for successful performance?

Heeks's conditions	Argentina's situation
Identification of demand-growth markets and synergies	Lack of knowledge about foreign markets
Ability to compete via costs or service innovation	Improved ability to compete via costs after the peso devaluation
	Lack of experience in innovation-based competition
Good marketing	Lack of marketing skills
Access to investment and working capital	Traditionally difficult, worsened after the banking system crisis
Access to programming, analysis and management skills	Good access to programming and analysis skills, but lack of management skills
Access to information technology	Good infrastructure, but difficulties in keeping up to date due to increased costs after the peso devaluation
Networking mechanisms, both intra-firm as well as with other software firms, potential or actual clients	Very weak
Finance (access to working and venture capital and tax incentives)	No access to venture capital
	Some tax incentives may be in place soon
Education and training	Good formation at the undergraduate level, but lack of high-level professionals (postgraduates) – and recently there is also a general shortage of professionals in this area
R&D	Weak R&D capabilities
Intellectual property rights protection	Lack of enforcement of copyright legislation
State procurement	Local firms (specially SMEs) have difficulty entering into tenders for the provision of SIS to the public sector ('short lists')
Infrastructure (telecommunications, Internet)	Same as information technology
'National vision'	So far, non-existent

Argentina has a large number of well-educated people and a cultural influence in Spanish-speaking Latin America. There are a large number of SIS firms that, in spite of the above-mentioned deficiencies, have managed to survive in a not very friendly environment during recent years, which implies that they have certain skills and capabilities that could be the basis of a new (and more outward-oriented) strategy for this sector.

An outward-oriented strategy should aim first at penetrating other Latin American markets as a way to learn how to export SIS. The US market, where at least two Argentine firms are already based, is also a potential key destination for SIS exports. To attain these objectives, domestic firms need not only to get information about the needs of those markets and incorporate modern quality systems, but also to define viable specialisation patterns.

A potentially promising strategy for Argentina's SIS sector may be based on the search for specialised niche markets for which services and semi-packages could be developed, as a first step to creating packages that can be sold in different countries with different degrees of customisation (see Heeks 1999).

The government should help this process through support measures aimed at facilitating private restructuring efforts and at helping to fulfil the above-mentioned conditions for successful performance in this sector. An environment full of incentives for young entrepreneurs to engage in this sector – for example, dismantling red tape and facilitating access to finance – should also be a major task for the government.

Finally, in the new post-devaluation scenario, *pari passu* the strengthening of the domestic SIS firms, the government should explore the possibility of attracting large international SIS firms in order to install in the country their regional basis for South America. In this regard, although the cost advantage derived from the devaluation may not be sustainable in the long run, it could be useful as an initial location advantage to attract investments. Such measures could improve Argentina's image as a potential provider of SIS as well as, in the long run, help to strengthen the development possibilities of the sector as a whole.

Notes

1 Information services include, among others, IT consulting, implementation services, IT training and education, processing services and IT support services (OECD 2002).
2 Both trade liberalisation as well as privatisation fostered the demand for SIS since they pushed for technological modernisation of Argentinean firms.
3 Fortunately, both the public authorities as well as the private sector are aware that the peso devaluation by itself is not enough to foster a sustained process

of exports growth, which requires the solution of the structural weaknesses inherited from the past.

4 See, among other studies, Weber *et al.* (2000) for Brazil, Zhang (2000) for Asian developing countries, Teubal *et al.* (2000) for Israel, Tallon and Kraemer (2000) and Coe (1999) for Ireland and Arora *et al.* (1999), D'Costa (2000, 2003) and Heeks (1996) for India.

5 In the case of India, for example, import substitution policies helped to establish a huge human resources base from the state-sponsored tertiary technical education system. The diaspora of skilled personnel also contributed to the development of the SIS sector as it became a conduit for exports from India (see D'Costa 2003).

6 Four firms, three of which are foreign owned, employed 40 per cent of the personnel with postgraduate degrees.

7 Two-thirds of surveyed firms' exports were made by the local affiliate of a German TNC.

8 Actually, Korea's exports are higher than those shown in available statistics since sizeable software exports are embodied in hardware and other devices sold abroad.

9 As is well known, most firms in this sector are engaged both in products as well as in services markets. In this chapter, we classify surveyed firms according to the kind of activity that is their main source of income (that is, local software products, foreign software products and information services).

10 Medium-sized firms were defined as those that have between 10 and 50 employees. Firms with less than 10 employees were defined as small, while big or large SIS firms are those that have more than 50 employees.

11 The low share of home users in the sales of the SIS sector is mainly due to the high piracy levels that exist in that segment of customers. Moreover, home customers mostly, if not exclusively, buy foreign software products.

12 According to Perazzo *et al.* (1999) Argentina has advantages to make inroads into these activities due to: (i) a relatively high educational level – at least by Latin American standards; (ii) domestic markets for these activities may reach significant dimensions – especially in agricultural and health applications, as well as in edutainment; (iii) information technologies are rather well diffused in the public sector – once more, compared with Latin American standards; (iv) the lack of linguistic barriers may facilitate the penetration in other Latin American countries.

13 The problem of access to finance is common to all SMEs in Argentina.

14 In fact, this is not something unusual for this sector, since the same has happened even with some successful European firms.

15 According to the Business Software Alliance, piracy rates in Argentina amounted to 62 per cent in 1998–99 (the respective figure was 80 per cent in 1994–95), against 36 per cent at world level and 59 per cent for the Latin American average.

References

Arora, A., V. S. Arunachalam, J. Asundi and R. Fernandes (1999) 'The Indian Software Services Industry', mimeo, Pittsburgh: Heinz School, Carnegie Mellon University.

Carmel, E. (2003) 'Taxonomy of New Software Exporting Nations', *The Electronic Journal of Information Systems in Developing Countries*, XIII.

Chudnovsky, D. (1999) 'Science and Technology Policy and the National Innovation System in Argentina', *CEPAL Review*, 67: 157–76.

Coe, N. M. (1999) 'Emulating the Celtic Tiger. A Comparison of the Software Industries of Singapore and Ireland', *Singapore Journal of Tropical Geography*, XX (1): 36–55.

Comité pro-Industria de Software (2000) 'Industria de software en Chile. Pilar de las Tecnologías de Información y Comunicación', Santiago de Chile, October.

Computerworld Chile (1999) *¿En qué está el software chileno?*, 196.

Correa, C. (1990) 'The Legal Protection of Software. Implications for Latecomer Strategies in Newly Industrializing Economies and Middle-income Economies', OECD Development Centre Technical Paper 26, Paris: OECD.

Correa, C. (1996) 'Strategies for Software Exports from Developing Countries', *World Development*, XXIV (1): 171–82.

D'Costa, A. P. (2000) 'Export Growth and Path-dependence. The Locking-in of Innovations in the Software Industry', presented at the 4th International Conference on Technology Policy and Innovation, Curitiba, August.

D'Costa, A. P. (2003) 'Uneven and Combined Development: Understanding India's Software Exports', *World Development*, 31 (1): 211–26.

Heeks, R. (1996) *India's Software Industry: State Policy, Liberalization, and Industrial Development*, New Delhi: Sage Publications.

Heeks, R. (1999) 'Software Strategies in Developing Countries', Working Paper Series 6, Manchester: IDPM, University of Manchester.

Lee, I. *et al.* (2001) 'IT Industry Outlook of Korea', Korea Information Society Development Institute, Seoul.

MIEM (Ministerio de Industria, Energía y Minería) (1999) 'Informe Sector Software', Montevideo: MIEM.

OECD (2002) *OECD Information Technology Outlook. ICTs and the Information Economy*, Paris: OECD.

Perazzo, R., M. Delbue, J. Ordoñez and A. Ridner (1999) 'Oportunidades para la producción y exportación argentina de software', Working Paper 9, Agencia Nacional de Promoción Científica y Tecnológica, Buenos Aires.

SECYT (Secretaría de Ciencia y Técnica-/Subsecretaría de Informática y Desarrollo) (1987) 'Producción y comercio de software en la Argentina', SID Paper 35, Buenos Aires.

Stamm, A. (2000) 'La industria argentina de software: perfil, opciones de desarrollo y recomendaciones de política para su fomento', draft, Buenos Aires.

Stolovich, L., G. Lescano and R. Pessano (2001) 'Las industrias del copyright en Uruguay', Projeto: Importancia Economica das Atividades Protegidas por Direitos Autorais dos Países do Mercosul e Chile, OMPI/UNICAMP.

Tallon, P. and K. Kraemer (2000) 'Ireland's Coming of Age with Lessons for Developing Countries', *Journal of Global IT Management*, III (2): 4–23.

Teubal, M., G. Avnimelech and G. Alon (2000) 'The Israeli Software Industry: Analysis of the Information Security Sector', draft, prepared for the TSER Project 'SME in Europe and Asia: Competition, Collaboration and Lessons for Policy Support'.

Weber, K., C. J. do Nascimento, D. da Silva Marinho and G. Durski (2000) 'Measurements of Quality and Systemic Productivity in the Brazilian Software Industry', presented at the International Productivity Symposium, Curitiba, May.

Zhang, G. (2000) 'Knowledge-based Industries in Asia', OECD, Science, Technology, Industry, Paris: OECD.

8
ICT Opportunities and Challenges for Development in the Arab Region

Samia Satti O. M. Nour

8.1 Introduction

The rapid progress in information and communications technology (ICT) and its impacts on the global economy have intensified in recent years, leading to a new economic system that has attracted a great deal of interest. It has also raised debate on the effects of ICT and the economic opportunities and the challenges that the ICT imposes on the world economy, particularly for developing countries.

More recently, the continuous move towards globalisation has made ICT one of the most important factors in achieving success as well as in seeking new markets, improving quality, providing better and faster customer service and bringing the flexibility needed to make changes quickly.

The role and impact of technical changes in economic growth and economic development have received particular interest in the recent literature focusing on economic growth. In particular, many of the recent studies have shed some light on the impact of IT on economic growth, productivity, employment, work organisation, competitiveness and human capital development.

Several studies have highlighted both the opportunities and the challenges that ICT has imposed on the world economy. For instance, some studies have analysed the implications of IT on productivity (cf. Brynjolfsson and Yang 1996; Hitt and Brynjolfsson 1996) and the effect on growth and development (cf. Jorgenson and Stiroh 1995; Mansell and Wehn 1998; Pohjola 2000, 2001). Other studies examined the effect on human capital development and skill upgrading (cf. Acemoglu 1998; Hwang 2000) and workplace organisation (cf. Bresnahan *et al.* 1999).

On the other hand, several studies discuss the hazards ICT creates for economic development. Most of this literature is based on the idea that technical change is a creative destruction process that creates opportunities for development, while also imposing certain restrictions on development, highlighted, for example, by the negative implications of ICT on employment and the labour market (cf. Aghion and Howitt 1998; Freeman and Soete 1985, 1994, 1997). Some of these studies raised the issue that, as with most other technical change, ICT or IT has a so-called labour-saving or skilled-biased effect through the displacement of unskilled labour that results from either the reduction or elimination of some basic non-skilled jobs.

It has also been hypothesised that ICT could impose adverse effects in the developing world because greater advantages will accrue to the industrialised world from global competitiveness than to the developing world, thus making it hard for the LDCs to compete on the international market. Furthermore, the rapid evolution in ICT will make it harder for the developing countries to bridge the already widening gap between the developed and developing world. ICT, by increasing inequality in income distribution and thus adding to the poverty of the poor, will have adverse results on the status of the poor.

The aim of this chapter is twofold; to analyse the status and the determinants of ICT diffusion in the Arab countries and, to review the potential opportunities and challenges that ICT is expected to create for development in the Arab region.[1] In particular we test the hypothesis that high economic growth and high human capital, schooling and women's schooling lead to the high use of ICT in the Arab region. The chapter will use the descriptive approach, utilising secondary data.

Section 8.2 reviews the status and properties of ICT diffusion in the Arab region. Section 8.3 examines the determinants of ICT diffusion in the region, while section 8.4 reviews the potential opportunities and challenges that ICT is expected to create for economic development in the Arab region. The summary and conclusions are given in section 8.5.

8.2 The status and properties of ICT in the Arab region

This section discusses the status and properties of ICT diffusion in the limited market of the Arab countries, and regional disparities characterising the diffusion of ICT in the region.

8.2.1 Growing but limited market for ICT in the Arab countries

The diffusion of ICT in the Arab region has increased significantly. As Table 8.1 illustrates, the growth rate of the total online population, population with access to telephone mainlines and cellular subscribers in the Arab countries during the period 2001–2, has been significant. Table 8.2 presents more recent indicators from the International Telecommunication Union (ITU 2004) and illustrates that despite a slowdown in terms of both cellular mobile and telephone landlines, compound average growth rates for the Arab region exceeded the world average over the period (1996–2003). Moreover, MADAR (2002b)[2] indicates that in the Arab world Internet penetration rate more than doubled from March 2001, and expected to exceed the 25 million mark by the end of 2005. Over the period (2002–5), Internet penetration in the Arab region showed high compound average growth rate (50 per cent) compared to the world average (18.5 per cent) (cf. MADAR 2002b: 8, 10).

Despite the positive growth trend, the market for ICT is limited in the Arab countries and this is apparent in the low demand, limited supply and restricted ICT spending. The Arab region embraces more than 299.6 million people, but shows low demand as appears from low ICT

Table 8.1 Growth of the 'online' population, telephone landlines and cellular subscribers worldwide, 2001–2

	Population accessing/ Internet users (per 1000 people)		Telephone mainlines (per 1000 people)		Cellular subscribers (per 1000 people)	
	2001	*2002*	*2001*	*2002*	*2001*	*2002*
OECD	332	383.1	523	516	539	588
East Asia and the Pacific	41.4	60.9	122	142	113	159
Central and Eastern Europe and CIS	42.8	71.8	224	226	120	189
Latin America and Caribbean	49	81.2	160	166	162	191
South Asia	6.3	14.9	38	41	7	13
Sub-Saharan Africa	7.8	9.6	15	15	28	39
World	79.6	99.4	169	175	153	184
Arab states	15.6	28.0	76	81	58	85

Source: UNDP (2004).

Table 8.2   Growth rate of cellular mobile and telephone landlines worldwide, 1996–2003 (%)

	Cellular mobile country average growth rate in subscribers			Telephone mainlines country average growth rate in subscribers		
	1996–2001	*1997–2002*	*1998–2003*	*1996–2001*	*1997–2002*	*1998–2003*
Average Arab states	89.3	80.6	80.3	11.3	10.4	10.0
Asia	48.5	43.3	38.1	13.7	13.2	13.6
Africa	85.6	74.6	65	9.4	9	8.5
Oceania	24.9	24.3	24.6	2.5	2.4	2.1
America	32.9	28.7	24.8	5.1	3.8	2.4
Europe	56.8	46.3	33.4	3.4	2.6	1.9
World	46.1	40.2	33.4	7.3	6.6	6.3

Source: ITU (2004).

expenditures per capita. Table 8.3 indicates that during 2001, ICT spending, software-to-hardware spending ratios, IT variables, ICT per GDP and ICT per capita in Saudi Arabia/Gulf states and Egypt were minimal in comparison to the USA, UK, Korea, Singapore and the world total. In addition, Table 8.4 indicates that the number of the population having access to telephone landlines, mobile phones, personal computers (PCs) and the Internet in the Arab region are low in comparison to the USA, Europe, Japan, Korea, Singapore and Malaysia.[3] The market is discouraged by the low demand, which can be attributed to high price, as is indicated in Table 8.4. Moreover, the average Arab countries' supply as indicated by the average number of Internet service providers (ISPs) is very low versus the USA, Japan and Europe. This limited supply can be attributed to inadequate investment and infrastructure as can be seen from the low expenditures on ICT as a percentage of GDP.[4]

The limited market and the low diffusion rate of ICT in the Arab region are exacerbated by many problems that can be interpreted from both supply and demand perspectives. From the supply side the major problems are inadequate investment; lack of infrastructure; insufficient R&D in ICT-related issues; deficient services due to low speed rate; disconnection; lack of networks system and the uncertainty/risk aversion because the limited demand discourages investment and expansion of the services. From the demand side the major obstacles are inadequate awareness of the importance of ICT in the new economy, particularly of the value/importance of the Internet and intranet in daily operations.

Table 8.3 ICT spending and IT variables in Egypt and Saudi Arabia/Gulf states compared to the USA, UK, Korea, Singapore and world total, 2001

	USA	UK	Korea	Singapore	World total	Saudi Arabia/ Gulf states	Egypt
ICT spending (US$m)							
IT hardware spending	136,051	21,287	8,816	1,777	376,119	1,043	417
IT software spending	96,556	13,798	1,027	656	196,237	302	124
IT services spending	199,203	27,354	2,803	1,152	425,660	922	245
IT internal spending	107,428	26,723	2,731	1,153	345,500	557	223
IT other office equipment spending	7,442	2,194	797	161	33,705	94	38
Total IT spending	546,681	91,356	16,174	4,899	1,377,221	2,918	1,046
Telecommunications spending	265,954	46,370	16,127	4,694	1,037,877	3,276	1,337
Total ICT spending	812,635	137,726	32,301	9,592	2,415,098	6,194	2,383
Economic ratios							
ICT/GDP (%)	7.9	9.7	7.4	9.9	7.6	3.6	2.5
ICT/capita (US$)	2,923.8	2,318.6	676.3	2,110.0	395.3	309.4	36.8
Software/hardware spending (%)	71.0	64.8	11.6	36.9	52.2	28.9	29.8
IT variables							
PCs installed in education	16,322,694	1,824,106	610,724	150,702	36,778,755	66,391	48,816
PCs installed in homes	80,943,489	10,201,092	5,266,395	495,847	204,483,990	220,386	147,827
PCs installed in business and government	129,868,818	8,906,587	5,366,097	1,274,419	299,914,464	618,054	454,441
Total PCs installed	227,135,001	20,931,785	11,243,831	1,920,968	541,177,209	904,831	651,084
Telephone lines/HH	1.98	1.50	1.48%	2.57	n.a.	1.12	0.34

Note: n.a. = data not available.

Source: WITSA (2002).

Table 8.4 Total population with access to ICT, 1996–2003

Countries	Population access (per 1000 people)[a(1)]				Internet total monthly price[a(1)]		ICT expenditures[a(1)]		
	Telephone landlines	Mobile phones	PCs	Internet	$ per 20 hours of use	% of monthly GNI per capita	% of GDP	Per capita (US$)	ISP[b(2)]
USA	621	543	658.9	551	15	0.5	8.8	3,309	7,800
Japan	472	679	382.2	483	21	0.8	7.4	2,489	73
UK	591	841	405.7	423	24	1.1	7.3	2,223	245
Netherlands	614	768	466.6	522	24	1.2	6.4	2,009	52
Singapore	450	852	622	509	11	0.6	10.5	2,254	n.a.
Korea, Republic of	538	701	558	610	10	1.2	6.7	842	n.a.
Malaysia	182	442	166.9	344	8	2.9	6.9	289	n.a.
Arab states	120.4	214.3	48.31	76.43	34.4	54.31	4.167	156	8.31

Notes:

[1] Figures for 2003.

[2] Figures for 1996–2000; CIA (2001) contains data collected during different time periods (i.e. 1996, 2000), and as a result, even though the countries are examined under the same data category, the data for the different countries may correspond to different years. This inconsistency can render the country comparison less reliable. However, this source is used here because it covers most of the Arab countries.

Sources: [a]WDI-ITU (2005); [b]CIA (2001).

In addition, the low demand from consumers can be attributed to the limited capacity/availability and efficiency of the services; high costs and the wide spread of illiteracy and poverty in some countries in the region. The high costs of the services discourage both the demand and supply sides; for instance, Tables 8.4 and 8.5 show that the prices and costs of Internet services in some Arab countries are far higher than in the USA, Europe, Japan, Korea and Singapore. Language problems caused by the preference for Arabic, or unfamiliarity with other languages, reduces the maximum benefit to be gained from the Internet, especially with regard to websites offered in other languages. This problem is emphasised by UNDP-AHDR (2002), which indicates language as a problem contributing to a digital divide within the Arab region and between the Arab and other countries in the world, mainly because most of the information currently on the Internet is in English, a language that much of the population do not know well (UNDP-AHDR 2002: 76).[5]

8.2.2 Market concentration and regional disparities

The diffusion of ICT in the Arab region is characterised by limited market size and market concentration in the Arab Gulf countries. Moreover, there is a wide gap between the Gulf countries and other countries of the region in terms of supply, demand, prices and intensity of the services.[6]

The limited market size and inequality/disparity in market size of ICT diffusion can probably be interpreted or attributed to the effects of inequality in income distribution, Human Development Index (HDI) and social and cultural legacies. For example, Table 8.7 (see section 8.3) indicates that high HDI and average years of schooling among the high-income Arab countries seem to have strongly encouraged high access to or use of ICT. The small rich Gulf countries probably managed to deal with social and cultural legacies when implementing ICT, because of high per capita income, HDI and average years of schooling and better resources offered to ICT, which probably facilitate high ICT diffusion, probably because they make transactions more transparent. Next to the Gulf countries, the medium-income countries such as Libya, Lebanon, Jordan and Tunisia display medium performance in terms of income level, HDI and the use of ICT. However, across countries comparison indicates that for example, Jordan shows an exceptional high performance in terms of average years of schooling but low in terms of the use of ICT compared to Bahrain and Kuwait.[7]

Table 8.5 shows that the Gulf countries account for around 11 per cent of the region's population. These countries account for 70, 59, 60 and

71 per cent of the total population with access to the Internet, PCs, telephone landlines and mobile telephones respectively. Moreover, Table 8.6 indicates that the Gulf countries account for 7.67 per cent of Internet service providers in the Arab region (see below). The wide differential between the Gulf countries and the other nations in the Arab region is obvious in the supply and demand, which can be measured by the percentage of population accessing the Internet, PCs purchasable by GDP per capita, ICT Use Index, prices and intensity of the services.

On the one hand, the differential in the demand is indicated by both the share of the population accessing the Internet and the ICT Use Index. Table 8.5, based on the WDI-ITU (2005) database, illustrates that the United Arab Emirates (UAE), Bahrain, Kuwait, Lebanon and Qatar have high ratios of the population with access to the three ICT modes (telephone, mobile telephones and Internet). The gap between these countries and the other nations of the region, especially the poverty-stricken Yemen and Sudan, is very wide.[8]

Moreover, Table 8.5 shows the variation in the cost/price of Internet services between the Arab countries. For instance, the UAE, Egypt and Tunisia have the lowest/cheapest prices, while both Sudan and Djibouti had the highest prices during 2003. Furthermore, there are differences in the intensity of the service, as indicated by the number of websites. For instance, according to the World Development Indicators (WDI: World Bank 2001), the UAE, Kuwait, Bahrain and Lebanon together have more websites (per 10,000 people) than Egypt, Jordan, Kuwait, Saudi Arabia and Oman. In particular, the Gulf countries account for 90.79 per cent of all websites in the Arab region, evidence of the wide gap that exists between the Gulf and other Arab countries.

Moreover, Table 8.6 illustrates that the demand for ICT as measured by the ICT Use Index and PCs purchasable by GDP per capita is unequally distributed and concentrated mainly in some countries in the region.[9] While the UAE, Gulf states, Lebanon, Tunisia and Jordan rank among the highest in terms of both ICT Use Index and PCs purchasable by GDP per capita, Yemen and Sudan are among the lowest. Moreover, difference across Arab countries also appears from the e-government index; for instance, the Gulf countries, mainly UAE, Kuwait and Bahrain together with Lebanon, show a high e-government index in the Arab region, while Yemen and Algeria show a low e-government index. In the Arab region, the UAE and Bahrain ranked first and second respectively in terms of e-government readiness, while Jordan and Tunisia ranked first and second respectively in terms of growth competitiveness (Kamli 2003).

Table 8.5 Access to ICT in the Arab countries, 2003

Countries	Population access (per 1000 people)				Internet total monthly price		ICT expenditures		Population, total	GDP Per capita (constant 2000 US$)
	Telephone mainlines	Mobile phones	PCs	Internet	$ per 20 hours of use	% of monthly GNI per capita	% of GDP	Per capita $		
Algeria	69	46	7.7	16	18	12	n.a.	n.a.	31,832,612	1,916
Bahrain	268	638	n.a.	216	39	4	2	n.a.	711,662	n.a.
Comoros	17	3	n.a.	6	67	206	n.a.	n.a.	600,142	365
Djibouti	15	34	n.a.	10	115	153	n.a.	n.a.	705,480	848
Egypt	127	84	21.9	39	5	5	1.2	15	67,559,040	1,622
Iraq	n.a.	3	8.3	1	n.a.	n.a.	n.a.	n.a.	24,699,542	n.a.
Jordan	114	242	44.7	81	26	18	8.8	164	5,307,895	1,801
Kuwait	198	578	162.8	228	25	2	1.7	304	2,396,417	16,738
Lebanon	n.a.	n.a.	80.5	117	37	11	n.a.	n.a.	4,497,669	3,925
Libya	136	23	23.4	29	19	4	n.a.	n.a.	5,559,289	n.a.
Mauritania	14	128	n.a.	4	39	113	n.a.	n.a.	2,847,869	372
Morocco	40	243	19.9	33	25	26	5.6	82	30,112,644	1,278
Oman	n.a.	229	35	71	24	4	n.a.	n.a.	2,598,832	n.a.
Qatar	261	533	n.a.	199	22	1	n.a.	n.a.	623,703	n.a.
Saudi Arabia	155	321	130.2	67	35	5	2.5	239	22,528,304	9,038
Somalia	n.a.	n.a.	n.a.	n.a.	n.a.	n.a.	n.a.	n.a.	9,625,918	n.a.
Sudan	27	20	6.1	9	161	551	n.a.	n.a.	33,545,726	433
Syria	n.a.	65	19.4	n.a.	55	59	n.a.	n.a.	17,384,492	1,135
Tunisia	118	192	40.5	64	17	10	5.2	132	9,895,201	2,214
UAE	281	736	129	275	13	1	n.a.	n.a.	4,041,000	n.a.
West Bank and Gaza	87	133	36.2	40	25	33	n.a.	n.a.	3,366,702	849
Yemen	n.a.	35	7.4	n.a.	31	75	3.3	n.a.	19,173,160	553
Average Arab states	120.4	214.3	48.31	86.67	39.9	64.65	4.167	156		2,872
Total Arab states	1927	4286	773	1505	798	1293	30.3	936	299,613,299	43,087
Total Gulf states	1163	3035	457	1056	158	17	6.2	543	32,899,918	25,776
% of the Gulf states to total Arab	60	71	59	70	20	1	20	58	11	60

Notes: n.a. = data not available; GNI = gross national income.

Source: WDI-ITU (2005).

Table 8.6 ICT Use Index and PC purchasing power, ISP and e-government index in Arab countries, 2002–4

Countries	End of 2002 ICT Use Index[a]	End of 2003 ICT Use Index[a]	End of 2004 ICT Use Index[b]	PC units purchasable by GDP per capita[a]	ISP 2002[c]	E-government index 2002[d]
Bahrain	1.15	1.26	1.67	11.39	1	2.04
Kuwait	0.95	1.17	1.32	15.13	21	2.12
Qatar	0.75	0.92	1.21	23.05	1	1.81
Oman	0.35	0.39	0.59	6.66	1	1.64
Saudi Arabia	0.50	0.61	0.8	7.90	21	1.86
UAE	1.40	1.50	1.66	18.19	1	2.17
Average Gulf	0.85	0.975	1.21	3.03	7.67	
Tunisia	0.25	0.4	0.6	2.35	12	1.36
Lebanon	0.52	0.54	0.58	4.30	14	2.00
Jordan	0.46	0.49	0.57	1.72	12	1.75
Palestine	0.31	0.4	0.52	0.81	10	
Morocco	0.27	0.3	0.38	1.28	150	1.47
Syria	0.15	0.23	0.31	1.20	2	
Egypt	0.21	0.26	0.31	1.11	80	1.73
Algeria	0.10	0.15	0.28	1.99	32	1.27
Libya	0.16	0.19	0.28	3.69	6	1.57
Iraq	0.04	0.06	0.16	1.32	1	
Yemen	0.05	0.09	0.11	0.54	1	1.30
Sudan	0.03	0.07	0.09	0.42	3	
Total Arab	0.22	0.27	0.35	2.27	369	

Sources: (a) MADAR (2004); (b) MADAR (2005); (c) MADAR (2002b: 5); (d) ESCWA (2003b: 101).

On the other hand, with regard to the supply of ICT, Table 8.6 shows that Morocco, Egypt, Algeria, Saudi Arabia, Kuwait and Lebanon have more than 300 ISPs while all other Arab countries together have less than 60 companies providing similar services.

8.3   The determinants of ICT diffusion in the Arab region

The discussion on the wide divergence in ICT diffusion in the Arab region is probably a reflection of the differences in both economic growth (income as measured by GDP per capita) and human capital development (educational attainment as measured by the average years of schooling). In this section we test the hypothesis that high economic growth and high human capital, schooling and women's schooling lead to high use of ICT in the Arab region.

For instance, Table 8.7 illustrates that the share of the population accessing the Internet in the Arab countries significantly increases with an improvement in GDP per capita. Thus, the richest Gulf countries like the UAE, Bahrain, Qatar and Kuwait, which have high GDP per capita,

also have a high ratio of the population online on the Internet, while Yemen and Sudan, with low GDP per capita, are accessing the Internet less. Similarly, Table 8.7 indicates that the share of the population accessing the Internet in the Arab countries increases with the rise in the average years of schooling. In particular, Bahrain and Kuwait, the richest Arab Gulf countries, have, on average, more years of schooling and thus a high percentage of the population online.

In addition, Table 8.7 indicates that high numbers of women participating in education (the definition herein being the average years of schooling, youth literacy rate, net enrolment in secondary and gross enrolment in tertiary education) among the high-income Arab countries seems to have encouraged high access to or high use of ICT. The Gulf countries have high income, HDI and women's participation in education, which probably contribute to women's development and thus probably facilitate ICT diffusion. Next to the Gulf countries, the medium-income countries such as Libya, Lebanon, Jordan and Tunisia show medium performance in terms of income level, HDI and the use of ICT. The major social implication from these results suggests that high income, high HDI and high women's participation in education are corresponding to better access to and use of ICT.[10]

Table 8.8 summarises the regression results of the percentage of population accessing the Internet as a dependent variable with respect to GDP per capita, average years of schooling and women's participation in education as independent (explanatory) variables. These results prove our earlier hypothesis and illustrate that the diffusion of IT – as measured by use of the Internet – in the Arab region significantly increases in relation to economic growth (as measured by GDP per capita). The use of the Internet is also positively correlated with human capital (as measured by average years of schooling) and women's development.

8.4 ICT opportunities and challenges for development in the Arab region

Like other modern technologies, ICT has the ability to impose the creative destruction effect by providing opportunities for development while simultaneously creating hazards to development, and equally so in the Arab region.

8.4.1 ICT opportunities for development

Similar to other countries, the Arab nations have the opportunity to benefit from the potential wide and fast diffusion of ICT to accelerate

Table 8.7 Total population, GDP per capita, average years of schooling, Human Development Index, female participation in education, ICT indicators: population access to the Internet, telephone and mobiles across the Arab countries, 2000–2 (defined by income level)

Countries	Total population (million)[a(1)]	GDP/per capita (PPP US$)[a(1)]	HDI (%)[a(1)]	Average years of schooling[b(2)]		Female ratio[a(3)] (%)			Access of population (per 1000 people)[a(1)] to:		
				All	Women	Youth literacy (% ages 15–24)	Net secondary enrolment	Gross tertiary enrolment	Internet	Telephone mainlines[a]	Cellular subscribers[a]
High income											
Bahrain	0.7	17,170	0.843	6.09	5.81	98.9	86	28	245	261	579
Kuwait	2.4	16,240	0.838	7.05	6.89	93.9	79	32	105.8	204	519
UAE	2.9	22,420	0.824	n.a.	n.a.	95.0	74	n.a.	313.2	291	647
Qatar	0.6	19,844	0.833	n.a.	n.a.	95.8	80	34	113.4	286	433
Average high income	6.6[(4)]	18,918.5	0.830	6.57	6.35	95.9	79.75	31.33	194.35	260.5	544.5
Medium income											
Oman	2.8	13,340	0.770	n.a.	n.a.	97.3	68	10	70.0	92	183
Saudi Arabia	23.5	12,650	0.768	n.a.	n.a.	91.6	51	26	64.6	151	228
Algeria	31.3	5,760	0.704	4.72	3.7	85.6	64	n.a.	16.0	61	13
Egypt	70.5	3,810	0.653	5.05	3.76	66.9	79	n.a.	28.2	110	67
Lebanon	3.6	4,360	0.758	n.a.	n.a.	n.a.	n.a.	48	117.1	199	227
Morocco	30.1	3,810	0.620	n.a.	n.a.	61.3	28	9	23.6	38	209
Syria	17.4	3,620	0.710	5.74	4.38	93.0	37	n.a.	12.9	123	23
Tunisia	9.7	6,760	0.745	4.2	3.26	90.6	69	21	51.7	117	52

Occupied Palestine Territories	3.4	n.a.	0.726	n.a.	n.a.	n.a.	83	30	30.4	87	93
Libyan Arab Jamahiriya	5.4	7,570	0.794	2.87	n.a.	94	n.a.	61	22.5	118	13
Djibouti	0.7	1,610	0.445	n.a.	n.a.	n.a.	13	1	6.9	15	23
Jordan	5.3	4,220	0.750	7.37	6.35	99.5	81	31	57.7	127	229
Iraq	24.51	n.a.	n.a.	4.34	3.25	n.a.	n.a.	n.a.	n.a.	n.a.	n.a.
Average medium income	228.21[4]	6137.27	0.700	4.89	4.11	86.64	57.3	26.33	41.8	103.17	113.33
Low income				1.91	1.35						
Sudan	32.9	1,820	0.505	n.a.	n.a.	74.2	n.a.	6	2.6	21	6
Somalia	9.48	n.a.	n.a.	n.a.	n.a.	n.a.	n.a.	n.a.	n.a.	n.a.	n.a.
Yemen	19.3	870	0.482	n.a.	n.a.	50.9	21	5	5.1	28	21
Mauritania	2.8	2,220	0.465	n.a.	n.a.	41.8	13	1	3.7	12	92
Comoros	0.7	1,690	0.530	n.a.	n.a.	52.2	n.a.	1	4.2	13	0.0
Average low income	65.18[4]	1,650	0.500	1.91	1.35	54.78	17	3.25	3.9	18.5	39.67
Average Arab states	296.6[4]	5,069	0.651	4.93	4.31	81.32	57.88	21.5	28.0	81	85

Notes: n.a. = data not available. (1) data refer to 2002; (2) data refer to 2000; (3) data refer to 2000/1; (4) figures refer to total.

Sources: (a) UNDP (2004), (b) Barro and Lee (2001) for the average years of schooling data.

Table 8.8   Determinants of IT diffusion: regression results for the period 2000–3

	IT Internet 2002[a(1)]				IT Internet 2003[b(2)]			
	Constant (t-value)	Coefficient (t-value)	R^2	N	Constant (t-value)	Coefficient (t-value)	R^2	N
GDP per capita UNDP 2002[a(1)]	−14.265 (−0.819)	0.010** (6.070)	0.684	19				
GDP per capita WDI 2003[b(2)]					17.673 (1.703)	0.012** (6.214)	0.778	13
Human capital (average years of schooling)[c(3)]	−46.110 (−0.425)	21.088 (1.082)	0.163	8	−118.624 (−1.248)	38.930** (2.212)	0.449	8
Women's average years of schooling[c(3)]	−75.475 (−0.702)	30.619 (1.441)	0.293	7	−135.746 (−1.811)	48.311** (3.181)	0.669	7
Women's youth literacy rate[a(1)]	−124.972 (−1.492)	2.361** (2.353)	0.270	17	−154.171 (−1.659)	2.947** (2.680)	0.356	15
Women's net enrolment in secondary education[a(1)]	−29.973 (−0.627)	1.758** (2.328)	0.279	16	−29.233 (−0.514)	2.019** (2.370)	0.319	14
Women's gross enrolment in tertiary education[a(1)]	23.589 (0.998)	1.590* (1.857)	0.198	16	34.118 (1.124)	1.953* (1.834)	0.206	15

Notes: (1) data refer to 2002; (2) data refer to 2003; (3) data refer to 2000; * correlation is significant at the 0.05 level (1-tailed), ** correlation is significant at the 0.01 level (1-tailed).

Sources: (a) UNDP (2004); (b) WDI-ITU (2005); (c) Barro and Lee (2001).

economic development in many ways (for instance D'Costa 2003, and D'Costa and Sridharan 2003, present several successful cases for the benefits from ICT use).

In particular, the increasing use of ICT has the potential to accelerate economic development in the region by facilitating the generation or creation of other sources of income and investment, thus enhancing sustainable development and promotion of economic growth in the Arab region. For instance, according to the WDI-ITU (2005) database, over the period 1988–2003 the average telephone revenues per landline for the Arab countries increased from US$1068 to US$2263 (see Figure 8.1).

In addition, the use of ICT can enhance employment opportunities by creating and initiating new jobs and increasing the employment rate of already existing jobs. For example, Figure 8.2 shows that the expected number of job opportunities for medium and high-skilled workers in the ICT sector in Egypt is expected to increase rapidly over the period 1999–2009. Moreover, ICT can be used to minimise poverty in the region by creating additional employment opportunities (cf. ESCWA

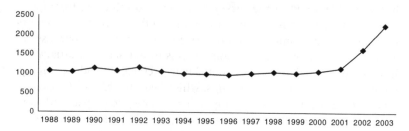

Figure 8.1 Average telephone revenues per landlines in the Arab region, 1988–2003 (current US$)

Source: Adapted from WDI-ITU (2005)

Figure 8.2 Expected number of job opportunities for high- and medium-skilled workers in Egypt, 1999–2009

Source: Adapted from Egypt Ministry of Communications and Information Technology (1999)

2004, 2005b). For instance, ESCWA (2005b) discusses a survey and examples of 48 ICT initiatives for employment creation and poverty alleviation that have been, or were being, implemented as of November 2004 in selected countries, namely Egypt, Jordan, Lebanon, Palestine, Syrian Arab Republic and Yemen. Jordan and Lebanon reported a higher number of initiatives as compared to other selected members. Most of the initiatives identified in the survey targeted youth and women, and were generally located in impoverished areas. The majority of ICT

initiatives identified in the survey as directly contributing to employment creation and poverty alleviation were in the form of training programmes or community centres established for the purpose of eradicating IT illiteracy or providing access to ICT services, usually the Internet. In general, initiatives offered many services including employment preparatory assistance groups, which refer to services that either link training efforts directly to employment or help to prepare individuals for job seeking. The report identifies the Professional Computer Association of Lebanon Internet Point of Presence and the Jordan Information Technology Community Centre as two successful initiative case studies that provide expansion strategies and sustainability that were launched by the private and public sectors respectively (cf. ESCWA 2005b: 14, 15–17).

The diffusion of ICT can be used to promote the degree and efficiency of the work organisation, to accelerate and facilitate the catching-up efforts to bridge the gap with advanced countries by building the knowledge-based economy. This can be achieved mainly through increasing the efficiency of the educational system and learning to benefit from long-distance teaching in the near future; by developing the communication system through the provision of cheaper, easier, faster and more efficient services, and upgrading skills and developing human resources through improved educational and training systems and enhancing the capability of people. For instance, according to UNDP-AHDR (2002) Egypt, Jordan, Saudi Arabia and the UAE have formulated ambitious plans to introduce computers at various stages of education (UNDP-AHDR 2002: 79). Moreover, a recent study reflecting the case of Egypt shows a corresponding increase in ICT-related university graduates from 2600 in 2000 to 3200 in 2002 (ESCWA 2003a: 17).

Moreover, ICT can encourage the advancement of R&D efforts by motivating and facilitating collaboration between research institutes and organisations in the region, thus promoting pan-Arab research activities. ESCWA (2003a: 35), reporting for Egypt, shows a corresponding improvement in capacity building related to ICT investment; over the period 2000–2, R&D expenditures in ICT as a percentage of GNI increased from 1.9 to 2.10, while scientists and engineers in R&D in ICT increased from 1674 to 1925.

Furthermore, ICT can be used to enhance gender equality in the Arab region by increasing both education and employment opportunities for women. ESCWA (2005b) indicates many programmes, such as the women's empowerment in impoverished communities programme that aims at improving the status of women in the region. Establishing

ICT-enabled national centres helps to combat poverty as well as illiteracy, bridges the education gap, provides access to women-relevant information and increases employability, economic welfare and the social integration of women (ESCWA 2005b: 38). Moreover, according to ITU (2004), the telecommunication sector offered 19 per cent of its employment opportunities to Arab women in 2001. However, this share of women telecom staff (19 per cent) in the Arab states lags behind compared to those of South Africa (22 per cent), Sweden (38 per cent) and the UK (25 per cent).

The diffusion of ICT can be useful for promoting e-commerce. Investments in ICT have the potential to push/enhance e-commerce. Both the Internet and the recent growth in e-commerce can help facilitate the fast delivery of products or services to large numbers of consumers within the Arab region and to new and different markets, thus improving commerce both within the Arab nations and with other countries outside the Arab region. This, in turn, will enable the region to generate further revenue from e-commerce. For instance, MADAR anticipated an increase in revenues from B2B and B2C e-commerce in Egypt, Saudi Arabia and UAE: for example, compound average growth rates in B2B and B2C e-commerce are expected to increase in Egypt by 100 and 65 per cent respectively and Saudi Arabia by 75 and 40 per cent over the period 2002–5, and in the UAE by 42 and 20 per cent over the period 2002–8 (MADAR 2002a: 14; 2002b: 13; 2003: 34).

8.4.2 ICT challenges for development

In addition to the potential opportunities ICT offers for development, it can also impose challenges to development in the Arab region. The adverse effects of ICT may become apparent in many ways.

One possible challenge of the use of ICT is related to increased competition. In order to be able to deliver competitive goods and high-quality services efficiently to global markets the Arab region needs not only to enhance its productive capacity but also to increase and accelerate its investment rates in ICT and related infrastructure. This, in turn, creates the need to enhance the technological capabilities of the region, to raise funds for R&D, to develop scientific research that matches both local and global needs and to promote collaborative research activities between Arab countries. The Arab countries face challenges to implement more effective policies to improve the competitiveness, liberalisation and privatisation of ICT sector. Table 8.9 shows the high level of monopoly and poor level of competitiveness and liberalisation in the ICT market in the Arab states compared to other countries.

Table 8.9 Level of competition and liberalisation of ICT market in the Arab states compared to world countries, 2003/4

Global region	Level of competition for basic services		Countries with partly or fully private incumbents (%)	Level of competition in cellular mobile services		Level of competition in Internet services	
	Competition	Monopoly		Competition	Monopoly	Competition	Monopoly
World	54	46	n.a.	n.a.	n.a.	91	9
Europe and CIS	77	23	77	94	6	100	0
Americas	49	51	74	75	25	90	10
Asia-Pacific	51	49	53	69	31	89	11
Arab states	15	85	43	69	31	71	29
Africa	52	48	42	92	8	92	8

Note: Europe refers to Europe and CIS.

Source: Adapted from ITU (2003-4: Figure 1).

Another possible challenge of ICT may be a growing unemployment rate. ICT is similar to other technologies in that it has the tendency to cause so-called labour-saving skill-biased effects by reducing employment either through the removal and elimination of jobs or through reduction of already existing jobs, particularly those for unskilled workers. The skill-biased technical change measured by the use of IT or ICT can lead to dual implications for employment and demand for skill by increasing unemployment or reducing the demand for unskilled workers as verified in the literature (Bound and Johnson 1992; Berman *et al.* 1994; Freeman and Soete 1994; Autor *et al.* 1998). There is no study to measure the extent of displacement of workers caused by the use of ICT in the Arab region, but given the high unemployment in the region – about 13.6 per cent of the total labour force – and the increasing use of ICT, the displacement in the demand for unskilled workers is predictable from the new growth literature and may contribute to increasing the unemployment level in the Arab region.[11]

Other challenges relate to widening regional disparities; ICT has the propensity to increase the already existing gap and disparity within the region. Table 8.10 indicates the disparity in the use of ICT and the digital divide according to income level in the Arab region.[12] While only 3 per cent of the total Arab population belong to the high-income group, they had around 71, 52 and 58 per cent of total Arab population access to the Internet, telephone landlines and cellular subscribers in 2003. The estimation from the WDI-ITU (2005) indicates an increase in the concentration of access to the Internet (from 45 to 71 per cent) and telephone landlines (from 47 to 52 per cent) in the Arab high-income band over the period 2002–3, but there is a relative decline with respect to cellular subscribers from 61 to 58 per cent. In contrast, when integrating the UNDP and the WDI-ITU (2005) database, we observe a decrease in the digital divide. For instance, we recognise the decline in the concentration of access to the Internet (from 81 to 71 per cent) over the period 2002–3 and access to both telephone landlines (from 78 to 52 per cent) and cellular subscribers (from 97 to 58 per cent) over the period 1990–2003 within the Arab high-income range.[13]

Another serious challenge is related to increased inequality and the rift between the Arab countries and the developed countries. ICT may have an adverse effect on the already existing gap that exists in ICT investment and infrastructure and technological capability (cf. Tables 8.1, 8.2, 8.3, 8.4 and 8.9). Moreover, the Arab region faces serious challenges with respect to progress in e-readiness, and growth competitiveness compared to the global community. For instance, the UN-DESA (2002)

Table 8.10 ICT disparities and the digital divide in the Arab region defined by income level

Share in Arab total(%)[a,b]	Total population		Population accessing/ Internet users (per 1000 people)			Telephone mainlines (per 1000 people)				Cellular subscribers (per 1000 people)			
	2002[a]	2002–3[b]	2002[a]	2002[b]	2003[b]	1990[a]	2002[a]	2002[b]	2003[b]	1990[a]	2002[a]	2002[b]	2003[b]
High income	2	3	81	45	71	78	68	47	52	97	78	61	58
Medium income	76	75	17	53	28	20	27	49	45	3	16	36	38
Low income	22	22	2	2	1	2	5	4	3	0	6	3	4

Sources: Author's calculation from (a) UNDP (2004), (b) WDI-ITU (2005).

report on global e-government readiness underlines the backwardness of Arab countries in terms of worldwide global rank: the UAE (38), Bahrain (46), Egypt (140), Sudan (146) and Yemen (151). The report concluded that Arab nations must exert greater efforts in order to bridge the digital gap with developed countries. In addition, the WEF (2003–4) report on global competitiveness indicates the backwardness of Arab countries in terms of worldwide global rank: Jordan (34), Tunisia (38), Egypt (58), Morocco (61) and Algeria (74). The competitiveness report suggests that Arab countries need to set in motion both economic and legal reforms, in order to raise their competitiveness with regard to the rest of the world (Kamli 2003).

Furthermore, other challenges related to the fact that the need for further public investment in ICT could create some difficulties, given the high proportion of poverty in the region, especially in the poor Arab countries – from 2 to 63.1 per cent (UNDP 2004),[14] where the allocation of public funding is targeted to meet different social needs, particularly to reduce the poverty rate, promote education, health and other infrastructure. Public funds and/or investment in these budget items are given special priority and therefore compete with public investments in ICT and related infrastructure.

ESCWA (2005b) identifies some challenges preventing impoverished communities from benefiting from the various applications of ICT to improve their human development level and gradually become an integral part of the knowledge society. These include restrictive government policies; the lack of enforcement mechanisms; lack of affordable communication services; high cost of ICT; irrelevant content; illiteracy; lack of sustainable projects and limited equitable access to ICT due to legal and regulatory barriers (ESCWA 2005b: 20–1).[15]

Moreover, the success and increase of e-commerce in the Arab region face several challenges or obstacles, such as the relative newness of online commerce and setting-up of e-commerce in the region and inadequate and slow Internet services. Additionally there are the high costs of building and managing websites, a lack of trust or inability to ensure and secure transactions due to the low level of electronic commercial transactions and low Internet user rates in the region.[16]

8.5 Conclusions

This chapter examines the status of ICT in the Arab region, and the opportunities and challenges ICT can trigger for the countries of the region. Section 8.2 shows that despite the recent growth in the demand

for ICT, the ICT market is very limited and lags far behind the advanced countries in terms of demand, supply and spending. The chapter illustrates the market concentration of ICT diffusion in the Arab Gulf countries and the wide disparities between these and the other Arab countries with regard to supply, demand (percentage of population accessing the Internet, telephones and mobiles, PCs and ICT Use Index), prices and intensity of the services. Section 8.3 illustrates that the richest Arab Gulf countries, with a higher GDP per capita and better average years of schooling, also have a higher percentage of people accessing the Internet. Poorer Arab countries with a lower GDP per capita and less schooling, also have a correspondingly smaller percentage of inhabitants accessing the Internet. The regression results prove our hypothesis that the diffusion of IT – as measured by the use of the Internet – in the Arab region significantly increases in relation to economic growth (as measured by GDP per capita). The use of the Internet is also positively correlated with human capital (as measured by average years of schooling) and women's development (as measured by their average years of schooling, youth literacy rate, net enrolment in secondary education and gross enrolment in tertiary education). Section 8.4 shows that ICT has the potential to accelerate economic development through increased employment opportunities, improved e-commerce, better human resources, upgraded skills and enhanced capabilities. However, ICT also has the potential to create obstacles to development by intensifying competition, eliminating certain jobs – particularly for unskilled workers – increasing regional disparities within the Arab region and, furthermore, escalating the already existing gap and inequality between the advanced countries and the Arab region.

UNDP-AHDR (2002) indicates the absence of national information policies; all Arab countries lack information policies that delineate targets and priorities, coordinate the various sectors and formulate strategic alternatives with regard to the creation of infrastructure and the development of human and information resources. The organisational and legislative frameworks for production and services institutions in various fields of information and communication are also lacking. Nevertheless, over the past few years, political leaderships in Egypt, Jordan, the Syrian Arab Republic and the UAE have shown interest in the information industry. This has led to the formulation of national plans to promote infrastructure, encourages foreign and local investment, provides Internet services to schools and establishes free zones for ICT technology, such as the Dubai Internet city, the Smart Village in Egypt and the Silicon Hills in Jordan (UNDP-AHDR 2002: 77).

According to ESCWA (2003b), in terms of ICT policies and strategies only two countries, Jordan and the UAE, have clear strategic goals or vision for ICT policies and ability to leverage strong local funding capabilities. They have operational ICT projects, recognised on a regional level, effective results in creating employment, generate revenues and attract FDI, which occur on a large scale in the case of the UAE. While Bahrain, Kuwait, Egypt, Oman and Qatar have, to varying degrees, planned ICT in their national economy, Iraq, Lebanon, the Palestine authority territories, Saudi Arabia, Syrian Arab Republic and Yemen do not have strategic plans (ESCWA 2003b: 14–15). ESCWA identifies the absence of serious commitment to implement operational plans and strategies and has recently issued several reports to contribute towards formulating a regional approach to implementing such strategies.

Notes

This is a revised version of the paper originally prepared for the UNU-WIDER Conference on the New Economy in Development, 10–11 May 2002, Helsinki, and an update of UNU-WIDER Discussion Paper 2002/83.

1 The Arab region is composed of 22 countries: Algeria, Bahrain, Comoros, Djibouti, Egypt, Iraq, Jordan, Kuwait, Lebanon, Libya, Mauritania, Morocco, Oman, Palestine, Qatar, Saudi Arabia, Somalia, Sudan, Syrian Arab Republic, Tunisia, the UAE and Yemen. The Middle East region includes all the Arab countries in addition to Iran, Turkey and Israel.
2 MADAR citations can be accessed via the website of the MADAR Research Group: www.madarresearch.com
3 For instance, 'Arab [world] represents 5 per cent of the world population but only 0.5 per cent of internet users' (Dewachi 2000). 'The Arab world is now home to almost five percent of the world population – but it has less than 1.3 per cent of the world internet users community' (MADAR 2002b: 8).
4 The Arab Gulf states are Bahrain, Kuwait, Oman, Qatar, Saudi Arabia and UAE.
5 According to ESCWA (2005a), the percentage of Internet users per language and the share of each language group in the world economy as of March 2004 indicates an almost perfect correlation between language groups of Internet users and their share in the world economy. Accordingly English has a high share but Arabic a low share in both (www.global-reach.biz/globstats/index.php3) (ESCWA 2005a: 23–4). According to ESCWA (2003c) digital Arabic content continue to be weak and online Arabic language users constitute less than 1 per cent of total online users in the world, despite the fact that the Arab population constitutes approximately 5 per cent of total world population (ESCWA 2005b: 10). According to MADAR (2002b), websites using only the English language constitute 42 and 49 per cent in Saudi Arabia and Bahrain respectively. Bilingual sites (using both English and Arabic) represent 34 and 48 per cent in Saudi Arabia and Bahrain respectively, while sites offering only Arabic language constitute only 24 and 3 per cent in Saudi Arabia and Bahrain respectively (MADAR 2002b: 18, 31).

6   One example of illiterate populations accessing the Internet for limited purposes that may be useful to serve as a model regarding ICT projects from developing countries can be observed from fishing in Saint Louis in Senegal; fishermen have been able to improve their safety and increase their revenues by accessing weather forecasts and transport schedules on the Internet before putting out to sea. In addition to providing vital weather forecasts to determine the best fishing times, the same website is used to advertise jobs to the community (ESCWA 2005b: 13).

7   These results have been confirmed by the UNDP-AHDR (2002: 76, 80) which indicates the digital divide in Arab countries according to the countries' HDI ranking and shows extreme disparities among Arab countries regarding informatics.

8   These results are consistent with the findings of MADAR (2002b: 3, 8).

9   The ICT Use Index covers four ICT parameters: PC installed base and the number of Internet users, mobile phones and fixed lines. The index is calculated by adding up the values of these four parameters and dividing the sum by the country's population figure. A higher index score indicates more aggressive ICT adoption in the country (MADAR 2004, 2005).

10   Our results should be interpreted carefully, since the comparison across individual Arab countries indicates inconclusive evidence for the correlation that high women's participation in education (youth literacy rate, net enrolment in secondary and gross enrolment in tertiary education) corresponds to high use of ICT. For example, Jordan shows high female participation in education as measured by women's youth literacy rate and average years of schooling but lags behind in the use of ICT compared to Bahrain. Moreover, both Libya and Lebanon have high women's participation in education (as measured by gross enrolment in tertiary education), but in the meantime in terms of the use of ICT they fall far behind the high-income Gulf countries, Bahrain, Kuwait and Qatar. In addition, the UAE ranks first in terms of the use of ICT, but falls behind Bahrain, Qatar and Jordan in terms of women's youth literacy rate and access to secondary education.

11   For instance, estimation from the IMF (2002) indicates that average unemployment as a percentage of total labour force in the Arab states was 13.06 in 2001.

12   According to the World Bank classification, the Arab high-income group includes only four countries: UAE, Qatar, Kuwait and Bahrain. The Arab medium-income group includes 13 countries: Saudi Arabia, Oman, Egypt, Algeria, Tunisia, Morocco, Syria, Lebanon, Jordan, Iraq, Libyan Arab Jamahiriya, Occupied Palestine Territories and Djibouti. The Arab low-income group includes five countries: Sudan, Somalia, Yemen, Comoros and Mauritania.

13   These results are consistent with the findings of MADAR (2002b: 9):

> Overall Internet penetration in the six Gulf nations is expected to grow from the current 9.23 per cent to 19.76 per cent by the end of 2005. Penetration in other Arab countries is foreseen to register a much higher growth rate – rising from 1.67 per cent to 19.76 per cent. This can be partly explained by the fact that the Gulf countries – with their more open and vibrant economies and exceedingly higher levels of per capita income – have been able to go through the 'initial boom-stage' much

faster than the rest of the Arab world. … Gulf Internet users – taken as a percentage of total Internet users in the Arab world – will be only 28 per cent by the end of 2005, compared to the current level of 42 per cent. This can be understood given the large population levels by which Arab countries outside the Gulf are characterized (almost nine fold the Gulf population) – also given that many of these countries have started to realize the economic importance of the Internet and are poised to go through the 'initial boom stage' of internet adoption.

14 For instance, UNDP (2004) shows that the percentage of population below the income poverty line during the period (1990–2002) is estimated between 2 and 63.1 per cent of the total population.
15 These results are consistent with the findings of MADAR Research (2002b: 4, 10).
16 For instance, a major impediment to B2C e-commerce in Egypt, besides the low Internet penetration, is the lack of a credit card culture in the country. There are only 600,000 credit cards in use by around 300,000 clients (MADAR 2002a:14). Similarly in the UAE the B2C e-commerce market is driven by a relatively conservative mindset and online culture, which has not yet opened up fully to online purchases and commerce. UAE payment card penetration at the end of 2003 was estimated at 54.4 per cent, despite the high rate of ICT penetration in the country (MADAR 2003: 34).

References

Acemoglu, D. (1998) 'Why do New Technologies Complement Skills? Directed Technical Change and Wage Inequality', *The Quarterly Journal of Economics*, 113 (4): 1055–89.

Aghion, P. and P. Howitt (1998) *Endogenous Growth Theory*, Cambridge, Mass.: MIT Press.

Autor, D. H., L. F. Katz and A. B. Krueger (1998) 'Computing Inequality: Have Computers Changed the Labour Market?', *The Quarterly Journal of Economics*, 113 (4): 1169–213.

Barro, R. J. and J. W. Lee (2001) 'International Data on Educational Attainment: Updates and Implications', *Oxford Economic Papers*, 53 (3): 541–63.

Berman, E., J. Bound and Z. Griliches (1994) 'Change in the Demand for Skilled Labour within U.S. Manufacturing Industries: Evidence from the Annual Survey of Manufacturing', *Quarterly Journal of Economics*, 109 (2): 367–98.

Bound, J. and G. Johnson (1992) 'Change in the Structure of Wages in the 1980s: an Evaluation of Alternative Explanations', *American Economic Review*, 82 (3): 371–92.

Bresnahan, T. F., E. Brynjolfsson and L. M. Hitt (1999) 'Information Technology, Workplace Organization, and the Demand for Skilled Labour: Firm Level Evidence', NBER Working Paper 7136, Cambridge, Mass.: National Bureau of Economic Research.

Brynjolfsson, E. and S. Yang (1996) 'Information Technology and Productivity: a Review of the Literature', *Advances in Computers*, 43: 179–214.

CIA (2001) *World Fact Book*. http://www.cia.gov/cia/publications/factbook/

D'Costa, A. P. (2003) 'Uneven and Combined Development: Understanding India's Software Exports', *World Development*, 31 (1): 211–26.

D'Costa, A. P. and E. Sridharan (eds) (2003) *India in the Global Software Industry: Innovation, Firms' Strategies, and Development*, Basingstoke: Palgrave Macmillan.

Dewachi, A. (2000) 'Information and Communication Infrastructures of the ESCWA Region', Beirut: ESCWA, 15–16 May.

Egypt Ministry of Communications and Information Technology (1999) 'National Plan for Communications and Information, December 1999', in ESCWA (2003a) *Profile of the Information Society in the Arab Republic of Egypt*, New York: UN.

ESCWA (2003a) *Profile of the Information Society in the Arab Republic of Egypt*, New York: UN, pp. 4, 17, 35.

ESCWA (2003b) *Regional Profile of the Information Society in Western Asia*, E/ESCWA/ICTD/2003/11, New York: UN, October, pp. 14, 15, 101, 107.

ESCWA (2003c) *Annual Review of Developments in Globalization and Regional Integration in the Countries of the ESCWA Region*, E/ESCWA/GRID/2003/41, New York: UN.

ESCWA (2004) *Using Information and Communication Technologies to Create Employment and Alleviate Poverty*, E/ESCWA/ICTD/2004/1, New York: UN.

ESCWA (2005a) *Information Society Indicators*, E/ESCWA/ICTD/2005/1, New York, UN, January, pp. 23–4.

ESCWA (2005b) *Information and Communication Technologies for Employment Creation and Poverty Alleviation in Selected ESCWA Member Countries*, E/ESCWA/ICTD/2005/2, New York: UN, April, pp. 10, 13, 14, 15–17, 20, 21, 38.

Freeman, C. and L. Soete (1985) *Information Technology and Employment: an Assessment*, Brighton, Sussex: SPRU.

Freeman, C. and L. Soete (1994) *Work for All or Mass Unemployment? Computerized Technical Change into the Twenty-first Century*, London: Printer.

Freeman, C. and L. Soete (1997) *The Economic of Industrial Innovation*, 3rd edn, London: Cassell.

Hitt, L. and E. Brynjolfsson (1996) 'Productivity, Business Profitability, and Consumer Surplus: Three Different Measures of Information Technology Value', *MIS Quarterly*, 20: 121–42.

Hwang, G-H. (2000) 'Diffusion of Information and Communication Technologies and Changes in Skills', Electronic Working Paper 48, Brighton, Sussex: SPRU.

IMF (2002) 'World Economic Outlook: the Middle East and North Africa Regional Outlook', September, Washington, DC: IMF.

ITU (2003–4) *World Telecommunication Regulatory Database* 'Europe's Telecommunication/ICT Markets and Trends 2003/2004', Geneva: ITU.

ITU (2004) *International Telecommunication Union Database 2004*, Geneva: ITU.

Jorgenson, D. W. and K. Stiroh (1995) 'Computers and Growth', *Economics of Innovation and New Technology*, 3: 295–316.

Kamli, A. (2003) 'E-Readiness and Growth Competitiveness', MADAR Research Group: http://www.madarresearch.com/archive/archive_edit.aspx?id=13

MADAR (2002a) 'eLANDSCAPE: Egypt's IT Market will be Worth $1.4 billion in 2005 as Software Industry Leads Growth', *MADAR Research Journal*, 1 (December 2002–January 2003).

MADAR (2002b) 'Knowledge Economy Research on the Middle East', *MADAR Research Journal*, 1 (October).

MADAR (2003) 'eLANDSCAPE: UAE Information Technology Market Forecast to Grow to $2.22 billion by End 2008, Led by Service Sector', *MADAR Research Journal*, 10 (December).

MADAR (2004) 'The Full End 2003 ICT Use Index Report', *MADAR Research Journal*, 2 (February–March).

MADAR (2005) 'The Full End 2005 ICT Use Index Report', *MADAR Research Journal*, 3 (May).

Mansell, R. and U. Wehn (eds) (1998) *Knowledge Societies: Information Technology for Sustainable Development*, Oxford: Oxford University Press.

Pohjola, M. (2000) 'Information Technology and Economic Growth: a Cross-country Analysis', Working Paper 173, Helsinki: UNU-WIDER.

Pohjola, M. (ed.) (2001) *Information Technology, Productivity and Economic Growth: International Evidence and Implications for Economic Growth*, Oxford: Oxford University Press for UNU-WIDER.

UN-DESA (2002) *Report on Global E-Government Readiness*: www.worldbank.org/publicsector/egov/2002eReadAss.pdf

UNDP (2004) *Human Development Report 2004 – Cultural Liberty in Today's Diverse World*, New York: UNDP.

UNDP-AHDR (2002) *Arab Human Development Report 2002: Creating Opportunities for Future Generations*, Regional Bureau for Arab States, New York and Amman: UNDP and AHDR.

WDI-ITU (2005) *World Development Indicators Database: the Information Age*, Washington, DC and Geneva: World Bank and ITU.

WEF (2003–4) *Report on Global Competitiveness (2003–2004)*, www.unpan.org/e-government/

WITSA (2002) *'Digital Planet 2002'*, *the Global Information Economy*, Vienna: World Information Technology and Services Alliance.

World Bank (2001) *World Development Indicators*, database, Washington, DC: World Bank.

9
Impact of Technology on Competitiveness: a Case Study of Indian Small Auto Component Units

T. A. Bhavani

9.1 Introduction

The phenomena of globalisation, liberalisation and rapid technological developments are changing business environments the world over. World economies, especially developing economies, have been shifting since the 1980s away from 'policy regulation' towards 'market orientation' through liberalisation of state controls on economic activities and also globalising in the sense of moving towards greater integration. Simultaneously, rapid technological developments are drastically changing the methods of doing business. At the base of technological progress is the revolution of information and communication technologies (ICT). The globalisation and liberalisation processes are not only exposing business enterprises to market competition to a greater extent but also intensifying that market competition.[1] Technological developments, on the other hand, are providing opportunities for enterprises to improve their competitive strength in order to deal with the challenges of open markets. Technology plays a significant role in promoting competitiveness and growth both at the macro- and microeconomic levels, much more so in these days of globalisation that is necessitating as well as allowing technological change. It is the competitiveness of microeconomic units like firms that explains most of the variations in macroeconomic growth (Porter and Christensen 1998).

In July 1991 India initiated systemic changes in its economic policies, involving a major shift in the development strategy towards greater integration with the world economy and liberalisation of restrictions on market transactions and private economic activities. Until then, India

had been for almost four decades a closed and heavily regulated market economy that insulated domestic markets. Within this generally insulated environment, small enterprises were further protected from the competition of large-scale enterprises through a set of protection policies, since the former were understood to provide employment and hence a source of income for millions of people. This policy-protected business environment did not provide any incentive for Indian small enterprises to upgrade technologically. Rather, it provided a perverse incentive to remain small. The result was that, after four decades of policy support, Indian small enterprises, in general, remained tiny, using traditional and older vintage technologies, and lacked competitive strength.[2] As the economy moves towards globalisation and liberalisation that limit the scope for policy protection and unleash the dynamic impulses of competition, small enterprises have to sustain themselves by their own competitive strength by successfully facing competition from large enterprises including multinationals. It is possible mainly through the adoption of later vintage technologies. Realising the situation, some small enterprises have upgraded their technologies (Bhavani 2005; also see note 19). Technological upgrading does not, however, improve the competitiveness of enterprises instantly or automatically. Absorption of new technologies requires technological capabilities that can be acquired only through the time-consuming process of learning (Dahlman *et al.* 1987; Lall 1992). With this background, the study of the impact of technology on the competitive strength of Indian small enterprises that were protected so long and hence did not have any incentive to acquire technological capabilities, assumes significance. This chapter attempts to examine the impact of technology including ICTs on the competitiveness of Indian small auto component enterprises.

The auto components industry has a good number of small-scale enterprises and it is one of the dynamic sectors of the Indian economy. With the entry of multinational corporations in the more liberalised and globalised 1990s, the industry is undergoing rapid transformation both in its structure and product composition. In addition, automobiles are one of the industries that is organised in the form of global commodity chains, forcing auto component enterprises to integrate with these chains. To get into the supply chain and to remain there, auto component enterprises have to be on a par with the other enterprises in the chain, including the multinational companies, in terms of technology and operational efficiency. It is interesting to find out how small enterprises are doing in this situation, which is what prompted us to select the auto component industry.

Two features of the study are interesting and deserve to be highlighted. One, the chapter takes technology in a comprehensive form by covering three dimensions of it, namely transformation, organisation and information at the enterprise level. Two, these three technology variables are directly included on the right side of the production function along with the conventional inputs of capital, labour and materials, to examine their impact on sales performance, a proxy for competitiveness, that is taken on the left side of the function. Our results show that the transformation technology (mechanisation) has a significant impact, along with the conventional inputs, on the competitiveness of the enterprises but not the organisation and information technologies. This is probably because these enterprises are yet to acquire mastery over the new organisation and information technologies.

The chapter is organised in six sections. Section 9.2 presents the analytical framework that has been used in the chapter to measure the impact of technology on the competitive strength of enterprises, along with the definition of competitiveness and technological change used in the literature. In section 9.3, we describe the Indian auto components industry structure and its likely future, with a special emphasis on small-scale enterprises. This is expected to provide us the relevant technology and other variables for the selected industry. Empirical analysis of the chapter is based on the data collected through the primary survey. Section 9.4 discusses the survey data in order to bring out the immediately relevant technology variables for empirical analysis of the study. Section 9.5 examines the empirical evidence relating to the impact of technology on the competitive strength of the small auto component enterprises. In the final section, we summarise the important features and findings of the study.

9.2   Analytical framework

Competitiveness of a firm can be taken as its ability to do better than comparable firms in sales or market shares or profitability (Lall 2001: 4). In a highly competitive market environment, the relative performance of a firm in sales or market shares or profitability depends primarily on technology. Technology enables higher sales in many ways: through the introduction of a new and superior product, by improving the quality of the existing products, through the efficient utilisation of resources (productivity improvements) and thus enabling cost reductions, by improving access to customers or any combination of these. In other words, technology enables firms to raise their sales by making it possible for them to supply increasing amounts of quality goods at cheaper prices and through the creation of new markets.

For the purpose of analysis, *competitiveness of the enterprises is proxied by their sales performance.* This is because we are dealing with small enterprises whose market shares are too minuscule to be known and their profit figures are either unavailable or unreliable. *Technology is taken to include the physical processes of transformation of inputs into output, organisational methods that structure these processes and information flows required to carry out these processes.* Thus, the study covers three dimensions of technology, namely transformation, organisation and information (Bhavani 2001).[3]

All three dimensions of technology have undergone major changes in the past few decades. In the case of transformation technology, mechanical devices were initially replaced by electrical, later by electronic and very recently by computerised machines. Microelectronics-based technologies drastically altered manufacturing processes by permitting automation of a wide range of operations in many industries. Production organisation methods too changed remarkably, and some of the recent developments in the area include total quality management (TQM) and just-in-time (JIT) (Mody *et al.* 1992: 1797). Exchange of information in business has traditionally been carried out through paper documents delivered by messengers or postal services and later by facsimile. With the advent of computer and communication technologies, more efficient alternatives are available nowadays. These new technologies not only enable firms to acquire any amount of information cheaper but also provide it faster and accurately. Timely availability of information is essential in this fast-changing world. Also, new technologies can store, process and retrieve a variety of data forms from simple numbers to video images (Mody and Dahlman 1992: 1703). In fact, it is the changes in information technologies that 'include computer and communication technologies as well as the associated software' (Mody and Dahlman 1992: 1703) that led to changes in transformation and organisation technologies. For example, computerised machines used in the production process directly originate from the revolution of information technology (IT). All these technological developments are making upgrading of technology at the enterprise level imperative by making the existing technologies unviable.

Empirical studies on technological change mostly covered changes in the physical processes of transformation including output characteristics, and typically associated these changes with innovations and studied them mostly in terms of patents, R&D expenditure or personnel (Bos and Cole 1994: 232; Teitel and Westphal 1984: 2; Patel and Pavitt 1995).[4] Changes in organisational methods are studied independently.

Although information is crucial to keep the production process on and also for decision-making in economic organisations, IT was not treated explicitly till recently (Hayek 1945; Mintzberg 1979). The faster developments in recent years in IT, however, led to a growing separate literature on the subject.

This chapter considers all three aspects of technology – transformation, organisation and information – as it enables us to disaggregate their contribution. Following the literature, we take the *transformation* technology broadly to include plant and machinery, tools, components, accessories, materials and products. The *organisation* aspect refers to the organisation of the production process that encompasses plant layout, materials management, production schedules, work allocation and quality management. The *information* aspect covers the means of communication with outside agents such as customers and suppliers as well as information (data) management – ways of storing, processing and exchange of information within the enterprise. Since our survey refers to one time point and technological changes mainly involve improvements in technology, we preferred to carry out the analysis in terms of differences in the levels of technology across enterprises.[5] In this respect, mechanical, electromechanical and electronic devices can be treated as three different levels of transformation technologies, with mechanical devices falling at the lower end of the scale and electronic devices positioned at the upper end and electromechanical lying in the middle. New organisational methods like TQM systems and new communication means like e-mail can be taken as superior levels in comparison with the traditional method of random quality check-ups and personal visits and phones.

Moving to the measurement of the impact of technology, neo-classical economics measures it *indirectly* in terms of the changes in factor productivities, especially total factor productivity (TFP), which is the ratio of production to the weighted average of all inputs used in the production process. The production function approach measures TFP as a derivative of the time variable without any assumptions such as constant returns to scale.[6] Total factor productivity growth (TFPG) was initially identified, in neo-classical economics, with technical change (progress) without differentiating the change in technology from its impact. Later studies considered technology as cause and TFPG as its effect by explicitly treating technical change as the primary determinant of TFPG, although it has been taken along with the other determinants such as labour skills, learning-by-doing, capacity utilisation and scale economies (see, for example, Ahluwalia 1991; Griliches 1996). Some of

these studies tried to decompose TFPG into different components to segregate the impact of technology from that of the other variables. In some other studies, technology has been taken as one of the many explanatory variables of productivity (Link 1987; McGuckin *et al.* 1996).

In this chapter, we are trying to measure the impact of technology *directly* by considering the technology variables explicitly in the production analysis.[7] To be specific, we introduce technology as one of the inputs along with the conventional inputs like capital, labour and materials in the production function. Further, we take sales turnover as a dependent variable instead of conventionally used production. It is because sales turnover represents the actual size of the market that the unit is catering to and hence its competitiveness, which is a much wider concept than the productive efficiency given by production. By taking sales as a dependent variable and technology as one of the explanatory variables, we can directly measure the impact of technology on the competitiveness of the units. We write the production function as

$$Y = A (T)f(K, L, M) \tag{9.1}$$

where Y = sales; K = capital; L = labour; M = materials; T = technology. Technology (T) is further expanded to cover transformation, organisation and information aspects. The production function given in (9.1) is rewritten by taking a simple Cobb-Douglas form with three conventional inputs of capital, labour and materials:

$$Y = AK^{\alpha}L^{\beta}M^{\gamma} \tag{9.2}$$

where

$$A = e^{\theta_1 T + \theta_2 O + \theta_3 I}$$

In the log-linear form, it is written as

$$\ln Y = C + \alpha \ln K + \beta \ln L + \gamma \ln M + \theta_1 T + \theta_2 O + \theta_3 I + \mu \tag{9.3}$$

Y, K, L and M are as defined in (9.1), T = transformation technology, O = organisation technology and I = information technology. All the technology variables are qualitative in nature. μ = a random error term.

We determine the unit-level characteristics representing the transformation, organisation and information technologies from the industry background and the survey data presented in the following sections.

9.3   Auto components industry in India

The auto components industry in India produces the entire range of parts required by the domestic automobile industry.[8] It caters to nearly 87 per cent of the domestic market demand while the remaining 13 per cent is served by imports.[9] Production of the auto components industry for the year 2002–3 was estimated as Rs 255,354 million (US$5430 million).[10] Of the total production of the industry, the organised sector[11] produces goods worth Rs 196,426 million (US$4179 million), accounting for 77 per cent. The unorganised small-scale sector is estimated to contribute nearly 23 per cent to the industry's total production (ACMA 2002–3: 29).

As regards the market for automotive components, a major portion (nearly 55 per cent) is the vehicle industry for original equipment. Replacement demand constitutes 35 per cent of domestic production. Exports account for the remaining 10 per cent (ICRA 1999: xi).[12] Exports mostly serve the replacement market abroad. Both the OEMs (original equipment manufacturers) market and replacement market demand have been growing since the 1980s owing to a rapid growth in the passenger car and two-wheeler segments and poor road conditions (ICRA 1999: 33–4, 110).[13]

Indian automotive components are a low-volume and fragmented industry.[14] It has nearly 400 firms in the organised sector and more than 5000 firms in the unorganised small-scale sector (ICRA 1999: 38).[15] The industry structure can be taken as a minor variant of 'dominant firm with a competitive fringe', which theoretically refers to an industry that has a single firm with a dominant share of the market and many fringe or small firms each with a trivial share of the market. A firm is dominant either because of superior product or lower costs or both. Further, the costs of a firm could be lower due to better technology and management, economies of scale and experience (Carlton and Perloff 1990: 180–5). In the automotive components industry of India, it is not a single firm but a few firms together that control the dominant share of the market, leaving a tiny share of this to numerous small firms. Three to five firms control more than 75 per cent of the market for almost all the products.[16]

A majority of the small-scale enterprises are located in Delhi and the surrounding areas like Faridabad and Gurgaon, which came into existence mainly due to Maruti Udyog Limited in the 1980s. Small-scale auto component units mostly produce the products that require simple production set-up like that of sheet metal products and products for

which excise duties are very high. It is because small-scale units are given an excise duty concession that the price of their products is lower. The unorganised small-scale sector mostly caters to replacement demand with a few exceptions like sheet metal components. In most of the cases, small units use manual machines and at times second-hand machinery. There is no quality control system in the small manufacturing sector at large.

The development and structure of the components industry are closely connected with those of the vehicle industry. Until the 1980s, the vehicle industry was characterised by small-scale operations, technological obsolescence and numerous government regulations that forced these units to go for in-house production of components, and component manufacturers started mainly to cater to the replacement demand (Narayana 1989: 10–12). In the 1980s, relaxation of government regulations especially on foreign collaboration that triggered the entry of many joint ventures including Maruti Udyog Limited, along with the programme of phased manufacturing, caused an upsurge in the components industry.[17] Foreign collaborations, technological upgrading and close relations with the buyers characterised the auto components industry during this period (ICRA 1999: 30; Narayana 1989: 44–6; Varadharajan and Kannan 1998: 299).

The new economic policy of liberalisation and globalisation of the 1990s changed the rules of the game in the industry once again. Following its endorsement of the WTO agreement, India has opened its economy to transnational corporations and imports, which has resulted in the entry of many international players like General Motors, Ford, Honda and Hyundai in the vehicle industry along with Delphi and Visteon in the components industry.[18] The domestic market has become more competitive, forcing the Indian automobile industry to restructure itself along the lines of global industry.

Compelled by severe competition that is forcing cost reductions, the global vehicle industry is going in for consolidation at the vehicle manufacturing level and hierarchical subcontracting arrangements in the component supply chains (ICRA 1999: 20–3). International vehicle manufacturers are consolidating their positions through acquisitions and mergers and trying to reduce their costs through rationalisation of their supply chains. Instead of buying individual components from the numerous component manufacturers and assembling them in their own premises, vehicle manufacturers have started purchasing systems like entire engines. These systems suppliers form a tier one company in the supply chain and are expected to play a significant role in the development

and production of the vehicle. Systems suppliers procure further subsystems or components from other suppliers. These other suppliers form either tier two or three in the supply chain.

To get into the supply chain, Indian auto component units have to acquire technological levels on a par with the parent company. The Indian component manufacturers including some of the smaller ones have already realised this.[19] These units are moving towards adopting better machinery like fully automatic machinery, superior organisational methods like total quality control systems like ISO9000 and information technologies. In particular, established small enterprises are increasingly going in for semi- and fully automatic machines from the level of manually operated machines. Accordingly, work is allotted to workers on a rotation basis and more than one job is assigned to them at a time. These units are also trying to have the quality check-up which was otherwise missing and are slowly adopting new means of communication with their customers such as corresponding through e-mail.[20] Thus, the immediate technological upgrading, at the industry level, is involving shifts towards numerically controlled or computerised machines, total quality management systems like ISO9000 and electronic means of communications and information processing.

9.4   Survey data

This chapter, as mentioned above, is considering transformation, organisation and information aspects of technology. Keeping the industry characteristics that are discussed in section 9.3 in mind, we have confined transformation technology mainly to mechanisation and considered three levels of machinery, namely manually operated machines, semi-automatic machines and numerically controlled/computer numerically controlled (NC/CNC) machines.[21] We have taken the organisation to include plant layout, materials management, quality management, production schedules and work allocations. Under materials management, we covered the suppliers of materials, methods of procuring and financing of materials, and inventories of materials. Quality management is studied in terms of having a TQM system like ISO9000, which is a necessary condition to get into the supply chains. Work allocations refer to the ways of assigning jobs to workers – whether jobs are fixed or rotating and whether a worker is given a single or multiple jobs at a time. IT is taken in terms of the means of communication with outside agents and data (information) management. These are further taken in terms of three means of communication that are person/post/phone,

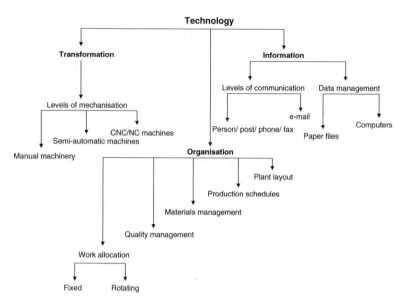

Figure 9.1 Firm-level characteristics representing technology

facsimile and e-mail, and two types of storing and processing data, namely paper files and computers. All these technology characteristics are summarised in Figure 9.1.

For the purpose of the survey, we have followed the official definition of small-scale units. In India, small-scale industrial units are defined in terms of a maximum ceiling on the original value of investment in plant and machinery, which was Rs 30 million (US$682,000) during the period of the field survey although later brought down to Rs 10 million (US$227,000).[22] A ceiling limit does not convey much about the small-scale sector, as 98 per cent of the small units fall in the category of 'tiny units' defined to have less than or equal to Rs 2.5 million (US$56,518) investment in plant and machinery and 90 per cent of them are proprietary units (Government of India 2002–3). Although the majority of the small units are started as a means of earning – basic in most of the cases and profit earning in a few cases and not as industrial units aspiring to grow and establish themselves in the concerned area of production over time – a small proportion of units that are established are going in for technological upgrading (Bhavani 2005). The main limiting factor for these units is their small size which does not allow scale economies, essential for the adoption of new technologies (D'Costa 2004). Any

study of Indian small-scale enterprises in general and the empirical results of the chapter in particular should be viewed in the light of these facts.

Our sample has been selected, within the set of officially defined small units, based on purposive sampling, from Delhi and its surrounding areas such as Faridabad, Gurgaon and NOIDA. This region, as mentioned previously, hosts numerous small-scale auto component units.[23]

Using purposive sampling, we selected the units in such a way that there is a high likelihood that at least some of the units have undergone technological change and have been using sophisticated technologies like numerically controlled (NC) machinery, and the selected units are willing to respond and provide reliable information.[24] Also, given the nature of informational requirements, sample size has to be smaller but richer in the relevant information. We tried to obtain a desirable sample by approaching the relevant government agencies like SIDBI (Small Industries Development Bank of India), industry associations like ACMA (Automotive Components Manufacturers Association) and FSIA (Faridabad Small Industries Association) and the informal networks of the industrial units. The questionnaire is completed through direct interviews with the owner-managers of the sample units. Along with the collection of the information through the completion of the structured questionnaire, we visited the plant of each selected unit to confirm the same.

In addition to the technology variables that are qualitative in nature, we collected quantitative information about production, capital, labour and materials. All the quantitative information related to the year 1998–99.[25]

For the purpose of the study, we surveyed 31 small-scale industrial units producing automotive components. Of the 31 sample units, a majority of the units (23) are original equipment manufacturers (OEMs) for the vehicle industry and 8 units cater to the replacement market. Except for two, all the surveyed units are engaged in the production of metal products such as sheet metal products, turned components and tubular parts. The production operations of these components mostly involved pressing, forging and machining. All these operations are possible at different levels of mechanisation in the sense that they can either be done by manually operated machines or by semi-automatic or numerically controlled machines.

Regarding sales performance, the annual sales turnover of the sample units ranges between Rs 1.5 million (US\$34,000) (minimum) and Rs 200 million (US\$4.5 million) (maximum) with a mean value of

Rs 22.22 million (US$505,000). The sample varies widely around the mean (174 per cent as given by the coefficient of variation). The annual sales turnover of 12 sample units is less than Rs 5 million in the reference year. The sales turnover of six units lies in-between Rs 5 and 10 million. The sales turnover of nine units comes in the range Rs 10–30 million. The remaining four units have sales turnover greater than Rs 30 million.

The original investment in plant and machinery, in the surveyed units, ranges between a minimum of Rs 0.08 million (US$18,182) and the maximum of Rs 30 million (US$682,000). The mean value of the sample units is Rs 4.9 million (US$111,000). The plant and machinery of the sample units vary 135 per cent around the mean. Many of the units (12) have an investment in plant and machinery that is less than or equal to Rs 1.5 million. Five units have invested amounts that range from Rs 1.5 to 2.5 million. Another six units have an investment in plant and machinery that varies between Rs 2.5 and 5 million. The remaining units are operating with an investment of greater than Rs 5 million in plant and machinery.

As regards employment in the sample units, it varies between 3 and 375 employees. The mean employment of the sample is almost 46. Employment in the sample units varies 151 per cent (coefficient of variation) around the mean employment. Of the 31 sample units, nine employed less than or equal to 10 employees, five units employed somewhere between 10 and 20 employees. The employment of another 11 units lies in-between 20 and 50 people. Only six units of the sample employed more than 50 people.

The value of materials consumed during the year by the sample units varies between Rs 0 and Rs 60 million (US$1.4 million). Two units that are doing job work show zero materials. Otherwise the minimum value is Rs 0.72 million (US$16,000). The mean value of the materials consumed by the sample units is around Rs 11 million (US$250,000). The coefficient of variation shows that the material value of the sample varies around the sample mean by 130 per cent. For 12 units, the annual consumption of materials is less than or equal to Rs 2 million. The yearly consumption of materials of seven sample units falls in the range Rs 2–10 million. The remaining 12 units show their material consumption to be more than Rs 10 million.

Descriptive statistics, i.e. minimum, maximum, mean and the coefficient of variation of the sales turnover, plant and machinery, number of employees and material consumption, are given in Table 9.1.

Let us now summarise the technology characteristics of the sample units, namely levels of mechanisation, plant layout, production schedules,

Table 9.1 Descriptive statistics for output and inputs

Variable	Mean	Minimum	Maximum	Coefficient of variation
Sales turnover (million rupees)	22.22	1.50	200.00	1.74
Plant and machinery (million rupees)	4.95	0.08	30.00	1.35
Total employment (no.)	46	3	375	1.51
Materials (million rupees)	11.07	0.00	60.00	1.30
No. of observations 31				

Source: Field survey.

materials management, presence of total quality system, nature of work allocation, means of communication with the customers and data management.

Of the 31 auto component units that were surveyed, 14 have only manually operated machinery. Nine units have some semi-automatic machines and another 8 units have numerically controlled machines in their plants in addition to the manually operated machines. Suppliers of machinery are the primary source of technology for our sample auto component units. Except for two units, all the sample units purchased first-hand machinery. Almost all the units bought Indian machinery. The presence of foreign machinery is negligible and mostly it is second-hand.

Most of the characteristics of the production organisation, i.e. plant lay-out, production schedules and materials management, turned out to be quite flexible in the sense that they can be easily adjusted as per the need of the hour. Accordingly, units buy materials depending on their need, availability, costs and the space available for their storage. Production schedules are extended towards late evenings without much difficulty if the orders need to be sent immediately. Hence, these characteristics are not considered in the empirical analysis. Only work allocation and quality management varied across the units surveyed. Work allocation is taken, as said earlier, in terms of assignments of fixed or rotating jobs to the workers. Twenty-one out of the 31 sample units rotate work assignments to their workers. The remaining 10 units fixed the job assignments for the workers. Most of the units that rotate jobs to workers also assign them multiple jobs. Quality management of the unit is studied in terms of acquisition of a quality management system like ISO9000 certification. The survey results show that only nine units obtained ISO9000 certification. The remaining 22 units have not adopted any such quality system.

As far as IT is concerned, we covered, as mentioned previously, the means of communication with customers and data management. On

the communication front, only 13 units started using e-mails in addition to traditional methods like personal visits and the phone. Some of these units, which are OEMs, have even provided mobile phones to their truck drivers to contact them on their way to parent companies with the supplies of components. Though 16 sample units have installed computers, a majority of them are still in the process of computerising their data. The remaining 15 units did not even have computers and hence still record their data in paper files.

In sum, we found the level of mechanisation, quality management, work allocations, communication and data management technologies empirically relevant for our sample auto component units in the small manufacturing sector. Accordingly in the next section we will be using these characteristics in our production function to measure the impact of technology on competitiveness.

9.5 Empirical evidence

We studied the impact of technology on competitiveness, as discussed in the earlier sections, by introducing the relevant technology variables directly in the production function along with the conventional inputs of capital, labour and materials. All the technology variables are taken in the production function as binary variables. Although we have information for three levels of mechanisation, namely manual machinery, semi-automatic machinery and NC machinery, for the purpose of estimating the production function, we regrouped them into two categories, namely NC machinery and others. This is because NC machines are substantially different from the other two (manual and semi-automatic machinery) in many respects such as speed of production, quality and precision of the product and skills required to operate it. Hence, we expect the usage of NC machines to lead to a distinctly higher degree of competitiveness of the units.[26]

Quality management is taken in terms of acquisition of ISO9000 certification. ISO9000 refers to the TQM system aiming at giving consistent quality product to customers. It involves the formalisation of operations by documenting the details of work instructions, quality records, quality procedures and policies. Formalisation and standardisation of operations ensure consistency in approach and thus consistent quality (Kanji and Asher 1996: 48–50). By enabling the production of consistent quality components, ISO9000 is expected to increase the market for these components. In fact, it has become a necessary condition to get into the international supply chains. Apart from the consistent quality

improvements, formalisation and standardisation of operations are expected to increase the speed of production and productivity, and hence the competitiveness of the units. Rotation of job assignments among the workers and assignment of multiple jobs at a given time are expected to raise labour efficiency and thus the competitiveness of the units. Work allocations, however, are highly related with the type of machinery. For instance, manual machinery requires a person continuously for its operation leading to tie-up of persons with single machines. On the other hand, NC machines require people to set up the operation. After that, it works on its own till the operation is over allowing staff to attend to other jobs in-between. For this reason, organisation is represented only by a quality management variable in the production function.

Modern means of communication like e-mail and data management methods involve the usage of computers and thus are highly related to each other. Of the two, we preferred to have means of communication for our analysis. A shift towards electronic methods of communication, which are superior to traditional methods in terms of speed and flexibility, quickens the process of finalising orders from customers/dealers and thus is expected to raise productivity by raising the level of capacity utilisation by reducing the communication gap.[27] Electronic methods of communication enable the units to reach their customers easily.

Regarding the conventional variables in the production function, we considered the original investment in plant and machinery as capital, the total number of employees as labour and the value of materials consumed during the year.

We took sales turnover, as mentioned earlier, as the dependent variable. It gives the actual size of the market that the unit concerned is serving. The differences in the sales turnover across firms can thus be taken as the differences in their competitiveness. In effect, we specify our production function as a six-input Cobb-Douglas function and write it in the log-linear form as follows:

$$\ln ST = C + \alpha \ln PM + \beta \ln LAB + \gamma \ln MAT + \theta_1 LOM$$
$$+ \theta_2 ISO + \theta_3 MCC + \mu \qquad (9.4)$$

where 'ln' refers to the logarithmic values of the variables, ST = annual sales turnover in million rupees, PM = original value of plant and machinery in million rupees, LAB = total number of employees, MAT = value of materials consumed during the year in million rupees, LOM = level of mechanisation (LOM1 for units with NC machines, LOM0 otherwise), ISO = quality management systems (ISO1 for units with

ISO9000 certification, ISO0 otherwise), MCC = means of communication (MCC1 for units with e-mail, MCC0 otherwise) and μ = a random error term.

Equation (9.4) has been estimated through the ordinary least squares (OLS) method using the Eviews software package. The estimated parameters are:[28]

$$
\begin{aligned}
\ln\ ST = {}& 0.8685 + 0.0957 \ln\ PM + 0.2015 \ln\ LAB \\
& (6.709)^* \quad (2.374)^* \qquad\qquad (2.912)^* \\
& + 0.6792 \ln\ MAT + 0.2471\ LOM \\
& \quad (14.371)^* \qquad\qquad (2.523)^* \\
& + 0.1325\ ISO - 0.1112\ MCC \\
& \quad (1.357) \qquad\quad (-1.204) \\
& N = 29, R^2 = 0.9827, F_{6,\,22} = 208.237
\end{aligned}
$$

Since we are dealing with cross-section data, we tested for the heteroscedasticity problem using White's method by regressing the residual squares on all explanatory variables, their squares and cross-products. Our estimates in this respect are $R^2 = 27.2373$ and F-statistic $= 2.5754$, which essentially accepts the basic hypothesis of homoscedasticity. In other words, data do not reveal the problem of heteroscedasticity.

The estimated coefficients presented above indicate that all the conventional variables, namely plant and machinery, labour, materials and the level of mechanisation, have a statistically significant and positive impact on sales turnover. ISO9000 certification and methods of communication with the customers do not statistically influence sales turnover.

As regards the variables that show statistically significant impact on sales turnover, all these variables yield positive coefficients as expected. Of these coefficients, the level of mechanisation shows the highest coefficient (1.07), followed by that of materials (0.6792), labour (0.2015) and plant and machinery (0.0957). In other words, the sensitivity of firms' sales turnover turns out to be the highest to the presence of NC machines. NC machinery that embodies advanced technology brings in both quality and productivity improvements and thus increases the sales turnover. This, juxtaposed with the result that the investment in plant and machinery yields a statistically significant but smaller magnitude of impact of sales, implies that it is the machine-embodied technology (or quality of machinery) than the stock of machinery, which matters more to increase sales turnover. Next in quantitative magnitude is the sensitivity of the firms' sales turnover to materials. It means that

the availability and quality of materials considerably influence the sales turnover of the auto component units.

ISO9000 certification, implying a total quality system, enables the units to produce products of consistent quality and hence increases scope for expansion. It seems that in the case of our sample of small-scale auto component units, the expansionary effects of consistent quality have not yet started working. It is also the case with the electronic means of communications given the fact that it has just started and yet to get established. Owner-managers use it along with traditional methods like the phone and personal visits. The statistically insignificant influence of these two technologies over competitiveness could be due to the fact that the fruits of these two technologies depend on the degree of mastery that the concerned units have obtained over these technologies. This, in turn, depends on the nature of small enterprises as well as the nature and degree of association with the customer companies. It may take some time for smaller units to tune in with the customer companies. More important is the nature of small-scale operations, which has a loose division of labour with little formalisation of behaviour. These enterprises make minimal use of planning, training and liaison devices. Coordination is attained largely through direct supervision by the owner-manager. The owner-manager manages both labour and customers/suppliers through direct, personal and informal links. Working of the total quality system like ISO9000 requires total change in this behaviour, which takes time. Regarding IT, e-mail is a preliminary step and there is a long way to go before it is expected to yield results in bringing improvements in competitiveness. Also, to be effective, the new organisation and information technologies require higher scale economies and hence larger production volumes than NC machines.

9.6   Summary and conclusions

In this study, we have tried to gauge the impact of technology on the competitiveness of Indian small auto component units. We recapitulate here the salient features of the study.

- Impact of technology is studied by directly introducing technology variables in the production function along with conventional inputs.
- Technology has been taken in its comprehensive form by including all three aspects of it, namely transformation, organisation and information.

- Study is based on the data collected through the primary survey of a sample of small auto component units located in and around Delhi.
- In our sample of small auto component units, level of mechanisation (transformation), quality management, work allocation (organisation), means of communication with the customers/dealers and data management turned out to be the empirically relevant technology variables. Most of the production organisation variables such as production schedules and materials procurement and inventories were found to be highly flexible in almost all the units. Both information technologies, namely means of communication and data management, are found in some of the units. However, their usage is not yet standardised.
- Of these, we took the level of mechanisation, ISO9000 certification and means of communication into our production function as proxies for the transformation, organisation and information technologies. All these technology variables are specified as dummy variables. In the case of mechanisation, the dummy variable takes the units having NC machines and units not having them. For the organisation, we have a dummy that takes units with ISO9000 and units not having it. IT is represented by a dummy variable that takes the units with electronic mail and units not having it.
- Added to these technology variables are the conventional inputs, namely original value of plant and machinery, total number of employees and the value of materials consumed. Sales turnover is taken as the dependent variable instead of production as it represents the competitiveness of the units.
- Finally, we specified our production function to be of the Cobb-Douglas type and estimated the same by the OLS method.
- Results show that the technology represented by the level of mechanisation, materials, labour, and plant and machinery has a significant positive impact on sales turnover. The benefits of the units having NC machines in terms of sales turnover are quite high in magnitude. It is followed by the coefficient of materials. The impact of plant and machinery on sales turnover is relatively smaller in magnitude. Both the organisation and information technologies are yet to yield results in terms of improving the competitive strength of the enterprises.

Based on the empirical results, we conclude that the usage of advanced technology embodied in sophisticated machinery such as NC machines is substantially improving the competitiveness of the small auto component units in relation to both organisation and communication

technology on the one hand and the conventional inputs on the other. To make use of new organisation and information technologies effectively, small enterprises have to reorient themselves towards formalisation and growth, which require a quantum leap in their size. It comes mainly through a revamp of the policy package away from protection and towards facilitation in terms of the availability of critical inputs such as finance.

Acknowledgements

This is a revised version of the paper presented at the UNU-WIDER conference on The New Economy in Development, held at Helsinki, Finland, on 10–11 May 2002. I would like to thank the Indo-Dutch Programme on Alternatives in Development (IDPAD) for financing the field survey. I am highly grateful to Professors K. L. Krishna and Suresh D. Tendulkar (Centre for Development Economics, Delhi School of Economics) for their encouragement and valuable suggestions. Professor Krishna's suggestions were of great help in shaping the paper (see also Krishna 1987). The comments of Professors Francesco Daveri and Anthony D'Costa are acknowledged with thanks. I accept sole responsibility for any errors and shortcomings that persist.

Notes

1 'Enterprise', 'firm' and 'unit' are used synonymously to refer to ownership or decision-making unit in the production of goods and services.
2 Ayyar (1994: 39), Government of India (1997: 151) and Tendulkar and Bhavani (1997: 50–1).
3 We have added the information aspect to the definition of technology given in Dahlman and Westphal (1982).
4 At the level of imitation that involves transfer of technology from the proprietor firm of technology to other firms, the literature is full of studies on the issue of international technology transfer.
5 In the initial stages of our survey, we tried to find benchmark technologies for each of the three dimensions, especially for the small enterprises, but did not succeed.
6 Growth accounting method: the alternative measure of TFP assumes constant returns to scale and perfect competition.
7 As far as we know, Griliches (1995) and Stiroh (2001) have taken technology variables directly in the production function.
8 An automobile consists of more than 20,000 components, each performing a different function (ICRA 1999: 31).
9 The percentages refer to 2002–3, the latest year for which published data were available. Domestic demand is calculated as the sum of domestic production and imports minus exports. The contribution of domestic industry is taken as the percentage of share of domestic production minus exports in domestic market demand. Domestic production, exports and imports of the auto components are given in ACMA (2002–3: 29, 99 and 162).

10 This and the next figure are arrived at using the exchange rate of US\$ = 47 rupees by ACMA of India.

11 Organised sector refers to the factory sector units. All those units which employ 10 or more employees if using power, 20 or more employees if not using power, are to be registered under the Factories Act 1948 and taken as factory units. The majority of our survey units are non-factory units and hence fall in the category of the unorganised sector.

12 Since exports given by ACMA constitute around 14 per cent in the year 2002–3, there will be some difference in the other two figures. However, it is difficult to obtain them as they are estimated irregularly by certain specialised agencies.

13 Poor road conditions increase the wear and tear on the auto components that need to be replaced more frequently.

14 In terms of turnover, it is only about one-tenth of the size of the world's largest automotive company, namely Delphi Automotive Systems Corporation of the USA (ICRA 1999: 36; AIAM 1999: 80).

15 These figures are likely guesstimates as they differ from study to study. See NCAER (1999: 2).

16 ICRA (1999: 32, 40), Narayana (1989: 39–40), Gumaste (1988: 70), Gokarn and Vaidya (2004). ICRA (1999) discusses the industry leaders of many automotive components.

17 Under the phased manufacturing programme (PMP) vehicle manufacturing firms were required to indigenise their import requirements within specified time limits. This programme was abandoned in the early 1990s.

18 Delphi and Visteon are controlled by General Motors and Ford respectively and these are the largest automotive component manufacturers in the world.

19 The author observed the same during her survey of the units and interactions with the relevant business associations and individuals.

20 New methods are used along with the existing means of phone and personal visits.

21 In the majority of cases, transformation technology changes occurred in terms of the changes in machinery. Although one finds product diversification in a few cases, it can easily be captured through the mechanisation variable as it involved a shift in the machinery. For example, one of the survey units producing metal components diversified into plastic components and bought a fully automatic machine to produce the latter.

22 Converted at the current exchange rate of US\$ = 44 Indian rupees. The subsequent figures are also converted at this rate.

23 In fact, Faridabad was the natural cluster of the auto component industry (Gulati 1997: 36–40).

24 Indian small-scale units are known to be notorious in all these respects. Only a few of the growing units started using NC machines. Their response rate to surveys is poor and the majority of the small units are not in a position to provide quantitative information as very few of these units maintain records. The recent census of small industries conducted by the DCSSI for the year 2001–2 shows that around 26 per cent of the registered (as a small unit with any one of the government agencies) small units maintain records. The same census reports that hardly 7 per cent of the unregistered units maintain records. One must note that unregistered units dominate the sector in terms of numbers.

25   Although industry has been undergoing restructuring and hence some of the small units in the recent years, we feel things have not changed much if one takes the small-scale sector in general and hence our results still hold good.

26   Regrouping is partly done for reasons of estimation. The small sample size constrained us to have only a few variables.

27   In the case of the majority of the small-scale units, the production process is not continuous with three shifts. Rather, it is batch production with large time gaps between batches owing not only to lack of orders but also due to time gaps in communication.

28   Figures in parentheses are *t*-values and * indicates the statistical significance of the relevant variables.

References

ACMA (2002–3) *ACMA: Facts and Figures 2002–03*. Automotive Components Manufacturers Association: http://www.acmainfo.com/.

Ahluwalia, I. J. (1991) *Productivity and Growth in Indian Manufacturing*, Delhi: Oxford University Press.

AIAM (1999) *Recommendations for Developing Indian Automotive Policy*, New Delhi: Association of Indian Automobile Manufacturers.

Ayyar, S. R. S. (1994) 'New Emerging Challenges and Opportunities for Small and Medium Enterprises through Technological Upgradation and Better Financial Management', *Small Industry Bulletin for Asia and Pacific*, 29: 38–40.

Bhavani, T. A. (2001) 'Towards Developing an Analytical Framework to Study Technological Change in the Small Units of the Developing Nations', Working Paper Series E/216/2001, Delhi: Institute of Economic Growth.

Bhavani, T. A. (2005) *Technological Change in the Indian Small Scale Industries*, New Delhi: Ane Books.

Bos, A. and W. Cole (1994) 'Management Systems as Technology: Japanese, US and National Firms in the Brazilian Electronic Sector', *World Development*, 22 (2): 225–36.

Carlton, D. W. and J. M. Perloff (1990) *Modern Industrial Organisation*, Glenview: Scott, Foresman and Co.

Dahlman, C. and L. Westphal (1982) 'Technological Effort in Industrial Development', in F. Stewart and J. James (eds) *The Economics of New Technology in Developing Countries*, London: Pinter, pp. 105–37.

Dahlman, C., B. Ross-Larson and L. Westphal (1987) 'Managing Technological Development: Lessons from the Newly Industrialising Countries', *World Development*, 15 (6): 759–75.

D'Costa, A. P. (2004) 'Flexible Institutions for Mass Production Goals: Economic Governance in the Indian Automotive Industry', *Industrial and Corporate Change*, 13 (2): 335–67.

Gokarn, S. and R. R. Vaidya (2004) 'The Automobile Components Industry', in S. Gokarn, A. Sen and R. R. Vaidya (eds) *The Structure of Indian Industry*, Delhi: Oxford University Press, pp. 281–314.

Government of India (1997) *Report of the Expert Committee on Small Scale Enterprises* (Abid Hussain Committee), Delhi: Government of India.

Government of India (2002–3) *Third All India Census of Small Scale Industries,* Delhi: DCSSI, Government of India.

Griliches, Z. (1995) 'R&D and Productivity: Econometric Results and Measurement Issues', in P. Stoneman (ed.) *Handbook of the Economics of Innovation and Technological Change,* Oxford: Blackwell.

Griliches, Z. (1996) 'The Discovery of the Residual: a Historical Note', *Journal of Economic Literature,* XXXIV: 1324–30.

Gulati, M. (1997) *Restructuring and Modernisation of Small Medium Enterprise Clusters in India: a Report,* New Delhi: UNIDO.

Gumaste, V. M. (1988) *Technological Self Reliance in the Automobile and Ancillary Industries in India,* Madras: Institute for Financial Management and Research.

Hayek, F. A. (1945) 'The Use of Knowledge in Society', *American Economic Review,* 35 (4): 519–30.

ICRA (1999) *The Indian Automotive Components Industry,* ICRA Industry Watch Series, New Delhi: ICRA.

Kanji, G. K. and M. Asher (1996) *100 Methods for Total Quality Management,* New Delhi: Sage.

Krishna, K. L. (1987) 'Industrial Growth and Productivity in India', in P. R. Brahmananda and V. R. Panchamukhi (eds) *The Development Process of the Indian Economy,* Delhi: Himalaya Publishing House.

Lall, S. (1992) 'Technological Capabilities and Industrialization', *World Development,* 20 (2): 165–86.

Lall, S. (2001) *Competitiveness, Technology and Skills,* Cheltenham: Edward Elgar.

Link, A. N. (1987) *Technological Change and Productivity Growth,* London: Harwood Academic Publishers.

McGuckin, R. H., M. L. Streitwieser and M. E. Doms (1996) 'The Effect of Technology Use on Productivity Growth', Discussion Papers, Washington, DC: Centre for Economic Studies.

Mintzberg, H. (1979) *The Structuring of Organizations,* Englewood Cliffs, NJ: Prentice-Hall.

Mody, A. and C. Dahlman (1992) 'Performance and Potential Information Technology: an International Perspective', *World Development,* 20 (12): 1703–19.

Mody, A., R. Suri and J. Sanders (1992) 'Keeping Pace with Change: Organizational and Technological Imperatives', *World Development,* 20 (12): 1797–816.

Narayana, D. (1989) 'The Motor Vehicle Industry in India', Occasional Paper Series, Trivandrum: Centre for Development Studies.

NCAER (1999) *Spurious Automotive Components: Market Size and Consequences,* sponsored by the Automotive Components Manufacturers Association, New Delhi.

Patel, P. and K. Pavitt (1995) 'Patterns of Technological Activity: Their Measurement and Interpretation', in P. Stoneman (ed.) *Handbook of Economics of Innovation and Technological Change,* Oxford: Blackwell, pp. 14–51.

Porter, M. E. and C. R. Christensen (1998) 'Measuring the Microeconomic Foundations of Economic Development', *The Global Competitiveness Report,* Geneva: WEF.

Stiroh, K. J. (2001) *Information Technology and the U.S. Productivity Revival: What Do the Industry Data Say?,* New York: Federal Reserve Bank of New York.

Teitel, S. and L. E. Westphal (1984) 'Introduction' to the Symposium on Technological Change and Industrial Development, *Journal of Development Economics*, 16 (1–2): 1–12.

Tendulkar, S. D. and T. A. Bhavani (1997) 'Policy on Modern Small Scale Industries: a Case of Government Failure', *Indian Economic Review*, 32 (1): 39–64.

Varadharajan, S. and S. Kannan (1998) 'Brimming with Challenges', in *The Hindu Survey of Indian Industry*, Chennai: *The Hindu*.

10
How to Solve the 'Hotmail Problem': Global–Local Interfaces and Filipino Technopreneurs

Czarina Saloma-Akpedonu

10.1 Introduction

How does the Philippines come to terms with its history of acquiring mostly Western phenomena? Given its long history of borrowing and copying from the West, what does hybridisation mean in relation to technological creativity and innovation? I examine pinoymail.com, a Filipino free e-mail service patterned after hotmail.com,[1] for some answers.

The 'Westernisation' in the Philippines is the result of a long history of global integration. This came in different forms over the centuries: contact with Arab and Chinese traders since the tenth century, the export of tobacco and other agricultural products during Spanish colonial times, the migration of Filipinos to work as labourers in Hawaiian sugar and pineapple fields in the 1900s, and the export of semiconductor and electronics parts and the migration of information technology (IT) professionals almost a century later. Over the centuries, long-distance cross-cultural trade, colonialism, neo-colonialism and, these days, globalisation, integrated the Philippines, in itself full of diversity, into other distinct societies.

At no other historical point do views on the consequences of integration into the world stage vary more strongly than in discussions of the most current mode, globalisation. One view presents globalisation in terms of dichotomies that come along with the happy conclusion that globalisation is about homogenisation, that is, the West 'winning over' the others (see, for example, Barber 1996; Fukuyama 1989; Huntington 1993). For Filipinos, globalisation as a homogenising process or

condition can be experienced as the phenomenon of Filipinos singing perfect renditions of American pop songs.

The other view presents globalisation as a process or condition of hybridisation. Few Filipinos would agree that we are simply borrowing from the West or that borrowing from the West is the ideal path for everyone. The sense is that, far from being homogenising or even heterogenising, globalisation does not follow a single path to a terminal condition but rather occurs as interfaces between the global and the local.

In referring to the interfaces between the global and the local, I prefer the concept of glocalisation. The main point in the discussion of glocalisation is that globalisation involves the 'simultaneity and the interpenetration of what are conventionally called the global and the local or – in more abstract terms – the universal and the particular' (Robertson 1995: 30). It connotes a global outlook adapted to local conditions and implies adapting one's techniques to local conditions and making improvements on what has been borrowed. Thus my sense is that many Filipinos take upon the 'foreign' in the spirit of 'copying plus'. Filipino pop singer Gary Valenciano dances and reaches for the high notes like Michael Jackson, but he does so with materials he himself composed or those by a Filipino composer.

This chapter illuminates the principles that inform the practices and relations in the creation of information and communication technology (ICT) products in a so-called developing country. I look at the phenomenon of 'copying plus' to make sense of what glocalisation means to the Philippine ICT industry. It consists of four main sections. In the first, I describe the contexts for creating ICT products in the Philippines. I focus in particular on a group of IT professionals who I refer to as intermediate developers. In the second section, I examine the sites of glocalisation. I focus in particular on two types of imagined technological communities: the epistemic and ethnobusiness communities within the ICT industry. In the third, I present the different modes by which glocalisation takes place. In conclusion, I present some insights into how the work of intermediate developers in a country can challenge old notions of an international division of labour which mainly view so-called developing countries like Philippines as a site of routine assembly work.

10.2   The Philippine ICT industry

The information and communication technology industry in the Philippines is inextricably linked to the global ICT industry. This industry

is organised into three groups of ICT companies and professionals: first, a group of ICT companies and professionals who provide the framework and infrastructure that allow other individuals to develop products on their own; second, a group of ICT companies and professionals who develop products needed by everyday users using the framework and infrastructure created by the first group; and third, a group of consumers in various localities. The first group develops frameworks and infrastructures such as operating systems (e.g. Linux and Microsoft) and programming languages (e.g. C++). Their products allow a second group of individuals to create other applications for a wider audience. Given its position in the creation and consumption chain of ICT products, I refer to members of the second group as the 'intermediate developers'. Intermediate developers in the Philippine ICT industry include hardware and software developers, web designers, technopreneurs (i.e. technology entrepreneurs), and individuals who work in content processing and call centre companies. They develop products for everyday users and provide ICT-enabled support services.

Claims about Filipinos being 'the best in the world' are a da capo, not only but most especially in Philippine government pronouncements.[2] The so-called Y2K brain drain indicated that the country's ICT industry had also borne such claims.[3] A number of statistics lend credence to national self-depictions. Consider the 'Global New Economy Index', a tool that measures the technological production and potential of countries.[4] In 2000, the Philippines ranked first in 'knowledge jobs' and joined other top scorers such as Japan, Finland and the US in categories of innovation, economic dynamism, globalisation and movement towards a digital economy. This rank in terms of IT skills and knowledge was also affirmed by the Institute for Management Development (IMD 2000) ranking of countries according to their ability to provide an environment that sustains the competitiveness of enterprises.[5] In the category 'availability of IT skills', the report ranked the Philippines second only to India. The usual conclusion being made from these surveys is that the Philippines can and has managed to beat developed countries in certain areas of the ICT industry. Such conclusions have long preceded these rankings. In 1997, the Ramos government presented 'IT21' or 'The National Information Technology Plan for the 21st Century', a document announcing the vision and broad strategy to make the Philippines 'a knowledge centre in Asia' (National Information Technology Council 1997: 5).

Yet, the scientific and technological gap remains between industrial and developing countries, as well as among developing countries. In the

overall ranking of countries in the aforementioned reports, the Philippines was still at the tail end of the distribution (for example, it was number 37 in the IMD overall scoreboard for 47 countries). Moreover, subsequent public statements appear to downscale or contradict the grand visions of IT21. A news item in December 2000, for example, posits that the country aspires to become a 'call centre' capital (*Philippine Star* 2000). Call centre services vary according to skill requirements, but services such as data capture and processing, customer call centres for routine queries, order taking and referrals, hotel or rental car reservation and virtual services centres such as home delivery companies do not require technical training, problem-solving skills, specific expertise and managerial authority (Mitter 2004). Not all call centre activities, therefore, correspond to more complex tasks and high-value-added products characteristic of a knowledge society. A year later, the Philippine Senate President Pro Tempore said that, 'no foreign investments are forthcoming ... and the best bet is through agriculture' (*Philippine Star* 2001). The succeeding Estrada government (1998–2001), while not completely neglecting the ICT drive initiated by the preceding administration, put more emphasis on anti-poverty programmes (e.g. agriculture and fisheries modernisation). Clear support for the development of the ICT industry is also not evident from the Arroyo government that followed the Estrada government. Consequently, the Philippines seemed unable to maintain its position in global ICT rankings. In 2004, the Philippines was number 52 in the IMD overall scoreboard for 60 countries and regions. In 2003, the Philippines ranked 49 in the list.

Thus, the Philippine experience shows that creativity and ingenuity prosper despite the lack of governance structures, although state-regulated policy and implementation mechanisms are needed to make the most of such creativity and ingenuity.

10.3   Imagined technological communities

I suggest that glocalisation is observable in the mental maps of intermediate developers in the Philippine ICT industry. The concept of a mental map refers to the everyday lifeworld navigated by actors through a 'social stock of knowledge', the ready-made, standardised scheme for understanding the society one is born or reared into (Schutz and Luckmann 1973: 8). Mental maps, drawn from the 'social stock of knowledge', enable intermediate developers to take the world in which they live for granted. The taken-for-grantedness of each situation in the lifeworld is important to the concept of the local.

The mental maps of Filipino intermediate developers are of unusual interest because their global–local positions allow an insight into which contexts particular maps are drawn. At one point in time, intermediate developers think in terms of the needs of clients in the Philippines; at another point, they think in terms of global technologies and technology providers. Thus, looking at mental maps of intermediate developers, particularly the mental map of the founder of Pinoymail.com, a free Filipino web-based e-mail service, enables one to detect the phases and various logics that precede the glocal product or service, which more often comes to consumers with the aura of a ready-made object.

I met DD, Pinoymail's founder, a few months after a local holding firm invested US$2.5 million in Pinoymail and made him the first dot.com multimillionaire in the Philippines. I visited the Pinoymail website whose main page promptly announced it to be 'for Filipinos and their friends in the Philippines and everywhere else in the world', e-mailed DD, and met him one afternoon in his office at the Ortigas Business Centre.[6]

> As a technical company, we are pretty much global. We belong to a community of users of an operating system called Linux. This is called an open source community. I put my trust in a company called Digital Nation of Virginia, USA. I trust them to provide my public or my audience with 100 percent 'up service'. I haven't seen how my servers look like. I haven't seen if they really are what they claim they are. What I do know is that I never had any downtime with them. ... I actually have Argentinean programmers. And once in a while, I have Hong Kong consultants. But you know what? I never met anyone of them. ... On our first launching on March 9 [1998] we just went to the chat rooms, asked the chat room operator to announce it and presto!, we had 2000 users the next day. Mostly, it was through word of mouth. I think that is the phrase, word of mouth: chats, forwarding e-mails.... In a classic environment, word of mouth is whispering to you. On the Net it is possible, it is also word of mouth. I go to a chat room and see that the announced topic of the day is 'get your free Pinoymail at this time'. And you begin talking about it, that's word of mouth. And then you say, 'I want to shift to this from my Hotmail account', and then you send it to your friends: 'Hey, there's something new, this is ours.' (DD, founder of pinoymail. com, interview, 10 April 2000)

In introducing the notion of 'imagined communities' of nationality, Benedict Anderson (1985: 15) sees 'all communities larger than primordial villages of face-to-face contact [as] imagined'. Similar to the

imagining of the nation, DD sees himself as part of a wider group and his everyday lifeworld shared by many other IT professionals (e.g. local and foreign consultants and programmers) and artefacts (e.g. servers) which may not be physically present. The subscribers of Pinoymail also perform a social act performed with other subscribers who are drawn by the marker *pinoy*, Pinoymail's unique identifier on the Internet. Thus in addition to the community of IT professionals, a community of consumers is formed. Like the members of even the smallest nation, these professionals and subscribers will, in Anderson's (1985: 15) words, 'never know most of their fellow members, meet them, or even hear of them, yet in the minds of each lives the image of their communion'. Regardless of the heterogeneity and the social inequality that may prevail in each of these communities, each member feels a sense of comradeship that is similar to the imagining of the nation.

For Anderson, communities are to be distinguished according to how they are imagined. In this chapter, I focus on two imagined communities that shed light on the 'doing' of ICT in a developing country. In both communities, technology is either a medium or fodder for the communion of members. Both exist as online communities even as their traditional, offline forms remain. Both communities run on principles of glocalisation. But both differ in how each one is constituted. One is constituted through the need to know what consumers want, an essential element in the application of ICT knowledge into the practical context of business; the other is formed through the need for continuous access to ICT knowledge, a rationale behind encounters with fellow IT professionals.

The idea that imagined communities are technological is not a recent one. Anderson's imagined communities of the nation were partly made possible by the development of print technology in the first half of the sixteenth century. The sense of connectedness being accomplished by the newspaper and the book is now being accomplished by one of the newest forms of the imagination of the collective: the online communities, whether they are a loose community where the technology is mostly used for e-mailing or better organised communities with their own websites. To emphasise the primacy of both ICT and ICT professionals in ethnobusiness and epistemic communities, I refer to both as imagined technological communities.

10.3.1   Ethnobusiness communities

The ICT industry is one arena where globalisation strongly manifests itself as a homogenising process and condition. The application of information technologies into areas of social life such as business is also governed by

a similar rule: the product that is able to have the widest audience in the shortest time possible, achieved through marketing strategies, is the product that would set the standards. When Pinoymail came in, Hotmail had already established itself as the standard in free web-based e-mail services. Nevertheless, the barriers of entry in the development of business applications based on information technologies are not as high compared to those in hardware and standard software development.

This factor gives rise to ethnobusinesses. An ethnobusiness is a type of business that is based on an entrepreneur's common-sense knowledge and understanding of what works with consumers who share the entrepreneur's common-sense knowledge and understanding of a certain cultural or ethnic background. It is about local markets, and with ICT applications that consider local needs and capabilities, local technopreneurs have a comparative advantage over global and even national players. Because of the costs of, and the proximity requirements in, the development of certain ICT products (e.g. web design and business applications software), business establishments in Philippine provinces take the services of local service providers.

In response, many multinational companies providing business applications software in the Philippines therefore use the prestige and reliability argument in order to get contracts with Filipino companies. Metro Manila-based Filipino professional web business solutions providers also use the reliability argument in winning clients from the provinces by arguing that freelance and provincial-based web designers may not provide expertise on web business development and the documentation services essential for updating projects. The localisation of global companies, through the establishment of local bases in the Philippines, may appear to nullify the advantages and lessen the sustainability of ethnobusinesses. Nevertheless, the number of localities and client groups keeps on expanding. Ethnobusiness is business that is based on strategies built upon an entrepreneur's lifeworldly stock of knowledge. Viewed in this sense, glocalisation is the underlying principle of ethnobusiness. As a response to existing global variation in consumers, glocalisation involves the 'construction of increasingly differentiated consumers and "invention" of consumer traditions' (Robertson 1995: 29).

Ethnobusiness also explains why the so-called first-mover advantage in global standard markets does not work all the time – the global world comprises localities that seem unlimited:

In my Internet café in 1997, Pinoymail was born. I put up a paid e-mail service. After all, I thought some people would pay, but hell,

no one was paying me. Well, only a hundred persons subscribed. And the reason was that this company, Hotmail.com was giving everybody and anybody who wants, free e-mail. And I was so stumped. How can I solve the Hotmail problem? The solution I came up with was to copy it (laughs). Copy the model and put a *pinoy* touch to it.... The term '*pinoy*' has a pulling power.... Look at where our subscribers come from. Mostly from the Philippines, yes, but 10 percent would come from abroad. These are Filipinos from abroad, of course, because after all *pinoy* would not make sense to a person from the US or Japan. They would not know what *pinoy* means unless they have a relationship with *Pinoys*. (DD, founder of pinoymail.com, interview, 10 April 2000)

DD's social stock of knowledge enables him to turn fellow Filipinos who share and shape his stock of knowledge into consumers. It tells him that Filipinos would be willing to pay for an e-mail service that gives them some form of identity in the Internet unlike a generic Hotmail address. It also allows him recalibrate his initial and erroneous understanding of what appeals to fellow actors who share his lifeworld (e.g. the willingness to pay for a 'personal' e-mail address). Moreover, this social stock of knowledge enables him to arrive at three important insights crucial to the transformation of fellow actors in his lifeworld into consumers: one, fellow actors are to be differentiated into Filipinos in the Philippines, Filipinos abroad and the friends of Filipinos; two, these fellow actors form a community for whom subscription to Pinoymail is not just a solution to a technical need (e.g. to be able to send and receive e-mails) but for whom consumption is an imagining and a marker or a representation of 'Filipino-ness'; and three, fellow actors are great reproducers of one's own culture.

Pinoymail shows that intermediate developers can become nodes of international communicative networks and institutions of cultural ties, which link emigrants to their countries of origins. It works within the realities of migration and the attendant need of the relocated group for contact with the homeland. DD's knowledge of his lifeworld includes the knowledge that the culture of migration in the Philippines creates a diasporic consciousness which make Filipino migrants want to retain links with their homeland.

An ethnobusiness like Pinoymail is built upon an idea that appeals to local needs and interests. Nevertheless, its execution depends on its ability to access appropriate technology and to form partnerships with

technological providers and users all over the world. In the next section, I examine epistemic communities that function as a source and mode of technological transfer.

10.3.2 Epistemic communities

Besides imagining a community of consumers, DD also engages in what Knorr Cetina (1999) calls epistemic communities. These communities play host to knowledge creation, technical and scientific knowledge, as well as knowledge of work cultures, and are repositories of both ready-to-be-used and mutable knowledge. Moreover, they are not only limited to the laboratories of science but are also found in the new economy of globalised knowledge societies (Evers 2000: 11). They include universities, research institutions, industries, business entities, development agencies and 'open source' communities.

The epistemic communities in which Filipino intermediate developers partake are of two kinds. One is characterised by members' engagement with knowledge systems as reproduced by established cultural makers such as schools, media and global corporations. This type of epistemic community heavily relies on ready-to-be-used knowledge. The other corresponds to a new mode of knowledge production characterised by the expansion of the number of potential knowledge producers so that knowledge production is no longer limited to universities but is taking place in other settings. This type of epistemic community promotes the horizontal diffusion of knowledge. The newest of such settings are online epistemic communities that have a defined focus and provide a site of communication among people linked by interest and expertise. A software architect explained of the members of the communities he frequented:

> Individuals are only as good as the quality of their ideas on specific topics at a given time. I could be a focal point, the 'expert', say, on a specific design pattern. However, that's likely to last only for a discussion thread. On another thread, the person who picked up on my ideas and perhaps improved them, emerges as the expert. (RT, a Filipino software architect working in the US, e-mail, 2 February 2001)

Because of the existence of online epistemic communities, DD did not have to know the whole range of technological repertoire in order to develop Pinoymail. He relied on online epistemic communities to complement his knowledge gaps.

10.4   Modes of glocalisation

Pinoymail illustrates the relational notion of the local and the global that is based on the criteria of, one, a sense of belonging and two, the possession of detailed knowledge. For DD the local takes the form of whatever it is that he knows about fellow Filipinos as potential consumers of an e-mail service. The local also takes the form of a geographic territory (e.g. 'Filipinos in the Philippines'). DD's everyday use of the term 'global' provides a geographic definition of the 'global' as a community that includes members and elements outside of the space marked as 'the Philippines' (e.g. Filipinos and their friends around the world).

The notion of glocalisation draws attention to how Filipino intermediate developers deal with the local and the global in the context of imagined technological communities. There are two modes involved. In the first mode, glocalisation is about the promotion and the anchoring of the global within the local. In the second, glocalisation is achieved by highlighting the local within the global.

10.4.1   The global within the local

There are at least two ways in which the promotion of the global within the local is being expressed. One is in the dissolution of the marker of locality, the nation; the other is in the establishment of relations of trust. If Anderson had coupled the notion of imagined communities to the birth of the nation, imagined technological communities are to be coupled with the blurring of national lines. DD explains how the blurring of national lines happens in imagined technological communities:

> You are all anonymous, and when you are anonymous, you can basically have another name. I go there as Nikki, another colleague goes there as *pusacat*, another as Mark which is a real name.[7] And we talk about how to put up a mail server, we talk about the pros and cons of a line operating system ... without regard for anything but the topic, without regard for anything but technical know-how. You think about what your objective is for the day, which is, for example, to put up a server. You go into this chat room and discover what you can still do, and you don't know if you are talking to a white or black American. You talk the same language, the same jargon. There is nothing Filipino about it. (DD, founder of pinoymail.com, interview, 10 April 2000)

The marginal role being played by national boundaries in imagined epistemic communities shows the deterritorialisation of imagined

technological communities. In this case, deterritorialisation implies that there is *no* one locality. It also means communities where interactions among community members are independent of hierarchical social locations such as nationality and reputational structures.

When I met DD in his office, the setting of concrete, steel, glass and busy streets invited the question of the importance of locality for business practices built on ICT. I asked why Pinoymail moved office to the Ortigas Business Centre instead of remaining in his house or at the university shopping centre where he had first opened his Internet café:

> It's the decision of our new majority owner because all the other companies that he owns are also located nearby. We could be anywhere. We were in my house for a long time and it did not matter to the users. What matters to them is that I wake up and I get my e-mail and I am able to send. That's all that matters to them. It did not matter if it's just being run from a *sala* [living room]. Or does it matter to be in a fancy office like this? It does not matter. We have people selling advertising. We have people doing the marketing…. What matters to our advertisers is that we can deliver. (DD, founder of pinoymail.com, interview, 10 April 2000)

How important then is locality for business practices built on ICT? DD's description of Pinoymail as a company that 'could be anywhere' decouples the notion of 'modern' or 'high tech' from specific urban centres. Although most ICT companies choose to be in business centres where they are close to suppliers, banks, trade associations, clients, among others, the creation of ICT products is not specific to one area in the city. 'Being anywhere' also implies having a choice about locales. Although it is possible to get the technological services it needs from Philippine-based providers, Pinoymail is not keeping its technological facilities in the Philippines. In all these cases, deterritoriality implies that there is *no* one locality.

The second way in which the 'global within the local' is expressed is in the anchoring of global relations with the norms of locality. DD's description of the interaction in open-source and online communities as 'without regard for anything but the topic, without regard for anything but technical know-how' points to an initial view of these communities as global. Yet, although global, imagined technological communities are anchored on an everyday lifeworld. Technology providers and technologies inhabit DD's everyday lifeworld via shared knowledge and skills such as a language that is both generalist

(e.g. English as a medium of everyday communication) and specialist (English as programming language). The interactions within online communities create social capital, defined as the 'features of social organization such as networks, norms, ... trust that facilitate coordination and cooperation for mutual benefit' (Putnam 1993: 35ff). How DD found global technology providers illustrates how local characteristics are developed from what is putatively thought of as global in everyday life:

> I just read reviews, technical testing routes.... I inspect the other sites that they host. I found out that these sites looked good. And I made the determination all in front of a computer. So the milieu that you are talking about is very virtual. The milieu is quite large... we have a vendor–vendee relationship. They sell Internet presence, we pay them according to their prices.... It has something to do with your track record, what other people say about you. This is one thing good on the Internet. People tell on you if you don't do your thing, especially if you are bordering on the criminal aspect.... Information about who are bad providers gets around. It is also trial and error. We had had a bad provider. (DD, founder of pinoymail.com, interview, 10 April 2000)

Bonds of trust are still – and can only be – created within local contexts. In online communities, 'people will tell on you' and the news spreads by 'word of mouth'. Each of these imaginative vocabularies – the formation, accumulation and invocation of social capital – refers to processes that characterise a local culture, where people engage in face-to-face relationships. Online communities, which provide access to global technologies, underscore a main point in the nature of social capital: one's membership in these communities implies the ability to draw on social resources that behave like monetary capital from networks and from norms of solidarity. Concrete personal relations generate trust.

10.4.2   The local within the global

'Being anywhere' can equally mean thriving in the local. At the start, DD was looking for technology and partnerships and his everyday lifeworld was anchored on a computer. 'You have a computer and you know how to do some hacking.... You appreciate configuring things, then you learn new stuff from the Internet: how to configure a mail server, how to put up a web site', he said. While Pinoymail's initial activities centre on global technologies and appear to be disembodied from the local, the whole project is essentially contingent on the local

because the search for technologies and partnerships revolves around a business idea that seeks to create profits from the idea of locality. It used the US$2.5 million investment it received to improve technical capacity and marketing strategies in order to attract and accommodate more subscribers. To attract subscribers, the locality was invoked. Just as the print industry made use of the market for works in the vernacular as the market for works in the Latin language was saturated (Anderson 1985, 42), Pinoymail used *pinoy* as its unique identifier on the Internet, and provided representation of the various cultural groups in the country. Where certain dialects were unsuccessful in the seventeenth century in insisting on their own print form, Pinoymail saw a business opportunity in the twentieth century: a community of consumers whose consumption is anchored on feelings of belonging to a nation. 'After all,' he said, '*pinoy* can be seen along national lines.'

What does 'national lines' mean? In the transnational spaces created by intermediate developers, interpersonal relationships increasingly take precedence over established ideas of the nation. Nevertheless, visions of society are not a priori categories but rather come out of a process of actors constructing and reconstructing existing visions. For example, the e-card service of Pinoymail seeks to mix consumption not only with the land in general but with the political through its cards on EDSA 2, the people power revolt that drove Joseph Estrada out of the presidency in January 2001. Thus the term 'national' in the context of Pinoymail is to be understood with respect to the cultural formations and visions of a society, a vision that includes, among others, promoting the Filipino identity in a global world. In this sense, the term 'identity' describes 'group-identifying symbols' that are used to create difference and construct boundaries between those who belong to a specific group and all those who do not.

But Pinoymail's mobilisation of locality in the processes of creating markets also parallels a particular aspect of the mobilisation of ethnicity in the processes of nation building. In this sense, the Philippine nation is local vis-à-vis the global, in the same manner that the different ethnic groups are local vis-à-vis the nation. Pinoymail has to deal with the global (Hotmail), but at the same time, with the diversity of the local (notions of Filipino-ness):

> Whether one likes it or not, there are already real communities on the Internet. There is a commonality that you identify yourself with.... What we are trying to do is to have an online community of Filipinos – whatever that means. It does not mean anything really except like a virtual something, like a virtual community of Filipinos.

There is a feeling of togetherness online and mind you, e-mails are the number one application. I can't think of anyone who will not appreciate a Pinoymail address and in that sense, we are focused on whatever is *Pinoy* today. (DD, founder of pinoymail.com, interview, 10 April 2000)

The collective identity of Filipinos subscribing to Pinoymail, which comes as a result of being faced by universal, global identifications of Hotmail.com, takes precedence over regional and linguistic identity. We-statements – 'we', 'our', 'ours', 'us' – indicate that these subscribers are bound by the traditions that are evoked in their consumption of Pinoymail. The condition of globalisation has given way to a unified concept of a community, with Filipinos being represented and increasingly representing themselves as a single global community. Yet, Pinoymail's promotion of the country's different cultural events suggests a consumption of locality that is not only geared towards the global world entranced by Hotmail.com but also towards cultural groups in the Philippines struggling with what can be done with the local culture.

'What made this company what it is right now,' DD told me, 'was really putting things together and branding it as "Pinoymail.com".' 'Putting things together' means mixing ideas and technologies, one that evolves into the appropriation and invention of the local. In its earlier phase, Pinoymail merely involved an appropriation of the local, a phase when, according to DD, 'Pinoymail [was] just a name' and a representation. Representation means to present something once again and DD presents *pinoy* as a marker of different senses of belonging to a land or nation, feelings that have always been there. The more challenging task, the invention of the local, which involves the (re)invention of traditions via the promotion of Filipino-ness in Pinoymail's products, had to wait until capital was available:

But, for lack of capital, we cannot put a *Pinoy* content into the site yet. It requires a server build-up. So right now, since we already have the capital, we are already partnering with Filipino content providers on the Internet: Inquirer interactive, Businessworld-online.... We have these content providers to sort of run a content subscription. If you have your Pinoymail, you can read your inquirer.net everyday in your mailbox. Something like that. (DD, founder of pinoymail.com, interview, 10 April 2000)

DD's invention of the local clarifies what is meant by mobilising tradition. Tradition is about collective memories, rituals, guardians, and

moral and emotional forces, where the past is continuously reshaped and reinterpreted based on the present (Giddens 1994: 63). An invention is particularly individual, but by sharing in the lifeworld of consumers, an invention is fundamentally social. DD invented the local by structuring feelings for the nation or the homeland. Pinoymail, for example, delivers the homepage of a local newspaper's Internet edition to the subscriber's mailbox, runs a card service through pinoycards, which features cards designed by the Samahang Kartunista ng Pilipinas, and provided a link to *Yehey!*, a local search engine. By saying that 'we are focused on whatever is Pinoy', DD clarified what was meant by his project of inventing locality. In this sense, he was 'acting for' and Pinoymail was 'standing for' 'whatever is Filipino'. He disclaimed a proactive role in the invention of Filipino traditions of consumption. Instead he implied that other people in the public world are creating a protean Filipino identity. Yet, by providing services that enable a Filipino to enact the argument 'if you are a Filipino, you have to have a Filipino e-mail address', DD invented consumption of Pinoymail as a way to define 'Filipino-ness'. Pinoymail subscribers took up this invention as a way of making space for the Filipino social identity in cyberspace. His invention of 'whatever is Filipino' gained legitimacy via the market.

DD's representations of 'whatever is Filipino' may be vague, largely simplified and generalised. But this performs a function in relation to familiarity and strangeness. Thus a new experience is not necessarily a novel one; it may be new, but the individual is still familiar to its type. Pinoymail is a new experience but not totally alienating from a previous experience with 'whatever is Filipino'. Pinoymail's generalised representations of 'whatever is Filipino' ensure that Filipinos of as many cultural predispositions can identify with the product. The resemblance of the website's general features to that of Hotmail's (e.g. predominant colour scheme, dialogue boxes) means that a user goes through a smooth transition when getting a second free-mail account from Pinoymail or altogether changing from a Hotmail account to a Pinoymail account.

However, the comparative advantage of ethnobusiness over its global counterpart is compromised by the requirements of capital and markets. Pinoymail as an ethnobusiness may benefit from the promotion of locality, but the site of its production of locality is embedded in the dynamics of asymmetrical global relations. DD admits:

> there is something Filipino about this. I am a Filipino and I try to get a capitalist to invest in my company, and I will have a harder time than a Chinese or an American because investors think, it's in the business side that you have a problem. In the technical side there is

no problem. It is frictionless. But when the business side comes in there are many problems about being a Filipino. There is friction when it comes to business because first, there are few Internet users here and that makes for a smaller market than let us say, the US. And in the real world where you do marketing and communication, you deliver commercial messages and if you are able to deliver your messages to a larger audience, you are more valuable. But, in our situation, where we only have one million users, that is too small an audience and for the businessman, it does not mean a good investment. (DD, founder of pinoymail.com, interview 10 April 2000)

The problems encountered by ethnobusinesses therefore do not seem to lie in the capacity of intermediate developers to absorb current technologies, but rather in the capacity of these businesses to accumulate capital, where the size of the market is a key factor. Even when an Internet user is defined as someone who has access to the Internet either through his or her own PC, corporate facilities, schools, Internet cafés, among others, the estimate of the number of Filipino Internet users rises to only 2 million.[8]

I wish to return to the question I raised at the beginning of this chapter. How do we come to terms with our long history of being *manggagaya*?[9] What can we conclude from DD's solution to the 'Hotmail problem'?

> *Manggagaya Reconsidered*
>
> Bakit kaya tayo ay ganito?
> Bakit manggagaya
> Meron naman tayo?
> Tayo'y mga Pinoy
> Tayo'y hindi Kano
> 'Wag kang mahihiya
> Kung ang ilong mo ay pango.
> [Why are we like this?
> Why copy
> When we have our own?
> We are Filipinos.
> We are not Americans.
> Do not be ashamed
> If your nose is flat.]
>
> > > Heber Bartolome,
> > > 'Tayo'y mga Pinoy',
> > > a 1970s song

A number of writings about contemporary society and cultural globalisation make references to the sculptures of Amedeo Modigliani and to
the paintings of Oskar Kokoschka (Hannerz 1996; Knorr Cetina 1999).
The Filipino way of copying, however, is more Warhol than Modigliani.
Andy Warhol's works, like the work of the Filipino technological elite,
suggest something of what I have in mind about the work of Filipino
intermediate developers. Using silkscreen printing technology and
media images (e.g. magazine and newspaper pictures of celebrities such
as Jackie Kennedy and Marilyn Monroe, and of events such as a car
crash), as well as real-life consumer goods (e.g. a can of Campbell soup
or a bottle of Coca-Cola), Warhol brings to life new ways of presenting
these images. His 250 editions of Marilyn Monroe done in different
colours successfully show 250 versions of one image. Curators for the
Warhol collection on display at the Tate Modern in London,[10] explain
that a Warhol creation is about:

> hiding individual authorship behind appropriated photographs and
> the mechanics of silkscreen printing, ... a disinterested observer of
> history, merely recording the world around him, provocatively
> juxtaposing images drawn from newspapers, advertising, television
> and film. (Grunenberg and Beudert 2002, wall poster, to accompany
> Warhol collection)

Pinoymail, an application of ICT to various aspects of social life such as
business and media, is an example of how a global phenomenon is
appropriated in the Philippines. Like most Filipino cultural acquisitions,
it is inspired and supported by a global precursor. In particular,
American technological leadership and global competition help define
Pinoymail as a company that has access to the best and/or imported
technologies at a reasonable cost.

For Filipinos, the 'outside' world is 'a place of power, wealth, cleanliness,
beauty, glamour and enjoyment' (Cannell 1995: 223) and the US
stands at the centre of this world. It is a common view that a lack of economic opportunities within the country conditions this outward-
directed orientation, but Filipinos of all classes seem to have this mental
orientation.

In imagined technological communities, the attraction to the outside
is not only driven by aesthetics or religious values but by a goal-oriented
rationality, where the choice of an American product is being made on
account of technological leadership, cost and speed. This type of rationality calls for a rereading of the country's relationship with the US as

a hegemonic power and a rethinking of what is generally meant by the so-called Filipino outward orientation. Pinoymail's mixing of local elements with global technologies indicates that the influence of the outside involves multidirectional cultural flows and when done within the framework of online epistemic communities, even dialogic. At the very least, this 'outward orientation', which also implies a tradition of getting along with strangers, culturally predisposed Filipinos towards the new economy, particularly on the way the Internet helps create its own social capital. At its fullest potential, this 'outward orientation' becomes a type of mixing that shows that the Filipino 'outward orientation' is not simply about outside influence that is imposed or willingly absorbed. Anderson (1985: 15) exhorts readers to think of nationalism as an invention, not in the sense of falsity but rather in the sense of imagining and creation.

In this view, Pinoymail is to be seen as 'copying plus'. By mixing globally accessible technologies (e.g. Linux operating system) and various cultural ingredients such as symbols (e.g. *pinoy*) and ritualised procedures (playing out minor differences between the Filipino and the rest of the world), the mixed end-product is at once distinct and not distinct from the original model. The interplay of this dualism, for example, is reflected in the way Pinoymail is being written about in a Philippine newspaper column, namely, as a 'free e-mail service similar to hotmail.com'. In this sense, Hotmail provides the comparative optics through which the hybrid, Pinoymail, swings between a promotion of the local and therefore distinct from Hotmail (e.g. 'this is ours') and a promotion of the global, and therefore one that is not distinct from established models (e.g. 'pinoymail.com is similar to hotmail.com'). In some instances being a Filipino does not matter: because DD looks for technological solutions far and wide, he does not need to have Filipino programmers or Filipino technology providers. Yet in other instances, being a Filipino matters: because the barriers of entry in ethnobusiness are low, DD's mental maps of the local provide him with a comparative advantage. Being a Filipino can also matter, albeit in a less positive sense: because the size of investment depends on the size of the market, DD has to reckon with the fact that while the significance of consumption of information technologies is increasing in the Philippines, it does not compare with global figures. The alternation between distinction and non-distinction of Filipino-ness is the essence of glocalisation.

The current form of globalisation is best described as glocalisation. This chapter examines a case of practical glocalisation. Pinoymail.com, a Filipino free e-mail service inspired by hotmail.com, comprehends

a whole range of acts and insights concerning the mixing of local elements (e.g. appropriation and invention of Filipino cultural formations) and global information technologies and formations (e.g. open-source software, US-based servers, Argentine consultants and Hong Kong programmers). It generates two variations of an imagined technological community. One is constituted according to what could be called principles and elements of ethnobusiness. The other, according to what could be called an epistemic community. Alongside Pinoymail's imagined community of consumers are communities of technology providers that are permeated with the culture of knowledge creation. Within these Filipino imagined technological communities, glocalisation occurs as a promotion of the global within the local and the promotion of the local within the global. By dissecting glocalisation into these two modes, one arrives at a view of Filipino acquisition of global phenomena as a reflexive and creative process and, despite the persistence of unequal social stratification, is far from being a process of Americanisation or Westernisation, which implies truncated, disembodied and imposed cultural borrowings. The challenge now lies in how to create an environment conducive to the emergence of more intermediate developers whose creativity and ingenuity can make the most of global–local interfaces.

Acknowledgements

An earlier version of this chapter appeared in the *Philippine Sociological Review*, 49 (2001): 1–17, while a fuller version is available in my book, *Possible Worlds in Possible Spaces: Knowledge, Globality, Gender and Information Technology in the Philippines* (Ateneo de Manila University Press, forthcoming). I am grateful to Professor Dr Gudrun Lachenmann (University of Bielefeld) to whom I owe so many insights.

Notes

1 Hotmail is a free, advertiser-supported e-mail service from Microsoft Network (MSN) that provides a permanent e-mail address that can be accessed from any web browser. It was developed in 1996 by Sabeer Bhatia, an Indian national who studied and worked in the US. Patterned after Hotmail, Pinoymail was launched in March 1998. Pinoymail announces itself as 'the world's first and largest free Filipino e-mail service'.
2 These claims are invariably expressed as a preference for Filipinos over other nationalities in fields such as nursing, maritime, entertainment and domestic services.
3 There are no official figures, but the Philippine ICT industry claimed it had lost a considerable number of programmers who were recruited for Y2K jobs

abroad such as changing 'two-digit years' to 'four-digit years'. This particular lack of programmers in the country was especially felt in 1997 and 1998.

4   An annual index presented by the Meta Group, a US-based research and consulting firm on IT and business transformation strategies. It is based on the following criteria: knowledge jobs (e.g. number of qualified engineers, senior managers and higher education students), technological innovation (e.g. average number of annual patents), movement towards a digital economy (e.g. telecommunications investment as percentage of the GDP), globalisation (e.g. direct investment flows abroad) and economic dynamism (e.g. corporate financial health) (Costello 2000: www.idg.net/crd_meta_193682.html).

5   IMD is a Switzerland-based business school for executive development. Its annual study, published as the *World Competitiveness Yearbook*, measures the national environment according to four main factors: economic perform-ance, government efficiency business efficiency and infrastructure. 'Availability of IT skills' is a subfactor under 'infrastructure' (IMD 2000, 2004).

6   Metro Manila is dotted with financial and business centres, each of which is an ensemble of skyscrapers. Some of these centres are found in Makati (i.e. the Ayala Business Centre), Manila (e.g. Binondo area), and Mandaluyong (i.e. the Ortigas Business Centre).

7   *Pusacat* is an example of a Filipino penchant for playing with words. *Pusa* means cat in Filipino.

8   Internet cafés, which number about 1500 all over the country, provide the means for a great number of Filipino Internet users to be connected to the World Wide Web. It has been noted that compared to the users in Metro Manila, the Internet users in the countryside are more technologically sophisticated and come from all classes of Philippine society. This is brought about by cheap Internet café access in the provinces, ranging from PhP10 to 35 per hour (US$0.25–0.87) unlike in Manila where prices are from PhP30 to 150 per hour (US$0.75–3.75).

9   *Manggagaya* refers to the act of copying and someone who copies and connotes non-originality and falsity.

10 The Warhol collection was on display at the Tate Modern from 7 February to 1 April 2002.

References

Anderson, B. (1985 [1983]) *Imagined Communities: Reflections on the Origin and Spread of Nationalism*, London: Verso Editions.

Barber, B. (1996) *Jihad vs. McWorld: How Globalism and Tribalism are Re-shaping the World*, New York: Ballantine Books.

Cannell, F. (1995) 'The Power of Appearances: Beauty, Mimicry, and Transformation in Bicol', in V. Rafael (ed.) *Discrepant Histories: Translocal Essays on Filipino Culture*, Pasig City: Anvil Publishing, pp. 223–58.

Costello, S. (2000) *The Global New E-economy Index*, www.idg.net/crd_meta_193682.html

Evers, H.-D. (2000) 'Epistemic Cultures: Towards a New Sociology of Knowledge', Working Paper 330, University of Bielefeld: Sociology of Development Research Centre.

Fukuyama, F. (1989) 'The End of History?', *National Interest*, 16: 3–18.

Giddens, A. (1994) 'Living in a Post-traditional Society', in U. Beck, A. Giddens and S. Lash (eds) *Reflexive Modernization: Politics, Tradition and Aesthetics in the Modern Social Order*, Cambridge: Polity Press, pp. 56–107.

Hannerz, U. (1996) *Transnational Connections*, London and New York: Routledge.

Huntington, S. (1993) 'The Clash of Civilizations', *Foreign Affairs*, 72 (3): 22–49.

IMD (2000) *World Competitiveness Yearbook 2000*, Institute for Management Development, http://www01.imd.ch/wcy/ranking/pastresults.html

IMD (2004) *World Competitiveness Yearbook 2004*, Institute for Management Development, http://www01.imd.ch/wcy/ranking/pastresults.html

Knorr Cetina, K. (1999) *Epistemic Cultures: How the Sciences make Knowledge*, Cambridge, Mass. and London: Harvard University Press.

Mitter, S. (2004) 'Globalization, ICTs and Empowerment: a Feminist Critique', *Gender, Technology and Development*, 8(1): 5–30.

National Information Technology Council (1997) *IT21 Philippines: IT Action Agenda for the 21st Century*, Manila: National Information Technology Council.

Philippine Star (2000) 'RP Aspires to Become Call Center Capital', 28 January, www.philstar.com

Philippine Star (2001) 'Agri is RP's Best Bet, Says Villar', 1 December, www.philstar.com

Putnam, R. (1993) 'The Prosperous Community: Social Capital and Public Life', *The American Prospect*, 13: 35–42.

Robertson, R. (1995) 'Globalization: Time–Space Homogeneity–Heterogeneity', in M. Featherstone, S. Lash and R. Robertson (eds) *Global Modernities*, London, Thousand Oaks, New Delhi: Sage Publications, pp. 25–44.

Schutz, A. and T. Luckmann (1973) *The Structures of the Life-world*, vol. I, translated from German by R. Zaner and H. Tristram Engelhardt, Jr, Evanston Ill.: Northwestern University Press.

Index